OTHER BOOKS BY RICHARD J. GELLES AND MURRAY A. STRAUS

Behind Closed Doors: Violence in the American Family, with
Suzanne K. Steinmetz
The Dark Side of Families: Current Family Violence Research,
edited with David Finkelhor and Gerald T. Hotaling

BY RICHARD J. GELLES

The Violent Home
Family Violence
Intimate Violence in Families, with Claire Pedrick Cornell

BY MURRAY A. STRAUS

*Social Stress in the United States: Links to Regional Patterns in
Crime and Illness,* with Arnold S. Linsky
The Social Causes of Husband-Wife Violence, edited with Gerald T.
Hotaling
Violence in the Family, edited with Suzanne K. Steinmetz

INTIMATE
VIOLENCE

Richard J. Gelles, Ph.D.
Murray A. Straus, Ph.D.

SIMON AND SCHUSTER
New York London Toronto Sydney Tokyo

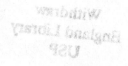
Published by the Simon & Schuster Trade Division

SIMON AND SCHUSTER and colophon are registered trademarks
of Simon & Schuster Inc.

Designed by Levavi & Levavi
Manufactured in the United States of America

10 9 8 7 6 5 4 3 2 1

Library of Congress Cataloging in Publication Data

Gelles, Richard J.
  Intimate violence.

  Includes index.
    1. Family violence—United States—Case studies.
  2. Family violence—United States—Prevention.
  I. Straus, Murray Arnold, date.   II. Title.
  HQ809.3.U5G4424   1988   362.8′2   88-3271
  ISBN 0-671-61752-4

ACKNOWLEDGMENTS

This book represents the results of more than fifteen years of re-search and study of family violence. Our two national surveys of family violence were supported by grants from the National Institute of Mental Health (MH 27557 and MH 40027). Dr. Saleem Shah, former Chief of the NIMH Center For Studies On Anti-Social and Violent Behavior and Thomas Lalley, former deputy chief of the center provided us support and guidance from our first tentative studies of family violence through our most recent investigation. They both had the foresight to see the importance of research on violent families long before child abuse and wife abuse were identi-fied as national social problems.

The design of the sample and the 6,002 interviews were conducted by Louis Harris and Associates. Dr. David Neft, a friend, valued colleague, and statistical expert, guided the formative stages of the study design. David was and remains always available, at work, at home, and at Larkin's Pond, to solve the trickiest sampling or statis-tical problems. Dr. John Boyle supervised the development of the complex interview schedule and kept the data collection on schedule.

We are indebted to Dr. John Harrop for coding the many compli-cated indexes and for getting our large and complicated data set to

run. John's exceptional attention to detail not only identified problems before they occurred but solved them with extraordinary in-
vestments of time and patience.

Ms. Jennifer Guckel provided able and constructive editorial comments and served as the prime research assistant on the initial stages
of the data analysis. Ms. Diane Hanscom helped us complete this
book by diligently tracking down the various reference sources and
statistics used in the book. She taught us the value of hiring a trained
library scientist.

The field of family violence research and treatment has grown
tremendously during the last decade. Those who have studied family
violence and attempted to unravel the complexities of this social
problem have had their endurance and faith tested by pain, suffering,
adversity, and tragedy. We have been fortunate to be able to draw
strength from many caring and compassionate colleagues as we have
had our own commitment challenged. The late C. Henry Kempe,
Bud Bolton, Eli and Carolyn Newberger, Robert Hampton, and
many other dedicated friends and colleagues inspired and motivated
us.

Our literary agent Robert Lescher helped us to move beyond our
traditional academic concerns and questions and conceptualize a
book that would help the public and policy makers understand family violence. Our editor, Bob Asahina and his assistant Rhonda Johnson let us write our book, and gently, but firmly, helped polish the
final product.

We have interviewed more than 10,000 individuals in the last
fifteen years. The specific cases which are described in this book have
been altered to protect the anonymity of our subjects. Names and
identifiable social descriptions have been altered. Many cases are
actually composites of a number of families. The persons we interviewed were kind enough to give us time and share some of their
lives. The victims of abuse and violence shared their suffering and
pain to help us provide insight into family violence so that others
would not have to suffer.

Finally, our families, Judy, Jason, and David Gelles and Jackie
Straus have always been beacons of light when we emerged from
studying and writing about the dark side of family life.

In memory of our fathers,
who gave us the gifts of
inspiration and compassion

CONTENTS

Part II: THE AFTERMATH:
OUT FROM THE SHADOWS TO SEEK HELP

PREFACE

"People are not for hitting." We began our research on intimate violence more than fifteen years ago with this deep conviction. Our research began in the 1970s when feelings about the Vietnam War were still running high. The country had been rocked by race riots and the assassinations of John F. Kennedy, Robert Kennedy, and Martin Luther King. We paid much too high a price for violence—fifty-five thousand young men in Vietnam, dreams of a bright and prosperous future snuffed out by the deaths of political and social leaders, and the suffering of countless victims of violent crime in the streets.

While others attended to public acts of violence, we were drawn to the more private acts. We thought that it was private violence that was at the root of public violence. At first we were frustrated. So little had been written on child abuse and wife abuse that the entire literature could be read at one sitting. Worse, much of what we read was flawed, biased, and unsound. Everything we read and all the advice of colleagues and friends suggested that we were looking up a blind alley; there just wasn't much family violence out there, we were told. We persisted. That it had not appeared in print did not mean it did not exist. We would find newspaper re-

11

ports on child abuse or family homicide each day. Something was out there.

Initially our involvement was purely scientific. Determining how to study child abuse and wife abuse represented a scientific puzzle to solve. Our job, we assumed, was to conduct sound scientific research so that others (clinicians and policy makers) could act to prevent and treat violence and abuse.

For a while we were able to keep our distance. We handed out surveys to college students. Later we ventured out into the community to interview people in their homes. Still, we were insulated by the scientific approach and the numbers. Always the numbers enabled us to remain detached.

But the distance could not be maintained. What started out as a short-term program of research has become life's work. Plans for other research were never realized. Family violence has taken hold of our lives just as it has the lives of most of the people who try to study, understand, and help the victims.

Slowly we came closer to the problem. Our seemingly dispassionate scholarly books and articles produced a few letters and some telephone calls from other researchers, clinicians, policy makers, and then finally, victims themselves. Friends and relatives began to take us aside and tell us about acts of family violence they had observed or committed. Speaking engagements produced more contacts, more firsthand experience, more sorrow from which we could no longer hide behind numbers. We lost some of our distance. We were forced to acknowledge our personal involvement. "How can this be?" we first asked. "What can we do?" we now ask.

To conduct research on intimate violence is to balance on a thin edge of emotion. On the one hand is the safety and security of scientific detachment. On the other hand is the agony of watching a baby, skull crushed from being thrown against a wall, wheeled into an emergency room. There is the near-total frustration of talking with a battered wife who wants help, while also knowing that there is practically no place she can go to escape the cycle of violence in which she finds herself. And there is anger—anger toward men who beat their wives, rage toward a parent who holds a child down in a scalding-hot bathtub, anger toward a political system whose budget for family violence is no more than the amount of a rounding error at the Pentagon, anger at clinicians who are too quick to take children away from parents, and equal anger at clinicians who wait too long.

Anger can become cynicism quickly. It is easy (and somewhat accurate) to conclude that family violence has always existed and that there is no evidence to suggest it will end or even diminish greatly in our lifetime. Cynicism, like scientific detachment, is a way of coping with the horror and tragedy of intimate abuse. Yet, even with some detachment and some cynicism, we are hopeful. We conduct our research, write our books and articles, and travel around the world to speak on this topic because we believe that human beings are basically nonviolent. We believe that parents and partners are not naturally mean and violent, but rather that violence arises our of social and psychological conditions that can change or be changed. We can choose to be nonviolent. We can raise a generation of nonviolent children who will never perceive violence as a legitimate means of self-expression or problem solving.

It was with these beliefs in mind that we began our research fifteen years ago; it was with these hopes in mind that we commenced the research that produced much of the information we report in this book. And it was with these ideals and aspirations that this book was written. Knowledge *can* make a difference. *People* can too.

PART I

VIOLENT

HOMES

1.

Because

They Can

From the time we are children we are taught that danger lurks in the streets at the hands of strangers. Walking to school or in the school-yard we are supposed to be wary of the stereotypical stranger in the old raincoat offering candy or a ride. As we grow older, we are warned not to run with the wrong crowd (presumably people our parents do not know). Dark alleys, strange cities, and the night are full of danger, ready to leap upon an innocent, unsuspecting victim. Women are taught a special brand of danger. Bars, dark alleys, hitch-hiking, and strange men hold the threat of rape.

Today, the fear of danger on the street at the hands of strangers is as strong as ever. Milk cartons and shopping bags carry pictures of missing children who have been snatched by strangers. Stories of abducted children spread like fire across a parched field of grass. One story tells of an infant girl who disappeared in a toy store. Her mother's screams attracted the attention of the store manager and other shoppers. After the store was locked and a search begun, the baby was allegedly found in a changing room, hair cut and dressed in boy's clothing. The mere telling of this story is enough to send a shiver down the back of a parent.

Today, parents selecting a day-care center or a summer camp not only have to consider the quality of the staff and the cleanliness of the facility; they also have to wrestle with the fear that a teacher or counselor is also a molester. With newspapers carrying a story about sexual abuse in day-care centers nearly every day, any informed parent will be a little hesitant when sending a child off to be cared for by strangers. The relief when the child returns home or ends the school year unharmed (hopefully) is just as profound as the fear.

Fear of violence in the United States cuts across age, social, and racial groups. The Figgie Report, a national survey on the fear of crime, sponsored by the brother of a victim of a violent crime, revealed that four out of five Americans are afraid of being assaulted, robbed, raped, or murdered. Nine out of ten Americans keep their doors locked. More than half say they dress plainly to avoid attracting the attention of a violent criminal. A significant number of people say they choose not to go places or do things because they fear for their personal safety. There are fifty-five million handguns lying around American homes—many no doubt purchased as a defense against violent intruders.

As real as the fear of violent crime is, so is the amount of crime. There is a very real danger in the streets. According to the United States Department of Justice, three Americans in a hundred are victims of violent crimes each year—this represents six million victims annually. But the cruel irony of staying home because one fears violence in the streets is that the real danger of personal attack *is in the home*. Offenders are not strangers climbing through windows, but loved ones, family members.

You are more likely to be physically assaulted, beaten, and killed in your own home at the hands of a loved one than anyplace else, or by anyone else in our society. Despite all the pictures of missing children on shopping bags and milk cartons, children are more likely to be kidnapped by their own parents than by strangers. Although the Federal Bureau of Investigation claims that there are 1.5 million children abducted each year, the agency actually investigated only sixty-seven cases of abduction in 1984. Experts outside the FBI say that there may be only six or seven hundred children abducted by strangers each year. On the other hand, hundreds of thousands of children are snatched by parents embroiled in custody disputes.

A somewhat grisly incident underscores the point that while the public is drawn to and fears instances of children being abducted or harmed by strangers, the real danger is in the home. In May 1985 a thirteen-year-old girl disappeared from her home in Minnesota.

Seven weeks of searching failed to turn up any sign of her. As a result of the disappearance, the community organized a group to help find missing children. The missing thirteen-year-old's father was chosen leader of the group. In the course of advancing the cause of the group that sought to search and find missing children, the father testified on a panel with Minnesota state attorney general Hubert H. Humphrey III. A week after the testimony, while police questioned him to aid in their investigation, the father broke down and admitted that he had killed his daughter. The father admitted that he had been sexually abusing his daughter for years. He admitted that when his daughter fought his sexual advances he had stabbed her to death. He hid her body for a few days and then buried it in a field.

Two questions beg for answers. First, if the home is so dangerous, why have we ignored the danger and focused our attention on violence in the streets? Second, if indeed the home is the scene of so much hurt, harm, and danger, why is it?

One of the saddest lessons we have learned in all of our years of research on family violence is that human beings can absorb outrageous violence over long periods of time with barely a whimper and rarely a cry for help. Every one of the women we have met who has slain her husband did so after years of cruel physical and mental punishment. We have talked with hundreds of middle-aged women who have been beaten regularly by their husbands for ten or even twenty years. Young women who come forward with allegations of sexual abuse will recount instances of abuse going back to their earliest memories at age five or even three. Countless people have come to us after one of our public presentations on family violence and described their injuries and experiences. What is sadder, is that many of these same individuals said they did not realize they had been abused until they compared their experiences with our dispassionate scientific descriptions of violence in the home.

We believe that human beings are less fearful of violence and injury than the violation of social order. What keeps people locked in homes, weapons hidden under mattresses, is not just the fear of harm, but rather the fear of an unpredictable world. Humans have a passion for social order. Our identity and very existence are tied to a notion of the world as a predictable place. That violence and harm could lurk in an alley, in a doorway, or somewhere else in the dark is what we fear the most.

Violence in the home, we have found, is not altogether unpredictable or unexpected. In our society, a person's earliest experiences with violence comes in the home—spankings and physical punishments from parents. We learn that there is always going to be a certain amount of violence that accompanies intimacy. Moreover, we learn that children "deserve" to be hit. That "sparing the rod spoils the child." We grow to accept violence as a way of solving problems. Violence is also considered an appropriate means of expressing oneself. Violence in the home is not the exception we fear; it is all too often the rule we live by.

Our society concentrates on violence in the streets because our goal is not just to eliminate violence but to enforce some kind of social order that renders the world predictable (and hopefully safe). We ignore violence in the home precisely because it is so predictable and because whatever harm it does cause is traded off against the safety and sanctity of the family. Thus, in answering our first question we set the stage for the somewhat paradoxical answer to the second. How can the group we turn to for love and understanding be so cruel and harmful? Because they can be.

PEOPLE HIT FAMILY MEMBERS BECAUSE THEY CAN

One of the first abusers we met was a middle-aged man who had been beating his wife on and off for most of their twenty-year marriage. Normally he was a mild-mannered person whose outward demeanor was a far cry from that of the stereotypical wife beater. Chet was not brawny, not macho, not visibly short-tempered. Yet, he freely admitted that he often lost his temper with his wife and that he beat her when this happened. Chet said that he became especially enraged when his wife, Margorie, did a poor job keeping the house neat. Margorie, also mild-mannered and conservatively middle class, had sought help because she wanted Chet to stop beating her. Yet, as Chet calmly explained the times when he lost his temper and hit Margorie, she nodded sadly and agreed that Chet had indeed been angry and this led directly to the beatings. "What can I do," she asked, "to keep him from getting angry and hitting me?"

We met David and Marie in the emergency room of a children's hospital. Their three-year-old son, Peter, was on his way to be X-rayed for a possible skull fracture. Peter, it seems, had accidentally knocked over David's new television set and the picture tube had shattered. David had saved for the set for more than a year, and had explained to little Peter that he should not touch the new TV. Peter, a typically curious toddler, had touched the screen and played with the dials. Each time, he had been slapped or spanked by David. Amid the shattered glass of the picture tube, David simply "lost it" and had slapped Peter harder than ever. Peter fell onto the coffee table, striking his head. The X ray would tell how much damage had been done. When we met David and Marie, the chief of the hospital child abuse team was explaining the state child abuse law and why she had to file a report to the state department of social services. David nodded that he understood. He was clearly distraught about the incident and repeated over and over that he wished he had not got so angry with little Peter.

The common thread that appears to run through both homes is that anger with a wife or a child led to loss of control and violence. This is not, however, an adequate explanation. Let us change the scenarios and see why.

Imagine that Chet is the manager of a medium-size office. The office employs a janitor who comes in the evenings to empty ashtrays, dust, vacuum, and clean the office. David runs an automobile agency. In the waiting room of the agency is a new television. One day, Chet comes to work and finds that although the janitor has been in, there is barely a sign that anything has been cleaned. That same day, a three-year-old overturns David's television. What is the outcome? Does Chet, finding his office a mess, pounce on his janitor and begin to pummel him? Unlikely. Does David slap, spank, or even beat the wayward three-year-old? Absurd. How is it that the very same situations at home can produce anger strong enough to lead to abusive violence? Why can Chet and David control their anger outside of the home, yet lose it with family members?

The answer is rather obvious. Let's suppose Chet grabs his janitor and begins to punch him. What could happen? Well, the janitor could hit back and beat up Chet. The janitor might not be able to do so, but he most surely would report the outburst to Chet's boss and perhaps call the police. Chet would stand a fairly good chance of being punished or even fired by his boss. The police would most certainly arrive on the scene quickly and probably arrest Chet for assault and battery. David would have major trouble on his hands. The three-year-old's parents would take a dim view of seeing their son hit by an auto salesperson. David could safely assume that the boy's parents would buy a car somewhere else, which would be the least of his problems. The little boy's father might attack David. Or, he could call the police. The police would soon arrive, and David, like Chet, would be subjected to arrest for assault and battery.

The unconscious knowledge that all these potential costs and punishments would await them if they struck strangers or fellow workers would constrain Chet's and David's anger. Anger that led to violence would surely result in significant costs for the violent perpetrators. The rewards would be slim. The best Chet could hope for would be that his janitor would clean better or quit. David would have little to gain by striking a three-year-old.

The anger and violence these two men exhibited in the home led to few costs. Margorie called the police the first couple of times Chet hit her. The police were slow to come to the house. When they did finally arrive they counseled Margorie to "kiss and make up" with Chet. Once they took Chet out and had him walk around the block a few times to "cool off." Margorie thought about divorcing Chet, but she said that she loved him and besides, "the black and blues go away, and he hasn't hit me in a couple of months." David and Marie spent an anxious hour in the emergency room waiting for Peter's X rays to be taken and read. Peter had a bad cut, and a bruise, but no fractures. The child abuse report was filed. A few days later, David and Marie were visited by a social worker who talked with them, looked over the house, and left. The social worker's report described David and Marie as a nice professional couple, who lived in a neat and attractive home. Both worked, neither had a drinking problem, and the incident appeared to be an aberration. Given that the department of social services had more than thirty cases of maltreatment per social worker, it did not appear that anything had to be done with David and Marie. They seemed to care genuinely for Peter. The case was closed with no recommendation for services or follow-up.

The proposition that people hit family members because they can is based on the principles of social exchange theory, which assumes that human interaction is guided by the pursuit of rewards and the avoidance of punishments and costs. When an individual provides services to another, he obliges the other to fulfill the obligation to reward him. When a reciprocal exchange of services and rewards occurs, the interaction will continue. If there is no reciprocity, the interaction will be broken off, since the costs of the exchange for the first person exceed the rewards. All take and no give is not a formula for happy or continued social interaction, unless one of the participants is a masochist.

Family behavior adds an important dimension to the normal assumptions of social exchange theory. Simply stated, it is not so easy to break off interaction with a family member, regardless of whether there is a reciprocal exchange of rewards or services. One can separate from or divorce a spouse, but almost always decisions about property, living space, and perhaps children are required. One can, with effort and typically with legal counsel, achieve the status of ex-wife or ex-husband. To become an ex-parent is typically impossible. Give-and-take with children is another dimension of exchange theory. Unable to break off inequitable social relations easily, individuals can become frustrated, angry, and resentful. Conflict is a common result. The principles of exchange theory suggest that people would only use violence toward family members when there are rewards for violent behavior and when the costs of violence do not outweigh the rewards. When we discussed the cases of Chet and David, we mentioned that there are relatively standard costs for being violent in our society, which are rarely paid by those violent in the home.

What about the police and the criminal justice system? Violence in the home, after all, is assault, and all fifty states have laws prohibiting child abuse. The simple fact is that the police tend to respond slower to a domestic disturbance call than to a public disturbance. There are a variety of reasons for the less than timely responses. First, and perhaps foremost, dealing with domestic disturbances can be dangerous work. The National Institute of Justice reports that between 1972 and 1984 there were 69 officers killed in domestic disturbances—thus accounting for 6 percent of all officers killed in the line of duty. This number is less than the 210 officers who died answering robbery calls, and less than the figure of 23 percent that has been quoted by numerous students of domestic violence. Yet, even this number is high when one considers the assumption that the streets pose much greater danger than homes. A second explanation for the reluctance of police officers to answer domestic disturbance calls is that this kind of police work is generally considered low prestige. Few police officers are rewarded or promoted for being especially effective in dealing with domestic assault. Arresting a battering husband or parent is considered less prestigious and less indicative of good police work than arresting a robber or drug dealer. The culture of the modern American police department simply does not place high esteem on one's ability to handle domestic calls.

What happens when the police do arrive? As we saw with Chet, arrest is not a common response in instances of wife abuse. Unless a victim of parental violence has been brutally tortured or slain, violence toward children almost always is treated as a child welfare and not a criminal justice matter. At present in the United States, the chances that a person will be arrested for hitting his partner or children are relatively slim. Our most recent national survey of family violence found that fewer than one in ten police interventions ended in the arrest of the offender. Thus, the cost of arrest, which is very real for public violence, is nearly nonexistent in cases of intimate violence and abuse.

In the rare case when a violent family member is arrested, what are the chances that there will be further costs paid? Again, the answer is slim. The criminal justice system is loath to break up families. Wives who press charges against their husbands are frequently advised to drop the charges. "After all," the prosecutor or judge may argue, "if he goes to jail, he will lose his job and you will have to go on welfare." The same line of reasoning is presented when a man batters his children. If the offender is a mother, the courts are even more reluctant to send women to jail, for fear of further harming the children. A second argument against jailing offenders is that the courts may fear that this will only further provoke or anger the violent individual. Battered wives are often told to go home and "kiss and make up." "You don't want to really make him mad, do you?" they are warned. Only the poorest offenders, those with inadequate legal counsel, or those who have committed the most outrageous crimes against partners and children are sentenced to jail.

The criminal justice system holds very little threat of cost for the average violent family member. Worse still, the very lack of real costs may actually encourage further violence. We spoke with a thirty-five-year-old woman who felt it was a drastic mistake to call the police. She had been the victim of gradually increasing violence over the first five years of her marriage. Finally, unable to bear more hitting, she called the police. She recounted the results:

> He threatened to beat me again, and I told him that if he tried I would call the cops. I forget what actually happened that night—I think the pizza was cold or something like that. Anyway, he threw a fork at me and started to chase me. I told him that I would call the cops if he didn't stop. Well, he didn't, so I called. The cops came pretty quick. Turns out that they knew Dan [her husband]. He had gotten into a couple of fights at Spenser's [a local bar]. They took him aside and told him he should try to calm down. They told him he had better go

for a walk, and they took him outside. One police officer told me that if I had trouble again to call. Well, Dan was back in about forty-five minutes. He had calmed down, but he had kind of a mean look on his face. When he came in he said, "Well, you played your ace—see what happened—nothing! Now you know who's out there to help you." Christ, calling the cops made it worse. Now he figured he could really beat the shit out of me and no one would do a thing.

Other battered women have sought restraining orders and all too frequently found that such orders offered little resistance to a violent man.

There are other possible costs. Using violence could lead to a loss of status, or to economic costs. Both Chet and David could lose their jobs for hitting a fellow worker or client. But, with few exceptions, there are practically no instances where a violent family member was fired because it became known he beat his wife or children.

SOCIAL ATTITUDES, PRIVACY, INEQUALITY, AND VIOLENCE

We can expand our first proposition that people hit family members because they can into three basic propositions:

1. Family members are more likely to use violence in the home when they expect the costs of being violent to be less than the rewards.
2. The absence of effective social controls (e.g., police intervention) over family relations decreases the costs of one family member being violent toward another.
3. Certain social and family structures reduce social controls in family relations and, therefore, reduce the costs and increase the rewards of being violent.

The social and family structures that are most important in reducing the costs of intimate violence and, to some degree, increasing the rewards are: (1) the social attitudes concerning violence and, more specifically, family violence; (2) the private nature of the modern household; and (3) the structural inequality that exists in the modern family.

Social Attitudes: The Marriage License as a Hitting License

Violence, the commentators tell us, is as American as apple pie. Violence is considered a socially appropriate means of solving interpersonal and international problems. Duels and fistfights have long been considered the manly way of resolving differences between gentlemen. Such a duel ended the life of the first treasurer of the United States, Alexander Hamilton (killed by the former vice president of the United States, Aaron Burr, in 1804). When fifty-two Americans were taken hostage in Iran in November 1979, one of the public reactions was that the United States should "bomb Iran back into the Stone Age" in order to obtain the release of the hostages. Force was also considered as a means of obtaining the release of Americans held hostage by Lebanese terrorists in a hijacked TWA airliner in the summer of 1985. More than 65 percent of Americans polled support the use of the death penalty as a legitimate means of punishing capital crimes. There are countless other signs of public support for violence. The legitimization of violence can be seen on Saturday morning cartoon shows, as when the wily coyote is regularly pummeled and crushed by the road runner. Culture heroes John Wayne, Clint Eastwood, and Charles Bronson all share the ability to be quick with their fists to right a wrong or defend the helpless.

Early in our research, we concluded that the level of violence in historical and contemporary families was sufficiently great to justify our calling the marriage license a hitting license. Numerous surveys have discovered that a large number of people believe that under certain circumstances, it is perfectly appropriate for a husband to hit his wife. Approval of using violence to raise and train children is practically universal.

The U.S. Commission on the Causes and Prevention of Violence conducted a national survey on violence in the United States during the late 1960s. The survey focused not just on public violence, but on attitudes toward private violence. Among the findings of the commission were that:

- One quarter of adult men and one in six adult women said they could think of circumstances in which it would be all right for a husband to hit his wife or the wife to hit her husband.
- Eighty-six percent of those polled said that young people needed "strong" discipline.
- Seven out of ten thought it was important for a boy to have a few fistfights while he was growing up.

Fifteen years after the U.S. Commission on the Causes and Prevention of Violence conducted their survey, we conducted our first national survey of violence in the home. We asked our national sample of more than two thousand subjects two questions that focused on their attitudes about violence between intimates. About one in four wives and about a third of the husbands we talked to thought that a couple slapping one another was at least somewhat necessary, normal, and good. More than 70 percent of those surveyed thought that slapping a twelve-year-old child was either necessary, normal, or good.

Parent-to-child violence is so common and so widely approved that one needs few case studies to make the point. In general, the large majority of Americans believes that good parenting requires some physical punishment. Over and over again, when we interview parents about hitting their children, we are told that kids "deserve to be hit" or "need to be hit." Among the thousands of people we have interviewed, it was *absence* of physical punishment that was thought to be deviant, not the hitting of children.

Even if violence is considered inappropriate by an individual, a group, or even by the society, the fact that violence is between family members means that most people will not want to intervene. One of our first research projects involved interviewing violent couples and their neighbors. Quite by chance we learned that the neighbors knew about the violence occurring next door. While neighbors might call the police, they almost never tried to get involved personally. Some feared for their own safety, but most simply said, "That's a family matter." Police officers, prosecutors, and judges have been known to say the same thing when confronted with domestic violence. When it comes to violence toward children, very few people try to intervene when a parent spanks or slaps a child in a supermarket or department store. While again, people might be hesitant because of fear for their own safety, by and large, even if one detests seeing a child hit, one tends to view it as the parent's own business.

Television also plays a role in perpetuating the support of private violence. Millions laughed (and still laugh) when Jackie Gleason rants, "Alice, you're going to the moon!" or, "One of these days, pow, right in the kisser!" while shaking his fist at his television wife on the popular program, "The Honeymooners."

For those who think that it is *just* television that portrays and supports family violence, a quick examination of fairy tales, folklore, and nursery rhymes will graphically illustrate that a variety of media has for many years supported intimate violence, abuse, and neglect.

Mother Goose's "Old Woman Who Lived in a Shoe" beat her children soundly when she sent them to bed. "Humpty Dumpty" is a thinly disguised metaphor of the fragility of children, and "Rock-a-Bye, Baby" is not even thinly disguised, with the baby and cradle falling from the tree. Wicked stepmothers abound in children's fairy tales. Snow White's stepmother had Snow White taken out into the woods to be beheaded by the huntsman. Hansel and Gretel's parents left them to starve in the woods because money was scarce.

A final means of making the marriage license a hitting license is to deny that the behavior is violent. Parents who hit children are not considered violent; they are thought to be properly disciplining their children. We have countless euphemisms such as "family matter" or "domestic disturbance" to serve as smokescreens for behaviors that would be considered assaults if committed by strangers. Denial also occurs when we create stereotyped images of what so-called "real violence" is. Stereotypical violence tortures, maims, or kills. For wife abuse, this has been labeled "burning bed" violence after the case of Francine Hughes, the Michigan housewife who endured years of violence before finally killing her husband by setting his bed on fire. In the case of child abuse, the stereotypical abuse is the 220-pound father punching his defenseless five-month-old son. There is little public support for these acts. Defining them as acts of "real violence" hides the more common forms of intimate violence, such as slaps, pushes, shoves, and occasional punches, behind closed doors.

Privacy

A number of years ago we attended a conference where the family and social change were being discussed. One of the aspects of social change that was on the program was our own presentation on child abuse and family violence. There was a general discussion of whether violence in the home was a new phenomenon or if we had simply not attended to a problem that had long existed in the family. The anthropologists in attendance were asked about their own observations of other cultures and societies. Beatrice Whiting, the eminent cultural anthropologist, observed that among the societies she had studied, violence between family members did not occur when families lived in communal residences. She concluded that, "when the walls [of separate houses] went up, the hitting started."

The social historian Barbara Laslett has studied the evolution of the modern family. A major distinction between the family in the

twentieth century and earlier families is the private nature of the
modern family and the public nature of the historical household.
These differences can be observed in terms of family size, residents
in the home, and the use of household space.

One major historical change is that today's mothers give birth to
fewer children than mothers two hundred years ago. Laslett notes
that privacy of the home is increased when there are fewer children
to serve as members of the family audience. A second change is the
reduction in the number of non-kin group residents in the home. In
the distant past, as well as the nineteenth century, the household
contained numerous categories of non-kin residents. Obviously, the
presence of a boarder, servant, or apprentice greatly reduced the
amount of privacy that existed in the home. The growth of a smoke-
stack economy and the factory system eliminated the apprentice
from the home. So, too, the development of a service society reduced
the need (and the cost-effectiveness) of live-in servants. Urbanization and the explosive growth of apartment-type housing removed
boarders and lodgers from the modern family. As the adult audience
dwindled, privacy increased.

Architecture and space usage further changed as the family
evolved. The medieval household was but one room. When dinner
was over, the dining table was moved away and the beds or mats set
out for sleeping. Anyone who has shared a motel room with children
can attest to the amount of privacy provided by a single room. The
historian John Demos described the typical colonial house in the
Plymouth Colony as a few rooms, with limited sources of heat.

The single-family detached house with which we are so familiar
did not evolve until the beginning of the nineteenth century. Increasing modernization—central heating, indoor plumbing, air-condi-
tioning, radio, and television—further influenced the space
utilization of the modern home.

In short, industrialization, urbanization, and modernization had a
consistant impact on the family, changing it from a public institution
with large and diverse audiences, to a private institution with the
regular audience limited to husband, wife, and one or two children.
Laslett explains that as the family became private, so too did it
become more insulated from social control. Although children are
not significant agents of social control, they do exert some—as anyone who has delayed an argument with a spouse until the children
have gone to bed can attest to. Non-kin residents were also possible
agents of control—implicitly by just "being around," and explicitly

by their ability to intervene in family conflict. The less observable family behavior is, the less opportunity exists for formal or informal social control.

What are the consequences of increased family privacy and decreased social control? The private nature of intimate violence shelters offenders and victims from an audience, public eyes, and social control. The multiroom architecture of the modern home means that partners can fight away from the eyes (and supposedly ears) of children. Sexual and physical abuse of children can be committed by one parent in a separate room from the nonabusive parent. While it is a bit naive to believe that the nonabusing parent is ignorant of the actions, it is not unrealistic to assume that separate rooms gives the nonabusing parent a justification for noninvolvement and not exercising social control. Quite inadvertently, the family has evolved over the years into a perfectly shielded setting for private violence.

Inequality

Social attitudes set the stage for violence as an acceptable means of solving problems and self-expression, and privacy shields the family from social control in circumstances when the violence may not be considered normative. The socially structured inequality of the family further reduces the costs to violent partners, parents, and even children. Sexual and generational inequality take on many forms. First and most obvious, are the physical size differences. Husbands are typically larger and stronger than their wives. Parents are almost always bigger and stronger than their young children. Such physical size differences are important. We learned in one of our early analyses of mothers' use of violence toward their children, that mothers of teenage children are less likely to hit their children than are mothers of younger children. When we talked to the mothers we learned that the reason for this was not that there were less conflicts between mothers and teenagers than between mothers and preadolescents; actually there are more. Rather, the mothers said they were afraid that their teenagers would hit back. These sentiments were expressed by a forty-seven-year-old mother of a teenaged son and daughter:

> I used to spank my two kids until they got to be about fourteen or fifteen. . . I still wanted to hit them but, you see, they got to be so big that I just was too afraid to hit them anymore. Why, if they even pushed me now they could really hurt me.

There is more to inequality than size. Men typically enjoy more social and economic status than do women. Because of their economic and social power, men can hit their wives without fear that their wives can extract a social or economic cost. By the same token, parents control the social and economic resources of their children.

Over and over again, the victims of family violence whom we have come to know say the same thing: The black and blue marks go away, the violence is only occasional, and they are willing to accept pain against the costs of trying to survive outside of the home with little money, credit, or experience.

The inequality we describe is part of a centuries-old legacy in which women are men's property and children are the property of their parents. The sociologist Lenore Weitzman finds that our traditional and still widely accepted conceptions about marriage can be traced back to tenth- and eleventh-century Anglo-American family law. One characteristic of traditional marriage was the husband being viewed as the head of the family with the wife and children subordinate. According to Weitzman, this hierarchy derived from the common-law doctrine of coverture, under which a husband and wife took a single legal identity at marriage—the identity of the husband. Although coverture was repealed in the nineteenth century, the assumption of a man as head remains embodied in statutory and case law in the United States.

The sociologists Russell and Rebecca Dobash have noted that there are very few historical references to women as important, powerful, and meaningful contributors to the lives and times of societies. There are, on the other hand, abundant legal, historical, literary, and religious writings that describe the subordinate and propertied status of women. Saint Augustine wrote that in marriage, "women ought to serve their husbands as unto God." The Roman father decided whether his newborn children would live or die, selected marital partners for his children, and could put an adulterous wife to death.

The legacy of women and children as property was carried forth with laws that allowed, under certain circumstances, the chastisement and physical punishment of women and children. The expression "rule of thumb" is said to come from old English common law which stated that a husband could beat his wife with a rod no thicker than his thumb. Colonial "stubborn child laws" gave Puritan parents the right to put unruly children to death, although there is little historical evidence that such a drastic punishment was ever meted out.

The sociologist Dair Gillespie points out that before the Civil War, American wives had many duties and few rights. Wives were not permitted to own property, even if they had inherited it. Husbands could collect and use their wives' wages, choose the education and religion of their children, and punish their wives if they displeased them. Husbands could even will children (born or unborn) to other guardians. If a divorce was granted, it was the husband who would decide who would have custody of the children. Husbands, according to Gillespie were their wives' companions, superiors, and masters.

The victims of violence in the home are disproportionately the smaller, the weaker, and the less powerful. Part of their weakness comes from hundreds of years of subordination and being treated as property. Part of the weakness is due to the current social organization of society which offers few places to which victims can flee and live life safely with adequate social resources. The stigma of being a runaway child or a single parent serves to imprison many victims of violence in their homes. In few, perhaps no other, social settings are the cards so stacked against victims of personal violence. Few victims of public violence have to think about trading off the rewards of a home, hearth, and relationship against the costs of being physically assaulted. If you patronize a bar where you get beat up every fourth time you go there, you can freely stop going or change bars. Such options are not typically available to victims of intimate violence.

THE REWARDS OF INTIMATE VIOLENCE

We have said that people hit family members because they can, and we have argued that they can because the costs of being a violent family member are so low. There is another side to the equation. There are also rewards for being violent. James Q. Wilson and Richard J. Herrnstein, in their book *Crime and Human Nature,* make the point that there are a number of rewards for crime and criminal violence: working off momentary anger, money, and having fun. Most importantly, these rewards are felt quite soon after the behavior. In the case of intimate violence, the rewards of working off momentary anger are immediate. Nowhere is this quite as obvious as in the use of force and violence against children. Childrearing can be an immensely frustrating task. Over and over again, parents explain the frustration of raising children and trying to enforce discipline. While many parents try diligently to use a reasoned and rational approach to training children, as often as not parents report that they resort to hitting because "hitting works." When we ask how they know the hitting works, they say, "because he, or she, or they stopped what they were doing." For example:

> My daughter is two and she gets into everything. Sometimes I try to explain to her that she could get hurt or break something that is valuable. But she is so little that she really doesn't understand. So I slap her wrist or hit her bottom. That she understands and she stops touching the stuff right away.

or,

> I know I shouldn't lose my temper and hit them [her children]. But I get so frustrated I just lose control. Besides, they do stop the things that got me mad in the first place.

It does little good to try to explain to parents that force and violence are not really effective ways of training and disciplining children.

It would do no good to explain to husbands that hitting their wives is not an effective means of encouraging conversation or debate. The reason for this is the rather immediate gratification the violent individual gets from hitting. For example, a husband described why he hit his wife: "She just nags and nags. I can't get her to stop and listen to me. So, I slap her in the face—that sure gets her attention and then she listens to me."

Violent parents or partners see immediately the reactions to the violence. If the force is sufficient to hurt a child or a spouse, they will most certainly stop whatever they were doing. Clearly, the immediate rewards of using violence to work off anger or frustration are quite valuable to some individuals who would rather not wait to see the longer-term benefits of more reasoned and rational discipline and conversation with their children or partners.

Power, control, and self-esteem are other rewards of family violence. The sociologist William Goode has stated that force or its threat is a fundamental part of all social systems, because all social systems are, to one degree or another, power systems. Force, or violence, Goode explains, is one of four major sets of resources by which people can move others to serve their ends. The four sets are: (1) economic factors (giving or withholding economic rewards or services); (2) prestige or respect; (3) likability, attractiveness, friendship, or love; and, (4) force and its threat. Once can exert influence on people using any of these systems. One can give money, offer respect, provide love or friendship, or threaten to do bodily injury. All of these factors are in operation in the family, and all are used because they can effectively control the behavior of loved ones.

You can hardly walk in a public place where there are parents and children without overhearing what has become the virtual motto of American parents: "You better watch out or you're going to get it!" Force is threatened because parents want to control the behavior of their children. Hardly anyone would intervene if they saw a parent spank a child who had just run out into the street. Here, force is considered a perfectly legitimate means of controlling the child's behavior and teaching the child a valuable lesson.

The consequences of intimate violence further increase the rewards for an individual who desires to control another. Repeated violence tends to beat down victims to the point where they will do anything, or say anything, to please their batterers and avoid violence. Betty, a thirty-five-year-old schoolteacher, said that after two years of violence she went to any length to please her husband:

> I would do anything. I would try to anticipate his moods. Cook his favorite dish. Dress the way he liked. I would have the kids washed and in bed when he got home from work so there wouldn't be any stress at home. I gave up my first job so I could be at home, but then he got too worried about money, so I got another job as a teacher. I think I spent twenty-four hours a day either doing things to please him or thinking ahead to prevent his getting mad.

For the person doing the controlling, the reward is not just control or power, but also self-esteem. Being in control, being master (or apparent master) of a situation, increases one's sense of self-worth. For men or parents whose sense of self-esteem may have been damaged or devalued by experiences outside of the home (losing a job, being humiliated by a boss or fellow worker, etc.), control at home is even more important. Over and over again we heard from men who first discussed how hard a time they had outside of the home and how they "had" to use hitting to keep their wives or kids in line. Obviously, the hitting served to make these men feel that they could control something in their lives.

One pattern of family violence we observed underscored the use of violence to control and increase self-esteem. It is not unusual to find a pattern of violence in a home where the husband hits his wife, the wife in turn uses violence toward her children, the older children use violence on the younger children, and the youngest child takes out his or her frustration on the family pet. One explanation for this pattern is that at each level the most powerful person is seeking to control the next least powerful person, and that this control is satisfying because it raises the hitter's feelings of self-worth.

A last reward for those who hit is revenge. "Revenge can be sweet," and one of the earliest patterns we identified in our study of intimate violence was that those who hit tended to do so after they felt that their self-worth had been attacked or threatened. Partners and parents are experts when it comes to understanding other family members' vulnerabilities. Conflict between intimates can quickly escalate because each person knows the other's most vulnerable points. If the conflict escalates the one partner goes for the other's jugular, violence may be the only way the partner can defend him- or herself. Wives often hit husbands and children strike their parents to extract some kind of revenge for a psychological or physical assault.

Our society and our families are organized to not only allow but often encourage violence between intimates. The combination of social attitudes (that sometimes encourage but often just simply allow violence), with the private nature of the modern family, and the socially structured inequality that is part of every household, makes for a tinderbox of emotions and possible violent outbursts.

If people are violent because they can be, and if the modern family and system of social control is organized in such a way as to provide minimal social control over family behavior, does this mean that all families are violent? The answer is yes and no. Yes, there probably is some hitting in almost every household at some time. Almost all children are hit by their parents. Virtually all brothers and sisters hit each other. Perhaps half of all husbands and wives will physically fight at some point in the marriage. And many children, young and old, strike their parents, young and old. The answer is no if one confines the definition of violence to the outrageous acts of abuse that we hear about in the news each day. Abuse is not a common act, probably because enough social control is exerted over most individuals and most households to keep minor hitting from escalating into major abuse. Where abuse occurs, more often than not it is because a combination of factors exist—low social control, perhaps due to social isolation, high stress and frustration, and attitudes that hitting and even violence that causes injury are appropriate ways to raise children and control wives.

2.

People Other Than Us:

Public Perceptions

of Family Violence

On an early morning in November 1987, Ms. Hedda Nussbaum called the New York City 911 emergency telephone number to report that her daughter, Elizabeth, was choking on food and was having trouble breathing. When police arrived at the fashionable Greenwich Village apartment that Ms. Nussbaum shared with attorney Joel Steinberg, they did not find the kind of medical emergency they expected. Instead they found six-year-old Elizabeth Steinberg physically abused and barely breathing. Elizabeth's eighteen-month-old brother, Mitchell, stood in urine-soaked clothes, tied to his playpen with some twine. Elizabeth Steinberg died later that week, and Joel Steinberg and Hedda Nussbaum were charged with murder.

Little Elizabeth's death set off an explosion of questions, anger, charges and countercharges, and media attention that was nearly unprecedented. For more than two weeks there was not a day when the sad and tragic story of Elizabeth Steinberg was not discussed in the newspapers, tabloids, newsmagazines, and on radio and television talk shows. Hundreds of New Yorkers, most of them strangers, attended Elizabeth's funeral. "How could such a horrible thing happen?" and "Couldn't Elizabeth have been saved?" were questions asked time and time again.

Why did the case of Elizabeth Steinberg rivet public attention to child abuse in a way that had not happened for a decade, if not longer? In many ways, the case of Elizabeth Steinberg was tragically similar to hundreds, if not thousands, of cases. More than one hundred children die as a result of child abuse in New York City each year. Nationally, nearly a thousand children are killed by their caretakers. Six-year-old Elizabeth was somewhat older than the average child who dies as a result of abuse. Much outrage focused on the fact that authorities had been warned about Elizabeth's condition many times. Neighbors and friends of the family told reporters that they had filed reports with New York State's child abuse hot line a number of times. City officials noted that they had investigated reports of Elizabeth's abuse and neglect a number of years earlier and deemed the reports unfounded. Again, this is sadly similar to other cases of child abuse. There is prior warning that a child is at risk in as many as 30 to 50 percent of all deaths of children due to abuse. One unusual aspect of the case was that although Steinberg and Nussbaum claimed to be Elizabeth's adoptive parents, there was a question as to whether the adoption was actually legal. Yet, here, too, this is not unusual enough to explain the fervor and the moral outrage that arose with the child's death.

Perhaps the reason why this case attacked the sensibilities of so many people was that it did not conform to the stereotype we have developed for abusive partners and families. Elizabeth Steinberg was white, and so were her abusers. Joel Steinberg is a forty-six-year old criminal lawyer. Hedda Nussbaum, who lived with Steinberg for seventeen years, was a former editor of children's books at Random House. Their apartment was not in an urban ghetto, but was an upscale building where Mark Twain had once lived. The case of Elizabeth Steinberg was one that hit close to home because she seemed so much like many of our daughters or our children's friends. If child abuse could happen to her, it could happen to anyone.

Media accounts of the Steinberg case attempted to distance the case from the middle-class mainstream. Steinberg was made to resemble a "Rasputin-like mad monk." Newspaper reports of his arraignment described him as being dressed with a black sport coat and slacks, but with no belt, no socks, and no tie. Nussbaum was treated for a broken jaw and fractured ribs and was seemingly cast in the role of the passive battered wife. Their apartment was described as dark and filthy. Newspaper reports also noted that drug paraphernalia, cocaine, and marijuana were found in the apartment.

The attention focused on intimate violence has illuminated a significant, tragic, and often deadly social problem. Attention has also generated public perceptions of the nature and causes of domestic violence that are often more conventional wisdoms and myths than facts or truth. The creation and perpetuation of these myths often serve a valuable social function. After hundreds of years of ignoring the problem of intimate violence, we are apparently still unable to face the true extent, patterns, and causes. While people are quite willing to attribute violence to mentally disturbed, unbalanced people, they are unwilling to see the violent home as an outgrowth of the very structure of our society and family. We willingly focus considerable attention on the most sensational and bizarre cases of violence—sexual abuse in day-care centers, children abducted by strangers, women who set fire to their husbands. By and large, we tend to think of abusers as people other than us. We believe that they are different, almost alien beings; victims are helpless, defenseless, innocents. This chapter explores the myths that have grown up around the topics of child abuse, wife abuse, and domestic violence.

THE WOOZLE EFFECT

A. A. Milne, in his popular children's book, *Winnie-the-Pooh*, describes how Winnie and Piglet go hunting and nearly catch a Woozle. One day Piglet observed Winnie walking around in circles. He called to him and asked what he was doing. Winnie replied that he was hunting. Winnie pointed to tracks on the ground. Piglet asked excitedly, "Do you think it's a Woozle?" Winnie began to walk, and then looked down, and, with a puzzled expression, noted that there seemed to be two sets of tracks now. Piglet joined Winnie, and they walked for a while, when suddenly Winnie noticed that there seemed to be three sets of tracks—the third one being smaller than the other two. They walked further around the tree, and then observed excitedly that there were now four sets of tracks. When Winnie and Piglet were worn from their tracking, they looked up in the tree they were under and saw Christopher Robin. Robin came down from the tree and explained the mystery of the Woozles. It seemed that Winnie had walked around the tree first looking for tracks, then finding his own, then finding two sets of his own. When Piglet joined in, he produced the third set. The Woozles were nothing more than their own tracks, repeated as they circled under the tree.

In the emotion-laden uncertainty of trying to study and help victims of family violence, we often construct our knowledge much in the same way that Winnie and Piglet track Woozles. There are indeed a growing number of Woozles in the study of domestic violence, and as we shall see in the next section, we often have built our "understanding" of the problem in much the same way that Winnie the Pooh hunted Woozles.

Myth 1: Family Violence: Rare or Epidemic

Public and professional attention to child abuse and wife abuse has skyrocketed since 1960. First child abuse, then wife abuse, and finally elder abuse became part of the public agenda. Social scientists have observed that one way a social issue becomes a social problem is for the public to become aware that the issue has a negative impact on a significant number of people. Thus, those who have studied intimate violence have expended considerable energy trying to measure and report on the extent of violence in the home. Sometimes their efforts have led to exaggerations, much in the same way Winnie and Piglet exaggerated how many Woozles they were tracking. For example, in 1962 Dr. C. Henry Kempe and his colleagues published their famous article, "The Battered-Child Syndrome" in the *Journal of the American Medical Association*. This article is viewed by nearly all professionals in the field as the benchmark of public and professional concern for child abuse. The article was accompanied by an editorial which said among other things, "it is likely that [the battered child syndrome] will be found to be a more frequent cause of death than such well recognized and thoroughly studied diseases as leukemia, cystic fibrosis, and muscular dystrophy." Soon after the publication of the editorial, politicians, journalists, and social activists began to quote it. First, the qualification, "it is likely" was dropped, then the quote was transformed to read that child abuse was the fifth most common killer of young children. The comparison between child abuse and other diseases has been repeated so often than it is accepted as fact.

A second example comes from our own work on wife abuse. In our first effort to study wife abuse we interviewed eighty families. At the time we were not sure how much violence occurred in the home, so we tried to find families in which a good chance existed that there was some violence between spouses. A private social service agency referred twenty couples to us. We obtained twenty more from a police department file of domestic disturbance and assault reports. In order to have a comparison group, we interviewed a neighbor of each family—thus forty neighbors were interviewed who had no public or private record of violence. Of the eighty families, 55 percent reported one instance of conjugal violence in the marriage. This was not unexpected, since half of the couples were selected because we thought they might be violent. Of the neighbors, about one in five were violent. It was the 55 percent figure, not the 20 percent estimate, that became widely cited in the public and professional literature. The statistic was cited without explanation or qualification. Most citations even failed to define violence, or worse, changed the term "violence" to "abuse." Finally, in 1977—a scant three years after we published the study—a trade book, titled *Wife Beating: The Silent Crisis*, written by the journalists Roger Langley and Richard Levy, reported that twenty-six to thirty million women were abused each year. The twenty-six to thirty million are roughly half of all married women. The Woozle had struck again.

A third example is the growth in official reports of child abuse. Because public attention has increased, there is the perception that the problem has increased. Thus, many researchers and social commentators have concluded that we are in the midst of an "epidemic of family violence."

Many people become confused over the various estimates of family violence that range from thousands to millions. There is a tendency to conclude that no one really knows how much violence there is in families. The political scientist, Barbara Nelson, in her book, *Making an Issue of Child Abuse*, explains that when experts provide widely varying estimates of the extent of child abuse, it is difficult to establish the legitimacy of the problem, allowing detractors to chip away at the claims for a place on the public agenda. In the end, the varying estimates from rare to epidemic probably result in many people concluding that the problem is not a problem at all, and that intimate violence is really not that extensive.

Myth 2: Abusers Are Aliens, Victims are Innocents

A number of years ago we were panelists on the David Susskind show. During the first hour and a half of the show Susskind interviewed six battered women from various parts of the country. Two were young and from blue-collar backgrounds, while the other four were in their thirties and from well-to-do households. Each described

the violence and abuse she had suffered over the years of her marriage. This was perhaps the first national television panel devoted to
wife battering, and David Susskind grew rather incredulous as the
interview progressed. Again and again he would ask, "But wasn't
your husband mentally disturbed?" Or, "aren't you convinced that
your husband was psychotic?" One woman explained that the husbands really were not mentally ill and that, had they been on the
show, they would have made most appealing guests. David Susskind
remained unconvinced and continued to press each woman as to the
mental status of her husband.

The enduring stereotype of family violence is that the abuser is
mentally disturbed or truly psychotic, and that the victim is a defenseless innocent. The typical reaction to a description of a case of
domestic violence or a photo of an abused woman or child is that
"only a sick person" would do such a thing. The stereotype is so
strong that unless the offender fits the profile of the mentally disturbed psychotic alien and the victim is portrayed as innocent and
defenseless there is a tendency not to view the event as abusive. Thus,
considerable public attention is focused on the most sensational
cases of intimate violence. Horrible torture of women and children,
sexual abuse in day-care centers, and the killing of babies and the
elderly make news not because they are unusual, but because they fit
the stereotype of what is family abuse.

We want to believe that the family is a safe, nurturant environment. We also do not want to see our own behavior, the behavior of
our friends, neighbors, and relatives as improper. Thus, most people
want to envision family violence as terrible acts, committed by horrible people against innocents. This allows us to construct a problem
that is carried out by "people other than us."

With the exception of a few television docudramas, the major
media support the portrayal of abusers as mentally disturbed aliens.
When we reviewed American fiction, television, and movies, we
found that family violence is infrequently portrayed. When violence
between family members is depicted, it almost always involves an act
committed by someone who is already a criminal (the violent son in
The Godfather), foreign (Andy Capp in the comic strip), or drunk
(Rhett Butler in Gone With the Wind). The media perpetuate the
message that normal people do not hit family members.

The theory that abusers are sick is often supported by a circular
argument. Some researchers note that one of the character disorders
that distinguishes child abusers is an "inability to control their

aggression." This seems a simple enough diagnosis. However, it is circular. How do we know that these people cannot control their aggression? Because they have abused their children. The abuse is thus the behavior to be explained and the means of explaining the behavior. When clinicians try to assess individuals without knowing whether or not they abused their offspring or spouses, they find that we can not accurately predict whether someone abused a family member based on his or her psychological profile. In fact, only about 10 percent of abusive incidents are caused by mental illness. The remaining 90 percent are not amenable to a psychological explanation.

Myth 3: Abuse Is Confined to Poor, Minority Families

All the research we have conducted, and the majority of the other clinical and survey investigations, find that intimate violence is more likely to occur in lower income or minority households. Official reports of child abuse and neglect include an overwhelming overrepresentation of the poor among reported abusers. Violence and abuse, however, *are not confined* to the poor or blacks. Middle- and upper-class parents and partners are violent. Japan's former Prime Minister Sato, a winner of the Nobel Peace Prize, was accused publicly of beating his wife. Aristotle Onassis, considered one the richest men in the world while he was alive, was accused of beating his mistress until he was forced to quit from exhaustion. The actor David Soul was profiled in *People* magazine as a former wife beater. The list of prominent wife beaters is quite long, yet not long enough to convince people that intimate violence occurs in all social groups.

We mentioned that the poor are overrepresented in official statistics on child abuse. In part, this is due to their greater likelihood of being violent. However, it is also due to the fact that the poor run the greatest risk of being accurately and inaccurately labeled "abusers." An injured child with poor parents is more likely to be labeled "abused" than a middle-class child with the same injuries. The sociologists Patrick Turbett and Richard O'Toole conducted an experiment with physicians and nurses. Each group was divided in half. One-half received a medical file that described a child, the child's injuries, and facts about the parents. Unbeknownst to the participants in the experiment, the files were systematically varied. For one-half of the subjects, the child's father was described as being a teacher, while the other half read that the father was a janitor. Even though the injury to the child was identical, the son of the janitor was more likely to be described as a victim of abuse than the son of the teacher. Turbett and O'Toole next kept the occupation and injury the same but varied the race of the child. Half of the subjects read that the child was black, while the other half had a file that described the child as white. The black children were more likely to be labeled as "abused."

Here again we see evidence that people want to see abuse as occurring in families "other than theirs." Seeing abuse as confined to poor or black families is yet another way people construct the acts of others as deviant and their own behavior as normal.

Myth 4: Alcohol and Drugs Are the Real Causes of Violence in the Home

When we first began our research on violence in the family we met with a number of police chiefs. We needed to get their assistance in locating families where the police had intervened in cases of domestic assault. We carefully justified our research and explained that we thought that if we could explain the causes of domestic violence we could aid the police in their work. The most frequent response of the police chiefs was that our research was not needed. They knew the real causes of child and wife abuse. The real cause was drinking.

The police chiefs' perceptions were accurate with regard to associations between drinking and violence. The research that we and others have conducted has found that almost half of all couples who engage in conjugal or parental violence report that it is associated with drinking by the one who is violent, by the victim, or both. Research on homicidal offenders has also found a high association between violence and alcohol.

Not only do the statistics bear out the perceptions of the police chiefs, so do the accounts of victims of family violence. Helen, the thirty-five-year old wife of a laborer, explains that the beatings occurred when her husband was drinking.

> When Larry was sober he was just the nicest person in the world. But when he was drunk . . . well, it was just like Dr. Jekyll and Mr. Hyde. He was irrational and ugly, and extremely violent to me and the kids. It was like living with two people, the nice and sober one and the drunk and evil one.

Again and again we have heard women and children tell us that the partners and parents would only be violent when they were drinking.

Nine out of ten times he hit me when he was drinking.

It was only when he was drinking . . .

When he had a couple of drinks under his belt he was the meanest son of a bitch in the world. He was really rough.

And, by and large, the victims believed that if the batterers' drinking problem was eliminated, the violence would stop.

Really, it was the liquor that was the cause of the whole problem. If he could have been treated, or counseled, or somehow just stopped drinking we would have had a happy life. I just know it because he was never abusive to me when he was sober. So, if the drinking had gone away, so would have the violence.

Although there is a consistent relationship between drinking and violence, it does not mean that alcohol is the *cause* of the violence. Those who believe that alcohol causes violent behavior base the belief on the notion that alcohol acts as a kind of "superego solvent." Drinking, the theory goes, breaks down people's inhibitions and leads to antisocial behavior. The evidence for this theory is that people behave differently when they are drinking than when they are sober.

There is a variety of evidence that undermines the explanation that it is the chemical property of alcohol which, when acting on the body, causes people to be violent. One important piece of evidence is an analysis of drinking patterns in various cultures. The analysis was conducted by the anthropologists Craig MacAndrew and Robert Edgerton and published in their book, *Drunken Comportment.* If it was the chemical property of alcohol that, when acting on the brain, made people violent, then drinking would lead to violence in cultures around the world. MacAndrew and Edgerton found that this was not the case. Drinking behavior was actually quite variable. In some societies people became violent and sexually promiscuous after drinking. In other cultures passivity and withdrawal were the typical drunken behaviors. MacAndrew and Edgerton argue that drunken comportment is situation-specific and essentially a learned affair. In our society, as well as many others, individuals learn that they will not be held responsible for their drunken behavior. There is in our culture, as MacAndrew and Edgerton learned, a "time-out" from the normal rules of behavior when people are drunk.

The "time-out" combines with a need to "hush up" or disavow responsibility for family violence. Thus, actually drinking (or claiming to be drunk) provides the perfect excuse for instances of domestic violence. "I didn't know what I was doing when I was drunk" is the most frequently heard excuse by those who counsel violent families. When women claim their husbands are like "Dr. Jekyll and Mr. Hyde" they are actually providing the excuse the husbands need to justify their violent behavior. In the end, violent parents and partners learn that if they do not want to be held responsible for their violence, they should either drink and hit, or at least say they were drunk.

A series of experiments conducted by the social psychologist Alan Lang and his colleagues, from Florida State University, put MacAndrew and Edgerton's findings to the test. Lang and his associates found that aggression was related to drinking only as a function of expectancy. In other words, the most aggressive individuals are those who think they are drinking alcohol, regardless of the actual content of the drinks!

Research by the psychologist Morton Bard also disputes the claim that alcohol causes violence. Bard noted, as have others, that about half of all men arrested for assaulting their wives claim to have been drinking at the time. However, when these same men are given blood tests, fewer than 20 percent have enough alcohol in their bloodstream to render them legally intoxicated.

Finally, our own investigations have discovered that it is moderate drinking that is most closely associated with domestic abuse. In our survey of family violence conducted in 1976 we found that individuals who never drank or got drunk often were the least abusive partners and parents.

Other drugs have been linked to violent behavior. The sociologist Howard Becker reports in his book, *Outsiders,* an instance where the U.S. commissioner of narcotics related an incident in 1937 in which an entire family was murdered by what the commissioner referred to as a "youthful marijuana addict." The police officers who arrived at the home found the youth staggering around in a "human slaughterhouse." He "seemed to be in a daze" with no recollection of what happened. The commissioner went on to note that the boy was ordinarily sane, but had recently taken up the habit of smoking marijuana.

More recently, the drug "crack" has been linked to family homicide. During the fall of 1986, a man walked into the Bridgeport,

Connecticut, city police headquarters and told detectives he had murdered the woman with whom he was living and her two children. The children, aged five and seven, had been stabbed numerous times. Their mother had been strangled. The man said he killed the three after using the drug, crack, a powerful derivative of cocaine, for two days.

As with discussion of the relationship between alcohol and violence, the topic of other drugs and their link to violent behavior is explosive and fact is often mixed with myth. One problem is that there are multiple drugs with varying physiological effects and equally varying social expectations for how these drugs affect human behavior.

Reviews of the different forms of drugs and their possible impact on violent behavior have found some consistent evidence. Opiates, such as heroin, are rarely associated with violence. Marijuana produces a euphoric effect. Contrary to the view of the U.S. commissioner of narcotics in 1937, Marijuana may actually reduce, not produce, violent behavior. Research on LSD also finds that the physiological effects of this drug are antithetical with violence. Amphetamine use, however, is quite another story. This is a drug that raises excitability and muscle tension. This may lead to impulsive behavior. The behavior that follows from amphetamine use is related to both the dosage and the pre-use personality of the user. High-dosage users who already have aggressive personalities are likely to become more aggressive when using this drug.

It is clearly difficult to establish a direct causal link between drug use and violence in the home. Type of drug, dosage, previous personality or character disorders, social setting, and social expectations all play a role in influencing the behavior of a substance user. Because of the ethical considerations that are involved in conducting research on drugs and violence, it is almost impossible to design a study that would disentangle all the possible factors that relate to drug use and violence.

Studies of nonhuman primates may help us understand the effect of certain drugs. The primatologists Neil Smith and Larry Byrd, of the Yerkes Regional Primate Research Center in Atlanta, Georgia, have studied the behavior of what they refer to as "captive group-living monkeys." The monkeys (stump-tailed macaques) were given a protocol of *d*-amphetamine and then observed. Those monkeys receiving the drug did increase in their aggressive behavior. Most remarkable, in terms of our concern with family violence, was that the aggression was more likely to be directed at kin-related monkeys than non-kin-related. More importantly it was the youngest kin monkeys who were the targets of the aggression. Smith and Byrd have applied their findings from nonhuman primate research to the human condition and estimate that perhaps as much as 5 percent of instances of physical child abuse are related to amphetamine use and abuse.

A single anecdotal case underscores the importance of Smith and Byrd's research, and the possible impact of amphetamine use on family violence. The book, *Fatal Vision,* tells the horrifying and grue-some story of Green Beret officer Dr. Jeffrey MacDonald who was convicted of the murder of his wife and two young daughters. The case captured public attention when MacDonald first claimed that the killings were committed by "drug-crazed hippies" in a copycat version of the Charles Manson cult murder of Sharon Tate. Nine years after the killings, it was MacDonald who was found guilty of bludgeoning to death his pregnant wife and two small daughters. It is almost incomprehensible that a husband and father would commit such a merciless crime. The book concludes with author Joseph McGinnis trying to make some sense of how the killings occurred. McGinnis draws a connection between the killings and MacDonald's use of pills to lose weight—amphetamines. Although one cannot make too much out of a single bizarre case of family violence, McGinnis's sorting of the case is consistent with the line of research that Smith and Byrd are pursuing that links amphetamine usage to violent behavior.

Except for the evidence that appears to link amphetamine use to violence, the picture of the alcohol- and drug-crazed violent individ-ual who lashes out impulsively at a wife and children is a distortion. If alcohol and other drugs are linked with violence at all, it is through a complicated set of individual, situational, and social factors.

One of the most unfortunate outcomes of accepting the myth of the drunk and drug-crazed abuser is the notion that curing the drug or alcohol problem would eliminate the violent behavior. Unfortu-nately, a large number of victims and even clinicians falsely raise hopes that treating substance abusers only for their substance abuse is also a treatment for the violence.

Myth 5: Children Who Are Abused Grow Up to Be Abusers

We are frequently called upon to lecture on the topics of child abuse, wife abuse, and family violence. At the end of each lecture we are usually approached by a number of individuals who have specific questions they would like to ask. On one occasion we were approached by a young man who was barely able to control his emotions. Tears were about to roll down his cheeks. Of all the speeches we have given, this was the only time someone came up to us in tears. "What seems to be the matter?" we asked. "Did we say something that disturbed you?" He responded by saying that he could not get married. We were puzzled. Our speeches evoked a range of responses, but this one was quite unlike any we had heard before. When we asked him what we had said that caused him to come to this conclusion, his response was, "You described the factors that were related to abuse. You said that people who are abused grow up to be abusers. Well, I was an abused child. I don't want to get married and grow up to abuse my children, so I will not get married!"

We had said that children who were abused *tend* to grow up to be abusive. But the young man, like many people who read or hear this statement, ignored the word "tend" and interpreted our statement to mean that *all* abusers grow up to be abusive.

There is absolutely no evidence to support the claim that people who are abused are *preprogrammed* to grow up to be abusers. Even the evidence that supports the claim that abused children tend to grow up to be abusers is blown out of proportion through countless repetition—much in the way Winnie and Piglet counted Woozles.

Myth 6: Battered Women Like Being Hit

Perhaps the cruelest of all the myths surrounding family violence is the one that claims that battered women like being hit. Common sense seems to argue that battered women should just pack up and leave if they want to escape abuse. If they do not leave, then they must somehow like abuse. The columnist Mike Royko once argued against the city of Chicago funding a shelter for battered women. Royko felt that a shelter would be a waste of taxpayers' money since the logical solution to women battering—women leaving their abusive husbands—was free.

There is another assumption about battered women that underlies the myth that they stay because they must somehow like being hit. A more sinister view of battered women is that they must do something to provoke their abuse, and therefore they deserve to be beaten.

Battered women have always failed to attract the same attention and sympathy directed toward abused children. Because women are not generally viewed as helpless innocents, the fact that they will remain with an assaultive partner is either viewed as a sign of their culpability or masochism. An examination of the dynamics of family violence and the social position of women in our society not only explodes the myth that battered women like being hit, but also details the conflicting double bind in which victims of wife abuse live day in and day out.

The increased attention to the problem of domestic violence has led people to assume that *all* victims of violence and abuse suffer unhappy and unfortunate consequences for life. The physicians Barton Schmitt and C. Henry Kempe claim that if abused children went untreated they would grow up to become the delinquents, murderers, and batterers of the next generation of children. Other researchers have suggested that battered children grow up to have higher rates of drug and alcohol abuse, criminal behavior, and psychiatric disturbances. So, too, battered women are thought to become depressed, deranged, or even suicidal. The public prognosis for victims of sexual abuse is especially pessimistic. Victims of sexual abuse are thought to suffer from a wide range of psycho/social/sexual dysfunctions.

There is every reason to believe that violence and abuse are harmful. At the moment it is almost impossible to predict how harmful it is. The 20/20 benefit of hindsight often allows us to find abuse and neglect in the background of someone who is emotionally disturbed or violent as an adult. However, researchers have not yet designed and carried out research on the consequences of abuse and violence that meets the normal standards of scientific evidence. Thus, while we have many clinical anecdotes about the consequences of child or wife abuse, we cannot precisely state what the actual chances are that a given victim will grow up to be a killer, delinquent, emotionally disturbed, or perfectly normal.

Myth 7: Violence and Love Are Incompatible

Most people find it difficult to believe that a battered child or a battered wife could still have some feelings for his or her attacker. In general, people tend to find love and violence incompatible. Thus, the truly unique and sad aspect of intimate violence is that violence is experienced by people who profess love for one another. We need to understand that many battered women have strong feelings for their partners. Most battered children, despite some fairly horrible beatings, still love their parents.

That violence and love can actually coexist in families is perhaps the most insidious aspect of intimate violence because it means that, unlike violence in the streets, we are tied to our abusers by the bonds of love, attachment, and affection. It is no wonder battered women do not automatically leave violent men, or that children suffer emotionally when they are taken from their abusive homes. Perhaps the greatest challenge to understanding intimate violence and devising adequate social policy is to see violence and love as coexisting in the same relationship.

It is difficult to abandon the simplistic thinking that leads to the creation and perpetuation of myths and conventional wisdoms. It is not only the myths that have to be abandoned, but the social function that they serve. The greatest function served by the seven myths we have discussed is that collectively they serve as a smokescreen that blinds us to our own potential for violence. Moreover, when our explanations focus on "kinds of people"—mentally disturbed, poor, alcoholics, drug abusers, etc.—we blind ourselves to the structural properties of the family as a social institution that makes it our most violent institution with the exception of the military in time of war.

3.

From Spankings to Murder:

Defining and Studying

Intimate Violence

United States Supreme Court Justice Potter Stewart once said about pornography that he could not define it, but that "I know it when I see it." One would think that behavior such as violence would be easy to define, and certainly easier to recognize, than something as subjective as pornography. On the contrary, our experience has been that violence, and especially abuse, are extremely difficult concepts to define. Even victims of severe violence and abuse do not always recognize it as such.

Lois is a thirty-five-year-old mother of three children. Her experiences are not atypical. Lois has been hit often, perhaps one or two times each year over the course of her fifteen-year marriage. She has never considered herself a "battered wife" and does not even view the times she was hit as violent episodes:

Now, as I look back, I think Jim [her husband] has pushed me or slapped me a couple of times. I don't recall that he ever really hurt me. I think maybe I have had a bruise or two, but never something as bad as a black eye. You see, Jim doesn't really have a bad temper. He's not really gentle, but not rough either. But sometimes, we get to fighting and he might push me, grab me, or even slap me. Once I think he punched me. But, he's not a violent man.

Others also tend not to define what they experience as violence. Richard, a thirty-eight-year-old lawyer, talked freely about his childhood. He characterized his childhood as a happy one, and had warm feelings for both his parents, who were still alive:

> I do recall that both my mother and father hit me. I guess they mostly spanked me, but I don't recall how often. I do remember some of the times they were really angry with me. I remember that my mother tried to hit me with her shoe. She threw a pot at me one time when I teased my brother. My father wasn't around too much, so he didn't get too involved in the discipline. Once, though, he did get real mad and I remember that he used his belt on my bottom. I guess it hurt. I don't remember how it felt, but I sure remember how mad he was. He had a real strange look in his eyes.

Not surprisingly, those who do the hitting often see their behavior as quite normal. They certainly do not define what they do as violent. Tim was a twenty-three-year-old college student when we interviewed him. He candidly discussed how, when, and why he hit his wife:

> I have hit her on occasion. I have slapped her face or hit her arm. I do have to slap her in the face a few times just to get her to shut up—of course, it's not what you might think. It's not an argument or in anger. But sometimes, especially when she has something go wrong with the kids, she just falls to pieces. She'll just fall apart. She doesn't know what to do. She goes wild, you see, and then I have to hit her to get her to calm down. It's not that I am mad at her. I am not trying to hurt her because of something she has done. I am trying to knock her to her senses, more or less. I just have to slap her to calm her down.

We need not spend a great deal of time illustrating how parents view the use of physical punishment. It goes without saying that spanking children is about as common, and viewed as equally normal, as Pampers. Parents have told us again and again that their kids "need to be hit" or "deserve to be hit."

Simply stated, the more normal hitting is perceived to be, the more the people doing the hitting and being hit view the act as legitimate, normal, and useful, the less likely those persons are to define the behavior as "violent." The public shares the view that so-called normal hitting is not violent. We found that it is difficult to arouse an indifferent public to viewing acts other than the most sensational and outrageous as violent. In our own research, we have always viewed violence as a continuum, beginning with slaps, grabs, and spankings, and extending up to murder. Yet, we are frequently criticized that such a broad definition dilutes our message and the possible impact of our research and recommendations. For our part, we think such criticisms are not only incorrect, but potentially harmful. Claiming that only outrageous and unusual acts represent violence serves to license the more normal slaps, spankings, and pushes. As we have said again and again, violence is possible if we fail to define it as wrong or improper. And, as we have found, permitting the so-called "normal" acts of violence sets the stage for a possible escalation to the more harmful and dangerous behaviors.

WHAT IS VIOLENCE AND ABUSE?

The earliest and most enduring problem in the study of child abuse, wife abuse, and family violence has been the development of useful, clear, acceptable (and accepted) definitions of "violence" and "abuse." Neither violence nor abuse is easily defined. Offenders' views differ from those of victims. Agents of social control (i.e., police or social workers) may have different perceptions than participants. Friends, neighbors, and bystanders offer additional perspectives. A key first question is whether or not one can reasonably and effectively differentiate spankings from shootings. Is it possible to differentiate force from violence?

Force and Violence

Is a spanking violent? Is it the same as punching, kicking, stabbing, or shooting someone? Is there some kind of line we could draw to distinguish between spankings and shootings? If one could draw a line, would it be based on the intent of the act, the consequence of the act, or some combination of both?

Our view is that it is impossible to differentiate between force and violence. Rather, all violent acts—from pushing and shoving to shooting and stabbing—properly belong under a single definition of violence.

Fifteen years ago, when we began our first survey of violence in the American family, we stated that violence was an act carried out with the intention, or perceived intention, of causing physical pain or injury to another person. The physical pain could range from the slight pain of a slap to murder. "Intent to hurt" can range from concern with a child's safety and welfare, as when a mother spanks a child who runs into the street, to hostility so intense that the victim's death is desired.

As we noted earlier, there are those who criticize this definition as being so broad that it dilutes the important message of our research. Implicit in this criticism is the notion that researchers, clinicians, and policy makers should only concentrate on severe and possible deadly beatings and burnings that occur in families.

In reality, true insight into the nature of domestic violence requires us to shed our stereotypes and blinders about routine spankings, normal pushings, and seemingly harmless grabbings, and to see these acts as part of the problem of intimate violence.

Abuse

In their seminal article, "The Battered-Child Syndrome," Kempe and his coauthors defined the "battered-child syndrome" as a clinical condition (meaning that diagnosable medical and physical symptoms existed) involving those who have been deliberately injured by a physical assault. Kempe's definition of abuse, which set the stage for the way in which abuse would be defined and studied for a decade, was restricted only to acts of physical violence that produce diagnosable injuries.

As the study of child abuse expanded, discussions of how to define abuse increased in scope and intensity. No conference on child abuse was complete without one or more sessions set aside to produce a definition of child abuse. Far from producing a clear definition, the discussions muddied the already turbid water. One set of debates focused on consequences. Did an act by a parent or caretaker have to produce an injury for it to be defined as abuse? The social policy expert and noted researcher on child abuse, David Gil, responded to this question anecdotally. Gil was the father of twin sons. As a response to the question about consequences, Gil posed another question. "Suppose," he said, "I hold one of my twin sons in each hand. I then throw them to the ground. The son in my right hand falls onto the concrete floor and fractures his skull. The son I hold in my left hand falls on a carpet and is not injured. Am I a right-handed abuser only?" Gil's question forced those in the field of child abuse to recognize that diagnosable injury was not the sine qua non of a

definition of abuse. Parents could inflict cruel and harsh treatment
on their children without necessarily producing a diagnosable clinical condition. Physicians and social workers were quick to recognize
that depending on diagnosable injury as the necessary and sufficient
condition by which to define an act as abuse would mean always
having to react to abuse. For the definition to be useful, it had to
allow diagnosis in advance of injury.

In general, most definitions of abuse require that the act be intentional. Our own definition of violence included the provision that
the act be intentional, or perceived as intentional. Intent, however, is
an internal state, and not readily or objectively measured. Are the
following instances examples of child abuse?

A small boy spills his milk on his father's new and expensive stereo
system. The system short-circuits. The father intends to slap the child
as punishment. As he moves to hit the child, the child turns. The blow
strikes the child's eye, severely injuring the eye.

A father takes his four-month old son to a neighborhood bar. The
father cannot get a baby-sitter that night, and he also wants to show
the child off to his friends. At the bar he shows off by tossing the child
in the air. Above the father is a ceiling fan. On one toss the child is
struck by the fan, severely lacerating the child's head.

The first case could be defined as abuse. Although a severe injury
was not the intent, the father did intend to strike the child and inflict
at least some pain. If we were to absolve parents from abuse because
they did not intend to cause the degree of pain or injury that resulted,
there would be few cases of abuse remaining to be treated.

The second case is more difficult. The father had no intention of
hurting his child. Yet, he clearly did not show wise judgment in
taking an infant to a bar and tossing it in the air. There are child
abuse experts who would agree that the father did not intend to
cause an injury, yet, the father's inability to properly protect the child
would lead many clinicians to label the father an abuser.

The third debate focuses on whether abuse is limited to acts of
physical violence. Henry Kempe did confine his classic definition of
the battered child syndrome to injuries caused by physical assault.
However, it was not long after Kempe published his article that
social service personnel began to argue quite strongly that physical
injury was not the only injury children suffered. Children are starved,

sent outdoors into freezing weather with inadequate clothing, deprived of medical attention and the opportunity for an education, medicated and sedated needlessly, subjected to cruel mental and emotional abuse, and are sexually victimized by adult caretakers.

The National Center on Child Abuse and Neglect defines child abuse as

> the physical or mental injury, sexual abuse, negligent treatment, or maltreatment of a child under the age of eighteen by a person who is responsible for the child's welfare under circumstances which indicate that the child's health or welfare is harmed or threatened thereby. (Public Law 93-237.)

David Gil takes this formal definition much further. For Gil, abuse is any acts of commission or omission by a parent or an individual, an institution, or by society as a whole which deprive a child of equal rights and liberty, and/or interfere with or constrains the child's ability to achieve his or her optimal developmental potential.

It is tempting to think that the years of debate and discussion have resulted in a conclusive definition of child abuse. Such is not the case. Debate still rages over the issues of consequence and intent. The broadening of the definition has produced as many problems as it has solved. For example, in the mid-1970s, after all fifty states had adopted definitions of child abuse that were similar to the definition provided by the National Center on Child Abuse and Neglect, a young child was removed from her home by child welfare authorities in a southern state. The authorities argued that the child was a victim of abuse because she was being forced to live in a depraved environment. The environment was labeled depraved because the child's mother was cohabiting with a man to whom she was not married.

Twenty years of discussion, debate, and action have led us to conclude that there will never be an accepted or acceptable definition of abuse, because abuse is not a scientific or clinical term. Rather, it is a political concept. Abuse is essentially any act that is considered deviant or harmful by a group large enough or with sufficient political power to enforce the definition. Abuse is a useful term for journalists who want to capture the attention of their readers or viewers. It is a useful political term because it carries such a strong pejorative connotation that it captures public attention. Unfortunately, there is no one set of objective acts that can be characterized as abusive. What is defined as abuse depends on a process of political negotiation. What is now considered child abuse and wife abuse is the product of a twenty-year effort to educate clinicians, policy makers, and the public about what acts and actions are harmful to women, children, and other family members.

Although there is typically consensus that certain physical acts are harmful, even here there is debate. On the one side of the debate are those who feel, as we do, that any act of violence, including a slap or a spanking, is harmful. On the other side are those who believe that sparing the rod spoils the child and that not using physical discipline is harmful to the welfare of children. With regard to sexual abuse, some feel that sexual acts with minor children who are not able to give informed consent are harmful irrespective of the physical or emotional consequences. Others claim that such sexual activity is actually beneficial to children and helps provide them with a healthy introduction to sex and sexuality. Defining neglect also produces debate and dissension that sometimes ends up in court. Each year there are a number of instances where Christian Scientist parents engage in battle with medical authorities over treatment of a dependent child. Some parents have had their parental rights terminated in order that physicians might be permitted to administer drugs or transfusions to ill children.

The newest and most recent battle emerged over treatment of newborns with severe medical disabilities. The classic case is that of Baby Jane Doe. Baby Jane Doe was born in 1983 on Long Island, New York, with spinabifida. Baby Doe's condition involved three major birth defects: an abnormally small head, an incomplete enclosure of the spine, and excess fluid on the brain. Baby Jane Doe's parents sought medical advice, and after receiving conflicting opinions, decided against corrective surgery. Without the surgery Baby Jane Doe would live for perhaps two years. With it she might live for two decades, but severely physically and mentally retarded. A Vermont right-to-life activist sued to force the surgery. The case was thrown out of a state appellate court. The federal government intervened, arguing that withholding surgery might violate the infant's civil rights. A federal judge ruled for the parents' decision against the surgery. That child abuse is a political concept was then underscored when Congress modified the definition of child abuse in 1984 to include instances of withholding of food or medical treatment from handicapped infants under the definition of abuse. Ultimately, even that definition was ruled unconstitutional and deleted from the Child Abuse Prevention and Treatment Act.

A final testimony to the politics of defining abuse is the raging debate over abortion. On one side is the so-called pro-life contingent which argues that abortion is child murder. On the other side are the pro-choice groups, the authors included, which believe that restricting access to abortion is an abuse of women in general and often results in the birth of unwanted children who run a very high risk of abuse and maltreatment.

We have found that a precise study of a political concept such as abuse is impossible. An intensive examination of the definitions of child abuse and neglect carried out by the social welfare researchers Jean Giovanonni and Rosina Becerra presented a series of vignettes to professionals and members of the public. Not surprisingly they found considerable variation in the behaviors defined as abuse across the various professional groups surveyed. Definitions of abuse also varied by race, social class, and occupation.

Although we have and will use the term "abuse," our proposed solution to the definitional problem is to focus on specific, definable acts of omission and commission that are harmful to individuals in families. Thus, our nearly twenty years of research and writing have focused on acts of physical violence. However, acts of physical violence do not exhaust the forms of family maltreatment.

FORMS OF VICTIMIZATION

The primary focus of this book is on violence toward wives and children. Many people believe that women and children are the only victims of intimate violence. Others believe that if young children and women are not the only victims, they are at least the more common victims. Neither point of view is correct. In point of fact, the most common form of intimate violence is between siblings. The most difficult to treat may be the abuse of the elderly. The most overlooked may be the violence directed at parents by their adolescent children. There is considerable consensus that violence toward women and children is a genuine social problem. Why and how this is the case will be examined at length in chapter 5. The purpose of this section is to briefly identify other forms of domestic violence and speculate on why they have yet to capture public attention as social problems.

Hidden Victims

Sibling Violence. Violence between siblings is the most common and most commonly overlooked form of family violence. It is perhaps so

much a part of family relations that this alone can explain why it is
overlooked. We expect a certain amount of sibling rivalry in families.
Moreover, we perhaps encourage such rivalry as a means of preparing our children for the dog-eat-dog competitive world in which they
will struggle as adults. As a result, we have developed a set of expectations and social norms which maintain that "boys will be boys"
and "kids will fight." Most parents view conflict between siblings as
an inevitable part of growing up.

The sociologist Suzanne Steinmetz was the first person to systematically examine violence between siblings. She had some difficulty
persuading parents to discuss sibling violence—not because they
were embarrassed or thought such violence wrong, but because it
was so routine they did not think it worth mentioning. One question
did seem to elicit comment. When Steinmetz asked, "How do your
children get along?" the responses were quick to follow:

"Terrible, they fight all the time!"

"Oh it [the fighting] is constant, but I understand that this is
normal."

Sibling violence is certainly not new. Cain's killing of Abel in the
Bible establishes the biblical dating of sibling rivalry and abuse. Our
own national survey of family violence measured how extensive sibling violence was. More than eight out of ten parents surveyed who
had two or more children at home between the ages of three and
seventeen said that there was at least one incident of sibling violence
in the previous year. This translates into more than thirty-six million
individual acts of sibling violence each year. Although most of these
incidents consisted of slaps, pushes, kicks, bites, and punches, there
was some fairly dangerous violent behavior occurring as well. Three
siblings in one hundred used weapons toward a brother or sister.
Extrapolated to children in the United States, this means that more
than a hundred thousand children annually face brothers or sisters
with guns or knives in their hands.

Teenage Victims. Although infants and preschoolers are frequent
targets of physical violence, abuse is not limited to very young children. Teenagers and very young children actually have the same high
rates of victimization. Since "helplessness" is often a criterion of who
is and is not considered a victim, it is not surprising that teenage
victims are among the missing persons of the official child abuse
reports compiled by each state. Teenage victims are not only victims
of physical violence, but of "victim blaming" as well. A three-month-

old victim of child abuse cannot be held responsible for provoking his or her parent. However many observers believe that teenagers precipitate or provoke their own victimization by outrageous or provocative behavior.

Parent Victims. One the other side of the coin of adolescent abuse are those parents of teenage children who are beaten and abused by their children. Most people assume that because mothers and fathers are typically larger than their children and command most, if not all, of the family's social and economic resources, they are immune to violence at the hands of their children. Such, however, is not the case. Clinicians have identified some severe and grievous injuries caused by children. The physician Henry Harbin and his colleague Dennis Madden report an instance in which an eleven-year-old boy became violent after being spanked by his mother. The child pushed his mother down, broke her coccyx, and then kicked her in the face while she was on the floor. The sociologist Carol Warren studied fifteen adolescents who were admitted to a psychiatric hospital. Although some of the children, as young as twelve years old, lacked physical strength, they more than compensated in speed and choice of weapons. One twelve-year-old poured gasoline in the bathroom while his mother was in there, threw down a match, and shut the door.

Our own survey of family violence found that almost one in ten parents reported that they had been hit at least once by one of their children. These figures include considerable biting and kicking done by young children. If we look only at children older than eleven years of age, we find that approximately 3 percent of parents report being victimized at least once by a severe form of violence. This translates into nearly 900,000 victims of serious violence each year.

Victims of parent abuse often find few services and little support in the community. Unless a child kills or maims a parent, it is unlikely that the child's violent behavior will come to public attention. There is a vicious cycle that is responsible for the lack of community and professional services. Parents are often ashamed to talk about the abuse they experience at the hands of their children. By and large, this is because they fear that if they talk about their victimization at home, they will be publicly victimized. Many of the parents to whom we talk report that they feel they will be blamed for their child's violent behavior. As a result, parents of abusive children suffer from tremendous anxiety, depression, and guilt that keep them psychological prisoners in their own home. Terrified of their violent children and fearful that they will be publicly blamed for their children's behavior, they cower at home. As a result, virtually no social or legal programs have been set up for battered parents. One battered parent whom we know has been trying to establish a support group for fellow victims. Although the victims have talked about their abuse on the telephone, thus far (and after six years of effort) no one has actually come forward for a meeting of the proposed support group.

Harbin and Madden note that victims of parent abuse establish a "veil of denial." Such parents try to avoid discussing violent episodes. If they do talk about the violence, they minimize the seriousness of the behavior, they avoid punishment for the abusive behavior, and they refuse to ask for outside help for themselves or their child. Sadly, the veil of denial only serves to license the child's violent behavior and perpetuate this form of hidden intimate violence.

Elder Abuse. The only form of hidden violence that has managed to emerge briefly from behind the closed doors of the violent home has been elder abuse. The aging of the population has resulted in increased concern for the problems of the elderly. The elderly receive recognition because a higher proportion of the elderly vote in local and national elections than other age groups.

Although the physical abuse and neglect of the elderly have received attention, the actual recognition and treatment of victims has been a difficult task. Unlike younger victims, older victims of family violence tend not to be linked to many social networks such as schools or work settings. Thus, the elderly are among the most isolated victims of violence, and their injuries may be shielded from public view. If a six-year-old is malnourished, it is likely to be recognized by someone in school. If the same child is tied to a chair in the home, someone from school may notice the child is missing. Malnourished elderly may be confined to the home without anyone but their abuser observing.

Identification of abuse victims is also hindered by the victim's unwillingness to report or confirm the abusive incident. A study of the reporting of elder abuse conducted by Legal Research and Services for the Elderly of Boston found that only one in four cases of abuse was reported by the victim. Victims of abuse are reluctant to report their victimization for a number of reasons. First and foremost, the most likely victims are infirm and suffer from physical and mental impairment. They may be incapable of reporting their cases or even leaving the home. Those who retain their physical and mental faculties may fear that they will be blamed for their own victimization. As with parent abuse, there is a tendency to blame parents for the behavior of the children. Victims may also fear retaliation from their attacker. Lastly, victims may accept abuse and neglect rather than the perceived risks of alternative living arrangements. Although most elderly are probably at greater risk from friends and relatives, there is the general belief among older victims of intimate violence that institutional care is the worst of all possible settings.

There are varying estimates of the extent of elder abuse—ranging from 500,000 cases per year to more than two million. The most recent and reliable study of the extent of elder abuse was carried out by the sociologists Karl A. Pillemer and David Finkelhor. Surveying more than two thousand elderly people living on their own in the Boston area, Pillemer and Finkelhor found that three in one hundred older Americans are victims of physical or verbal abuse each year. This means that between 700,000 and 1.1 million older Americans are subject to abuse. In all likelihood, the actual extent is more than this, since many victims may not have reported their situation to the researchers, and because the researchers did not study older Americans living in institutions. Surprisingly, nearly two-thirds of the victims were abused by their spouses, while less than one-fourth were abused by their children.

Experts feel that the most likely victim of elder abuse is a female of advanced age—eighty years old or older. As we noted earlier, victims tend to be those who suffer from physical and/or mental impairments. While many researchers also believe that increased dependency of older Americans makes them vulnerable to abuse, Karl Pillemer has found that it is the dependency of the abusive relative that leads to maltreatment. Abusers are more often than not the middle-aged daughters of the victims.

Courtship Violence. Most Americans tend to have romantic and nostalgic visions of dating and courtship. Moonlight cruises, the first kiss, flirtations and affections, and the occasional broken heart are all part of the American way of dating and courting. Unfortunately, so are hitting, beating, and abuse. A variety of studies of dating and violence find that between twenty-two and sixty-seven percent of dating relationships involve some kind of violence. While pushes, slaps, and shoves are the most common forms of violence, punches, kicks, and beatings have also been reported by victims. Researchers have found courtship violence among college students as well as among high-school daters.

The saddest aspect of courtship violence is its acceptability. The sociologist June Henton and her colleagues reported that more than one-fourth of the victims and three out of ten offenders interpreted violence in a dating relationship as a sign of love. This is a scary extension of the elementary school—yard scenario in which a little boy hits a little girl and she interprets his behavior as an indication of affection. Not only do love and violence coexist in intimate relationships, but apparently we are training our children to believe that love and violence should go together in intimate relationships.

Sexual Victimization

The physical abuse of family members is but one dimension of intimate victimization. A second dimension, one which until recently was the deepest, most emotional taboo in society, is the sexual abuse and misuse of family members.

The Sexual Abuse of Children. All societies have prohibitions against sexual relations between close family members. What is defined as close varies from society to society, but nearly every society prohibits sex between parents and their children. Yet, despite the taboos and prohibitions, sex between fathers and daughters, mothers and sons, and other adult members of households and dependent children does occur.

Kempe defined sexual abuse as "the involvement of dependent and developmentally immature children and adolescents in sexual activities that they do not fully comprehend, to which they are unable to give informed consent, or that violate social taboos of family roles." Implicit in this definition is that a child can be sexually victimized without sexual intercourse occurring.

As with the debate over whether a spanking is violent, there has emerged an intense and often furious debate over what is or is not sexual abuse. On one side of the debate are those who argue that any use or manipulation of a dependent child for purposes of sexual gratification of the adult is abusive. On the other side are those who feel that such a broad definition is abusive to adults. An editorial in *The New Republic* (May 13, 1985) begins with the provocative statement: "Have you hugged your child today? Careful, it's a trick question." The editorial cites a publication from the National Committee for Prevention of Child Abuse which stated that "excessive fondling" can be considered sexual abuse. The editorial makes two points: first, parents may be unfairly and unnecessarily accused of sexual abuse of their children; second, children may be made excessively anxious about touching and possible victimization at the hands of parents, teachers, baby-sitters, and strangers.

Social scientists, while trying to systematically study and draw attention to social problems, can be guilty of the kinds of excesses alluded to by *The New Republic*. The "accurate" definition of sexual abuse is somewhere between the broad "excessive fondling" and the most narrow view that only violent, forced sexual intercourse is abusive. David Finkelhor states that an appropriate definition of sexual abuse refers to activities involving the genitals that are for the gratification of at least one person.

The taboo against sex with children and the general unwillingness to discuss sexuality served to keep child sexual abuse hidden until quite recently. Its emergence as a social problem led to a general concern for the welfare of children. By the late 1970s there was an explosion of official reports of sexual abuse. The American Humane Association recorded nearly 2,000 reports of sexual abuse in 1976. The number of reports more than doubled to 4,327 in the next twelve months. There was a fivefold increase in the next five years, with more than 22,000 reports recorded in 1982. The Child Welfare League of America reported another significant jump in reporting of 59 percent between 1983 and 1984.

Official reports of sexual abuse reveal only the number of cases of abuse that come to public attention. It is likely that the massive increase in reporting reflects an increase in public awareness of sexual abuse and that it is not a symptom of an epidemic of abuse in America. It is also likely that only a fraction of the true number of cases of sexual victimization of children are coming to public attention, even with the increase in public awareness.

Various studies of sexual abuse of children reveal different estimates of the extent of the problem. The sociologist Diana Russell surveyed a representative sample of women in San Francisco and asked about sexual victimization as children and adults. Russell found that 28 percent of the 930 San Francisco women she surveyed reported victimization before the age of fourteen. Victimization was defined as experiencing unwanted sexual touching. Twelve percent of those sampled had been victimized by a relative. David Finkelhor surveyed college students and reported that 19 percent of all females and 9 percent of the males surveyed reported sexual victimization. Kinsey's famous survey of sexual behavior revealed that 9 percent of the more than four thousand females interviewed mentioned sexual contact with an adult before the age of fourteen.

There are many estimates and guesstimates of the extent of sexual abuse; however, there has yet to be a national survey that meets the normal standards of scientific evidence and can be used to determine a figure for frequency of sexual victimization of children. Assessing all the studies to date, Finkelhor suggests that perhaps as many as one in ten girls and two in one hundred boys are sexually abused before they are eighteen. This would mean that about 210,000 new cases of abuse occur each year in the United States.

Marital Rape. Children are not the only family members who are sexually victimized. Wives, too, are coerced and physically forced to engage in sexual acts with their husbands. It has been extremely difficult to assess the extent and nature of acts that we would normally call rape because most state rape laws specifically exclude forced sex between husband and wife from the rape statute. The so-called marital exclusion of rape has meant that women could not prosecute their husbands for forcing them to engage in sex. Moreover, the marital exclusion probably prevents women from seeing forced sex in marriage as a case of rape. We have interviewed many wives who have had forced sex with their husbands, but few defined the incident as rape.

> He thought I was a cold fish. He told everyone that I was frigid. Well, I suppose I was cold. I mean, after all, he would come home after being out the whole night and he was drunk and reeking of beer. I didn't feel like it [sexual intercourse]. But he wanted it. We didn't argue. He just got his way.

Violence and the threat of violence may also be part of forced sex in marriage.

> He put a shotgun to my head and told me that if I didn't have oral sex with him that the barrels of the gun were the last thing I would ever see. I believed him.

A handful of researchers have tried to study rape in marriage. Their task has been made somewhat easier by the increased publicity given to rape in marriage. Perhaps the first nationwide attention occurred when an Oregon housewife named Greta Rideout attempted to prosecute her husband for rape. John Rideout was acquitted, but the trial raised questions about whether a man has the right to rape his wife. Somewhat less sensational than the Rideout trial, but more effective, have been the efforts of women's groups across the country to overturn the marital exclusion in state rape statutes. Today, according to the National Clearinghouse on Marital Rape in Berkeley, California, twenty-eight states and the District of Columbia allow a husband to be prosecuted for rape even while he lives with his wife. Twenty-one states allow for prosecution if the partners are living apart, and one state, Alabama, retains the marital exclusion for married partners, irrespective of where they live.

David Finkelhor and Kersti Yllo interviewed 323 Boston-area women for their book, *License to Rape: Sexual Abuse of Wives*. Ten percent of the women said they had been forced to have sex with their husbands or partners. Violence accompanied the rape in about half of the instances. Diana Russell's survey in San Francisco was used as the basis of the estimate of marital rape published in her book, *Rape in Marriage*. Russell reports that 14 percent of the 644 married women reported one or more experiences of marital rape. Other investigators place the incidence between 3 and 10 percent of married women surveyed. If one adds all the additional instances in which wives are forced to engage in sexual acts they find objectionable, the extent of sexual victimization in marriage is much higher.

Emotional Abuse

The most hidden, most insidious, least researched, and perhaps in the long run most damaging form of intimate victimization may be the emotional abuse of loved ones. Defining physical or sexual abuse is relatively easy compared to the formidable task of setting forth what constitutes emotional abuse. Belittling, scorning, ignoring, tearing down, harping, criticizing, are all possible forms of emotional abuse. Such abuse takes many forms and the scars, while not always evident, tend to show through in discussions with victims of emotional battering. Tracy is a thirty-three-year-old woman with a husband and two children. She spoke to us in a soft, almost inaudible monotone about her husband.

> He rarely says a kind word to me. He is always critical. The food is too cold or it's too hot. The kids are too noisy. The house is a mess. I am a mess. He says I spend too much money and then complains that

I look like I got dressed in a used-clothing store. He says I am too fat or too skinny. No matter what I do he says it isn't any good. He tells me I am lucky he married me 'cause no one else would have me.

Sometimes the torment is more subtle than a direct verbal attack. One woman we interviewed told us how her husband bought gifts for his girlfriend. He brought the gifts home, showed them to his wife, and then said he would return after delivering the gifts—all this while the family was on welfare.

Children bear the brunt of emotional batterings that range from direct verbal attacks to outright brutal acts of cruelty. Many parents call their children dumb, stupid, fat little cows without so much as a thought to the effect of such taunts on the child. Other parents have destroyed children's toys or favorite objects. Some have gone further. We have talked with two young women each of whom told us that when her father was angry with her he killed her favorite pet. One girl told how her father put her dog out in twenty-below-zero-degree weather, and the dog froze to death. The other told of how her father killed a pet rabbit and then gutted the rabbit at the kitchen table while the young child watched silently.

There is little doubt that direct or indirect attacks on one's self-concept leave deep and long-lasting scars. Many of the people we talk to tell us that the physical scars of family violence fade, but the emotional wounds fester beneath the surface forever.

No one really knows how much emotional abuse exists in families. We know from our surveys that verbal violence almost always accompanies physical violence and abuse. Thus, there are no fewer victims of emotional abuse than there are victims of physical abuse. But the true extent may be many more times that of physical violence. We suspect that one reason so little research on emotional abuse has been conducted is that so many of us are guilty of occasional or even frequent emotional attacks on loved ones that the behavior is too close and too common to allow for objective research. Emotional abuse is not a case of "there but for the grace of God go I." Rather, as the late cartoonist Walt Kelly said so eloquently in his comic strip Pogo, "We have met the enemy and he is us."

Neglect

Acts of neglect represent the final form of intimate victimization. By and large, neglect is generally an act of omission rather than a physical act of commission. Parents may fail to adequately feed, clothe, or supervise their children. On a more passive level, parents may simply and completely be psychologically unavailable to their children, leaving their children psychological isolates in a complex and harsh world. As we noted earlier, acts of neglect include failing to properly seek and obtain medical treatment for an ill child. Medical neglect can also include acts of commission such as when a parent improperly medicates a child. Some overstressed parents have resorted to tranquilizing their children in order to calm them down. In other cases, some parents engage in the rather bizarre practice of Munchausen Syndrome by proxy and make their children sick, perhaps by injecting human feces into the children, so as to attract attention to their own problems.

The great dilemma in applying the term neglect to acts of omission or commission by parents is determining whether the parents neglected their children by choice, or simply did not have the financial or material resources to do better. It is certainly one thing to deliberately starve a child or fail to provide adequate clothing. However, many children suffer malnutrition because their parents simply do not have the resources to purchase food. It is not uncommon for families to fall through the cracks of the social service system and for their children to pay the price. In these cases society, not parents, is responsible for the harm done.

Again, as with emotional abuse, there are few adequate statistics that can be used to estimate how common neglect is. Our own best guess is that child neglect is about twice as frequent as are acts of physical abuse. This means that perhaps one in eleven children, or about four to five million children each year, suffers from some form of child neglect.

STUDYING INTIMATE VIOLENCE

The study of family violence is often governed more by the heart than the head. Emotions run high among those who have the responsibility for serving, treating, protecting, or understanding victims of violence and abuse. Because there is so much tragedy, anger, frustration, and ultimately cynicism involved in working with violent families, rational thought and logic are often left behind. The myths and woozles we identified in the second chapter of this book are nurtured by the emotional nature of the field.

When considering knowledge and facts about intimate violence, it is not enough to ask a researcher or clinician, "What do you know?" It is important also to ask, "How do you know it?" One constantly has to check and cross-check alleged statements of fact and truth against how well the statements meet the normal rules of logic and scientific evidence.

This final section of the chapter examines the various sources of information we have about the extent, nature, causes, and consequences of private violence. We look at the three major sources of information—clinical case records, official report data (police records or child abuse reports), and social surveys—and assess the advantages and disadvantages of each. In short, we will discuss how we know what we think we know about violence in the home.

Clinical Case Records

The earliest sources of information about battered children and battered wives were the clinical cases of psychiatrists, physicians, psychologists, and counselors. Pioneering studies of child abuse and wife abuse were based exclusively on an analysis of a handful of cases seen by clinicians either in their private practices or in a hospital or institutional setting. Henry Kempe's first article on the battered child syndrome was based on his experience with clinical cases of abuse at the Colorado Medical Center. The first published article on wife abuse was Leroy Schultz's 1960 paper, "The Wife Assaulter." Schultz selected four cases for analysis from a clinical caseload of fourteen spouse assaulters. Another clinical investigation was the 1964 article, "The Wifebeater's Wife: A Study of Family Interaction," written by John Snell, Richard Rosenwald, and Ames Robey. The clinic in which the authors worked has seen thirty-seven men charged with wife assault between 1957 and 1964. The authors studied twelve of the families, seeing both husbands and wives.

An office or hospital as a clinical setting provides ready access to victims and offenders. Researchers do not have to worry about the need to ask embarrassing questions such as, "Do you beat your wife?" The sad and graphic evidence of such beatings is readily apparent. Clinical data contain an abundance of medical, psychological, and social data about the families. Since the families tend to come back to the clinical setting, clinicians are able to follow violent couples or parents over a period of time. John Snell and his colleagues saw twelve families involved in wife abuse for three or more interviews. Four battered wives were followed for more than eighteen months.

The advantages of the wealth of information available in clinical settings are offset by significant disadvantages of such data. First and foremost, clinical case data are typically based on a rather small number of cases. Physicians Brandt F. Steele and Carl B. Pollock based one of the first published articles on the battered child syndrome on fifty-seven cases of abuse. The social welfare expert Elizabeth Elmer studied fifty families in her first examination of child abuse and neglect. The first two journal publications on battered women were based on clinical data on twelve victimized women and fourteen battering husbands.

In addition to small numbers of cases, clinical case data are quite selective. A number of books and articles on battered women have been based on data obtained from women who seek protection in shelters. The average shelter houses between ten and twenty women at a time. However, the ten to twenty women are far from a cross section of the population. A shelter in a predominantly black neighborhood is unlikely to attract many middle-class white victims. Where a shelter is located and how its services are publicized will determine the social characteristics of the women who seek refuge. It would be a mistake to assess the social characteristics of women in a shelter and use these data to generate a profile of battered women. Yet, this mistake is frequently made by researchers who gather data on battered women from shelters. Similarly, many studies of battered children draw data from clinical cases admitted to hospital emergency rooms. Since emergency room patients tend to be from lower social class groups, a profile of child batterers based on emergency room case records would be misleading.

In short, clinical data are rich in the quantity and quality of information. They cannot, however, be used to generalize information on the frequency of factors associated with private violence or the representativeness of the findings or conclusions. It is not uncommon for those who base their research on clinical data to totally lose sight of the forest while they fully and carefully examine the nature of a select sample of the trees.

Perhaps the major drawback of clinical studies is that they often fail to employ comparison groups; or if comparison groups are used, inappropriate cases are selected for comparison. If an investigator focuses only on cases of child or wife abuse and fails to include nonabusive families in his or her study, the researcher has no way of knowing whether the traits observed in the violent families are related to abuse, or whether the same traits occur with the same frequency in nonviolent families. A famous example of this problem is the theory of the "extra Y chromosome." During the late 1960s some researchers noticed that a number of men who had been convicted of violent crimes or confined to institutions for the criminally insane had an extra Y chromosome. Normal women have two XX chromosomes while the normal male has an X and a Y chromosome. The so-called extra Y chromosome was thought to generate "super-male syndrome," which could include more secondary sex characteristics—body hair, size, strength—as well as more aggressiveness. Clinical investigations focused on specific men who had the extra Y chromosomes and found many of them to be especially aggressive. A number of books and texts on violence note that Richard Speck, the man convicted of brutally murdering nine Chicago nurses in 1968, was an XYY male. Speck, it turned out, did not have the extra Y chromosome.

Unfortunately, few of the studies of the XYY chromosome males included comparison groups of nonviolent men in the research design. When Saleem Shah, the former chief of the National Institute of Mental Health Center for Studies on Antisocial and Violent Behavior, examined the theory of the extra Y chromosome, he concluded that, widespread publicity notwithstanding, there was no conclusive evidence that XYY males are more aggressive than a matched group of XY males.

The problems with clinical studies do not mean that such studies are useless, or that the results should not be taken seriously. Clinical studies are important because they often offer the only means of answering certain questions. One cannot test the effectiveness of specific treatments or interventions without using a clinical sample. The psychologist Lenore Walker's research on women who seek shelter provides us with rich data about these women. Data on the most severely battered women and children are only available from clinical studies. However, these data need to be read with caution since they do not pertain to all families who experience violence.

Official Statistics

Between 1965 and 1970 all fifty states enacted laws mandating the reporting of suspected child abuse and neglect. Reporting laws and the resulting central child abuse registries were manifestly designed to ensure that all children at risk come to public attention so they can be protected. The latent consequence of the child abuse reporting laws is that a large data base of officially reported and validated cases of child abuse became available for research and analysis.

Child abuse is not only tabulated at the state level; the American Humane Association has also been collecting and analyzing the state data for the last decade. The federal government fielded its own national examination of officially reported cases of child maltreatment in the late 1970s. There has not been a tradition of officially recording incidents of spouse abuse. Until recently there were few localities or states that recorded spouse abuse. In 1976 the state of Kentucky instituted an adult protection statute that mandated the reporting of any individual known or suspected of adult abuse, neglect, or exploitation. The statute was amended in 1978 to specifically include spouse abuse. Today, three states collect such data. Official report data provide useful information on an extremely large number of cases. The American Humane Association received more than one million reports of child maltreatment in 1984.

The major limitation of official report data is that the information is limited to only cases that come to official public attention, which represent only the tip of the iceberg of the problem of family violence. Moreover, official report data are biased in terms of who is reported, what is reported, and by whom it is reported. We have previously discussed the problem that poor minority families are more likely to be reported as abusers. Thus, official report data are useful for telling us about the personal and social factors that lead people to be publicly labeled "abusers" and "abused." Such data are not helpful in assessing the factors that actually cause violence and abuse.

Finally, official data are biased in terms of whose reports are given most consideration. We had an unusual opportunity to examine the child abuse registry for the state of Florida. Florida was the first state to institute a statewide telephone reporting system which included a twenty-four hour WATS line. The state also mounted an effective media campaign to spur reporting of child abuse and neglect. We examined reports that were considered valid and those that were classified invalid. Shortly after our study the state of Florida purged all invalid reports from the system. We assessed the type of reported abuse, the social characteristics of the alleged abuse victim and abuse, and the social characteristics of the person who filed the report. Surprisingly, type of abuse was unrelated to determination of validity. So, too, the characteristics of the abuser and victim were unrelated to classification of the report as valid by the state after an investigation. The only factor related to validity was the reporting party. If the report was filed by a professional, such as a physician, the chances were increased that the investigation would lead to a categorization of the case as valid. If the report was filed by a non-professional, friend, neighbor, or if it was anonymously reported, the incident was unlikely to be found valid. It is likely that many cases of serious abuse escape the attention and files of overworked protective service agencies because they are reported by sources not considered reliable.

Social Surveys

Twenty-five years ago researchers derived their knowledge either from clinical studies or from the scattered official statistics that were available on such as data on homicide. The criminologist Marvin Wolfgang studied data on criminal homicide in Philadelphia. He found that nearly a fourth of all the murders that occurred between 1948 and 1952 involved members of the same family in the roles of victim and offender. No one had carried out, or even thought plausible, the collection of information by conducting social surveys—interviews or questionnaires.

Three major hurdles were thought to stand in the way of survey research on family violence. First there was the problem of actually locating individuals who were involved in incidents of intimate violence. It was assumed that child abuse and wife abuse were rare. Accordingly many social scientists thought that it would be extremely difficult to identify a case of family violence outside of a clinical setting. Even if one could find an offender or a victim, there was no guarantee that an investigator could persuade the person to talk about violence in the home. One could count on one hand the number of researchers who wanted to ask the question, "Have you stopped beating your wife?" And no one believed that a researcher would receive a truthful answer to such a question anyway.

Private violence was not the only, or the first, taboo topic social researchers attempted to investigate. Sex researchers were also warned that few people would give them truthful answers. Yet Kinsey, Masters and Johnson, Shere Hite, and others successfully fielded large-scale surveys of sexual behavior. The sociologist Laud Humphreys was able to interview people about their homosexual behavior. Numerous social scientists have used survey research to study criminal behavior, and the National Institute of Justice surveys criminal victimization in the population each year.

We cleared the first hurdle by using the most accessible population available to us—the students enrolled in our classes. We passed out the first questionnaires on family violence to hundreds of our students. Later we identified families at risk of violence with the help of both a social welfare agency and a local police department. Finally, we surveyed large segments of the population using the techniques of representative sampling (for a complete view of our studies of family violence, see Appendix A). We overcame the second hurdle by developing the Conflict Tactics Scales. These scales asked subjects about various ways families went about trying to deal with conflicts in the home. Thus, rather than ask "have you ever abused your child?" we presented a list of various conflict tactics, ranging from calm discussion to abusive violence.

For all its virtues, survey research has some important limitations. These limitations, reviewed in detail in Appendix A, include limits on the amount of data that can be collected, biases in terms of which people are included and excluded by using survey sampling techniques, and biases arising from which individuals are willing to report on a questionnaire and which are willing to tell an interviewer.

There is no one best way of collecting information on intimate violence. For most of this book we rely on the data we collected in our surveys. Yet, many times we rely on information from official reports and clinical studies to make a point or provide a detailed look into the lives of violent families. In assessing results from the many studies of family violence, we have put the greatest faith in findings and conclusions that are confirmed by all three sources of information on family violence.

We often speak of child abuse, wife abuse, spouse abuse, or family violence as if it were a single generic phenomenon. Our discussion of the problems of defining words such as violence and abuse and our review of the many and varied forms of family victimization clearly illustrate that there is no one type of intimate violence and victimization.

The emotional nature of intimate violence pushes professionals and the public alike toward simple answers. Unfortunately the heart is not always logical, rational, or even particularly accurate. Researchers, clinicians, policy makers, and educated citizens need to be informed, critical consumers of the knowledge presented and the solutions proposed for dealing with abuse, violence, and victimization in the American family. Being informed means being aware of the strengths and limitations of different sources of information, and asking how well the information meets the normal standards of scientific evidence.

4.

Profiling

Violent Families

Each incident of family violence seems to be unique—an uncontrolled explosion of rage, a random expression of anger, an impulse, a volcanic eruption of sadism. Each abuser seems a bit different. The circumstances never seem to be the same. In one home a child may be attacked for talking back to a parent, in another the precipitating incident may be a broken lamp. Wives have been beaten because the food was cold, because the house was cold, because they were cold.

If we reject the notion that violence and abuse are the products of mental illness or intraindividual pathologies, than we implicitly accept the assumption that there is a social pattern that underlies intimate abuse. The public and the media recognize this underlying pattern. Perhaps the most frequently asked question by the press, public, and clinicians who treat cases of domestic abuse is, "What is the profile of a violent parent, husband, wife, family?" We mentioned in the opening chapter that humans have an innate desire for social order. They want to live in a predictable world. Even though violence in the home is more socially acceptable than violence in the street and thus, to a degree, more orderly, people still want to know what to look for. What are the signs, indicators, predictors of a battering parent, an abusive husband?

A profile of intimate violence must include at least three dimensions. First, we need to examine the social organization of families in general that contributes to the risk of violence in the home. Second, we review the characteristics of families in particular that make certain families high risk for violence. Third, we discuss the temporal and spatial patterns of intimate violence—where and when violence is most likely to occur.

VIOLENCE AND THE SOCIAL ORGANIZATION OF THE FAMILY

The myth that violence and love do not coexist in families disguises a great irony about intimacy and violence. There are a number of distinct organizational characteristics of the family that promote intimacy, but at the very same time contribute to the escalation of conflict to violence and injury. Sometimes, the very characteristics that make the family a warm, supportive, and intimate environment also lead to conflict and violence.

The time we spend with our family almost always exceeds the time we spend at work or with nonfamily members. This is particularly true for young children, men and women who are not in the work force, and the very old. From a strictly quantitative point of view, we are at greater risk in the home simply because we spend so much time there. But, time together is not sufficient to lead to violence. What goes on during these times is much more important than simply the minutes, hours, days, weeks, or years spent together.

Not only are we with our parents, partners, and children, but we interact with them over a wide range of activities and interests. Unless you live (and love) with someone, the total range of activities and interests you share are much narrower than intimate, family involvements. While the range of intimate interactions is great, so is the intensity. When the nature of intimate involvement is deep, the stakes of the involvement rise. Failures are more important. Slights, insults, and affronts hurt more. The pain of injury runs deeper. A cutting remark by a family member is likely to hurt more than the same remark in another setting.

We know more about members of our family than we know about any other individuals we ever deal with. We know their fears, wants, desires, frailties. We know what makes them happy, mad, frustrated, content. Likewise, they know the same about us. The depth of

knowledge that makes intimacy possible also reveals the vulnerabilities and frailties that make it possible to escalate conflict. If, for
instance, our spouse insults us, we know in an instant what to say to
get even. We know enough to quickly support a family member, or
to damage him. In no other setting is there a greater potential to
support and help, or hurt and harm, with a gesture, a phrase, or a
cutting remark. Over and over again, the people we talk to point to
an attack on their partner's vulnerabilities as precipitating violence:

> If I want to make her feel real bad, I tell her how stupid she is. She
> can't deal with this, and she hits me.

> We tear each other down all the time. He says things just to hurt me
> —like how I clean the house. I complain about his work—about how
> he doesn't make enough money to support us. He gets upset, I get
> upset, we hit each other.

> If I really want to get her, I call her dirty names or call her trash.

We found, in many of our interviews with members of violent families, that squabbles, arguments, and confrontations escalate rapidly
to violence when one partner focused on the other's vulnerabilities.
Jane, a thirty-two-year-old mother, found that criticizing her husband's child-care skills often moved an argument to violence:

> Well, we would argue about something, anything. If it was about our
> kids I would say, "But you shouldn't talk, because you don't even
> know how to take care of them." If I wanted to hurt him I would use
> that. We use the kids in our fights and it really gets bad. He [her
> husband] doesn't think the baby loves him. I guess I contribute to that
> a bit. When the baby start's fussin' my husband will say "Go to your
> mom." When I throw it up to him that the baby is afraid of him,
> that's when the fights really get goin'."

It is perhaps the greatest irony of family relations that the quality
that allows intimacy—intimate knowledge of social biographies, is
also a potential explosive, ready to be set off with the smallest fuse.
  The range of family activities includes deciding what television
program to watch, who uses the bathroom first, what house to buy,
what job to take, how to raise and discipline the children, or what
to have for dinner. Whether the activities are sublime or ridiculous,
the outcome is often "zero-sum" for the participants. Decisions and

decision making across the range of family activities often mean that one person (or group) will win, while another will lose. If a husband takes a new job in another city, his wife may have to give up her job, while the children may have to leave their friends. If her job and the children's friends are more important, then the husband will lose a chance for job advancement or a higher income. While the stakes over which television station to watch or which movie to go to may be smaller, the notion of winning and losing is still there. In fact, some of the most intense family conflicts are over what seem to be the most trivial choices. Joanne, a twenty-five-year-old mother of two toddlers, remembers violent fights over whether she and her husband would talk or watch television:

> When I was pregnant the violence was pretty regular. John would come home from work. I would want to talk with him, 'cause I had been cooped up in the house with the baby and being pregnant. He would just want to watch the TV. So he would have the TV on and he didn't want to listen to me. We'd have these big fights. He pushed me out of the way. I would get in front of the TV and he would just throw me on the floor.

We talked to one wife who, after a fight over the television, picked the TV up and threw it at her husband. For a short time at least, they did not have a television to fight over.

Zero-sum activities are not just those that require decisions or choices. Less obvious than choices or decisions, but equally or sometimes more important, are infringements of personal space or personal habits. The messy wife and the neat husband may engage in perpetual zero-sum conflict over the house, the bedroom, and even closet space. How should meals be served? When should the dishes be washed? Who left the hairbrush in the sink? How the toothpaste should be squeezed from the tube and a million other daily conflicts and confrontations end with a winner and a loser.

Imagine you have a co-worker who wears checkered ties with striped shirts, who cannot spell, whose personal hygiene leaves much to be desired. How likely are you to: (1) tell him that he should change his habits; (2) order him to change; (3) spank him, send him to his room, or cut off his paycheck until he does change? Probably never. Yet, were this person your partner, child, or even parent, you would think nothing of getting involved and trying to influence his behavior. While the odd behavior of a friend or co-worker may be cause for some embarrassment, we typically would not think of trying to influence this person unless we had a close relationship with him. Yet, family membership carries with it not only the right, but sometimes the obligation, to influence other members of the family. Consequently, we almost always get involved in interactions in the home that we would certainly ignore or make light of in other settings.

Few people notice that the social structure of the family is unique. First, the family has a balance of both males and females. Other settings have this quality—coeducational schools, for instance. But many of the social institutions we are involved in have an imbalance of males and females. Some settings—automobile assembly lines, for instance—may be predominantly male, while other groups—a typing pool, for instance—may be almost exclusively female. In addition to the fact that intimate settings almost always include males and females, families also typically include a range of ages. Half of all households have children under eighteen years of age in them. Thus the family, more so than almost any other social group or social setting, has the potential for both generational and sex differences and conflicts. The battle between the sexes and the generation gap have long been the source of intimate conflict.

Not only is the family made up of males and females with ages ranging from newborn to elderly, but the family is unique in how it assigns tasks and responsibilities. No other social group expects its members to take on jobs simply on the basis of their age or their sex. In the workplace, at school, and in virtually every other social setting, roles and responsibilities are primarily based on interest, experience, and ability. In the home, duties and responsibilities are primarily tied to age and gender. There are those who argue that there is a biological link between gender and task—that women make better parents than men. Also, the developmental abilities of children certainly preclude their taking on tasks or responsibilities that they are not ready for. But, by and large, the fact that roles and responsibilities are age- and gender-linked is a product of social organization and not biological determinism.

When someone is blocked from doing something that he or she is both interested in and capable of doing, this can be intensely frustrating. When the inequality is socially structured and sanctioned within a society that at the same time espouses equal opportunity and egalitarianism, it can lead to intense conflict and confrontation. Thus, we find that the potential for conflict and violence is especially high in a democratic and egalitarian society that sanctions and supports a male-dominated family system. Even if we did not have values that supported democracy and egalitarianism, the linking of task to gender would produce considerable conflict since not every man is capable of taking on the socially prescribed leadership role in the home; and not every woman is interested in and capable of assuming the primary responsibility for child care.

The greater the inequality, the more one person makes all the decisions and has all the power, the greater the risk of violence. Power, power confrontations, and perceived threats to domination, in fact, are underlying issues in almost all acts of family violence. One incident of nearly deadly family violence captures the meaning of power and power confrontations:

> My husband wanted to think of himself as the head of the household. He thought that the man should wear the pants in the family. Trouble was, he couldn't seem to get his pants on. He had trouble getting a job and almost never could keep one. If I didn't have my job as a waitress, we would have starved. Even though he didn't make no money, he still wanted to control the house and the kids. But it was my money, and I wasn't about to let him spend it on booze or gambling. This really used to tee him off. But he would get the maddest when the kids showed him no respect. He and I argued a lot. One day we argued in the kitchen and my little girl came in. She wanted to watch TV. My husband told her to go to her room. She said, "No, I don't have listen to you!" Well, my husband was red. He picked up a knife and threw it at my little girl. He missed. Then he threw a fork at her and it caught her in the chin. She was bloody and crying, and he was still mad and ran after her. I had to hit him with a chair to get him to stop. He ran out of the house and didn't come back for a week. My little girl still has a scar on her cheek.

You can choose whom to marry, and to a certain extent you may chose to end the marital relationship. Ending a marital relationship, even in the age of no-fault divorce, is not neat and simple. There are social expectations that marriage is a long-term commitment—"until death do us part." There are social pressures that one should "work on a relationship" or "keep the family together for the sake of the children." There are also emotional and financial constraints that keep families together or entrap one partner who would like to leave.

You can be an ex-husband or an ex-wife, but not an ex-parent or an ex-child. Birth relationships are quite obviously involuntary. You cannot choose you parents or your children (with the exception of adoption, and here your choices are still limited).

Faced with conflict, one can fight or flee. Because of the nature of family relations, it is not easy to choose the flight option when conflict erupts. Fighting, then, becomes a main option for resolving intimate conflict.

The organization of the family makes for stress. Some stress is simply developmental—the birth of a child, the maturation of children, the increasing costs of raising children as they grow older, illness, old age, and death. There are also voluntary transitions—taking a new job, a promotion, or moving. Stress occurring outside of the home is often brought into the home—unemployment, trouble with the police, trouble with friends at school, trouble with people at work. We expect a great deal from our families: love, warmth, understanding, nurturing, intimacy, and financial support. These expectations, when they cannot be fulfilled, add to the already high level of stress with which families must cope.

Privacy is the final structural element of modern families that makes them vulnerable to conflict, which can escalate into violence. We analyzed family privacy at length in the opening chapter of this book. The nuclear structure of the modern family, and the fact that it is the accepted norm that family relations are private relations, reduces the likelihood that someone will be available to prevent the escalation of family conflict to intimate violence.

We have identified the factors that contribute to the high level of conflict in families. These factors also allow conflicts to become violent and abusive interchanges. By phrasing the discussion differently, we could have presented these factors as also contributing to the closeness and intimacy that people seek in family relations. People who marry and have families seek to spend large amounts of time together, to have deep and long-lasting emotional involvement, to have an intimate and detailed knowledge of another person, and to be able to create some distance between their intimate private lives and the interventions of the outside world.

There are a number of conclusions one can draw from the analysis of the structural factors that raise the risk of conflict and violence in the family. First, there is a link between intimacy and violence. Second is the classic sociological truism—structures affect people. Implicit in the discussion of these factors is that one can explain part of the problem of violence in the home without focusing on the individual psychological status of the perpetrators of violence and abuse. Violence occurs, not just because it is committed by weird, bad, different, or alien people, but because the structure of the modern household is conducive to violent exchanges.

FAMILY AND INDIVIDUAL CHARACTERISTICS RELATED TO INTIMATE VIOLENCE

The structural arrangement of the family makes it possible for violence to occur in all households. However, not all homes are violent. A profile of intimate violence needs to analyze the characteristics of violent individuals and their families.

Volumes could be written inventorying the characteristics that are thought to be related to family violence. The earliest students of child and wife abuse focused on individual personality characteristics. Abusers were described as sadomasochistic, having poor emotional control, self-centered, hypersensitive, dependent, egocentric, narcissistic, and so on. Later, those who studied violence and abuse examined social and social psychological factors such as income, education, age, social stress, and social isolation. Other investigators focused on experience with and exposure to violence. Still others chose to study violence from the point of view of the family level of analysis, examining family size, family power, and family structure.

Sometimes investigators agree on specific characteristics that are believed to be associated with violence; other times the findings are contradictory. There is one thing that researchers agree on—there are a multitude of factors associated with violence in the home. Despite public clamor for a single-factor explanation, no one factor —not mental illness, not experience with violence, not poverty, not stress, and not alcohol or drugs—explains all or most acts of intimate violence.

Abusive Violence Toward Children

Most people who try to explain and understand individual acts of deviant or aberrant behavior such as child abuse immediately turn their focus on the perpetrator. Our culture has a definite "indiviudal level" bias when it comes to trying to explain seemingly unexplainable acts. When someone does something outrageous, weird, or bizarre, our immediate reaction is to look for the answer within that individual. A full understanding of abusive violence, however, requires an examination of not only the violent parent, but the child and family situation.

If one had to come up with a profile of the prototypical abusive parent, it would be a single parent who was young (under thirty), had been married for less than ten years, had his or her first child before the age of eighteen, and was unemployed or employed part-time. If he or she worked, it would be at a manual labor job. Studies show that women are slightly more likely to abuse their children than men. The reason is rather obvious: Women typically spend more time with children. But, even if mothers and fathers spend equal time with children (and this is rare), it is the woman who is typically given the responsibility of caring for and dealing with the children.

Economic adversity and worries about money pervade the typical violent home. Alicia, the thirty-four-year-old wife of an assembly-line worker, has beaten, kicked, and punched both her children. So has her husband Fred. She spoke about the economic problems that hung over their heads:

> He worries about what kind of a job he's going to get, or if he's going to get a job at all. He always worries about supporting the family. I think I worry about it more than he does. . . . It gets him angry and frustrated. He gets angry a lot. I think he gets angry at himself for not providing what he feels we need. He has to take it out on someone, and the kids and me are the most available ones.

We witnessed a more graphic example of the impact of economic stress during one of our in-home interviews with a violent couple. When we entered the living room to begin the interview we could not help but notice the holes in the living room walls. During the course of the interview, Jane, the twenty-four-year-old mother of three children, told us that her husband had been laid off from his job at a local shipyard and had come home, taken out his shotgun, and shot up the living room. Violence had not yet been directed at the children, but as we left and considered the family, we could not help but worry about the future targets of violent outbursts.

Stressful life circumstances are the hallmark of the violent family. The greater the stress individuals are under, the more likely they are to be violent toward their children. Our 1976 survey of violence in the American family included a measure of life stress. Subjects were asked if they had experienced any of a list of eighteen stressful events in the last year, ranging from problems at work, to death of a family member, to problems with children. Experience with stress ranged from households that experienced no stressful event to homes that had experienced thirteen of the eighteen items we discussed. The average experience with stress, however, was modest—about two stressful life events each year. Not surprisingly, the greater the number of stressful events experienced, the greater the rate of abusive violence toward children in the home. More than one out of three families that were unfortunate enough to encounter ten or more stressful events reported using abusive violence toward a child in the previous year. This rate was 100 percent greater than the rate for households experiencing only one stressful incident.

Violent parents are likely to have experienced or been exposed to violence as children. Although this does not predetermine that they will be violent (and likewise, some abusive parents grew up in nonviolent homes), there is the heightened risk that a violent past will lead to a violent future.

One of the more surprising outcomes of our first national survey of family violence was that there was no difference between blacks and whites in the rates of abusive violence toward children. This should not have been the case. First, most official reports of child abuse indicate that blacks are overrepresented in the reports. Also, blacks in the United States have higher rates of unemployment than whites and lower annual incomes—two factors that we know lead to higher risk of abuse. That blacks and whites had the same rate of abusive violence was one of the great mysteries of the survey. A careful examination of the data collected unraveled the apparent mystery. While blacks did indeed encounter economic problems and life stresses at greater rates than whites, they also were more involved in family and community activities than white families. Blacks reported more contact with their relatives and more use of their relatives for financial support and child care. It was apparent that the extensive social networks that black families develop and maintain insulate them from the severe economic stresses they also experience, and thus reduce what otherwise would have been a higher rate of parental violence.

Most of the cases of child abuse we hear about involve very young children. There is nothing that provokes greater sadness and outrage than seeing the battered body of a defenseless infant. The youngest victims evoke the most sympathy and anger, best fit the stereotype of the innocent victim, and are more likely to be publicly identified as victims of abuse. The youngest children are indeed the most likely to be beaten and hurt.

However, the myth that only innocents are victims of abuse hides the teenage victim. Teenagers are equally likely to be abused as children under three years of age. Why are the youngest children and teenagers at the greatest risk of abusive violence? When we explain why the youngest children are likely victims the answer seems to be that they are demanding, produce considerable stress, and cannot be reasoned with verbally. Parents of teenagers offer the same explanation for why they think teenagers as a group are at equally high risk.

Among the younger victims of violence and abuse, there are a number of factors that make them at risk. Low birth weight babies, premature children, handicapped, retarded, and developmentally disabled children run high life-long risk violence and abuse. In fact, the risk is great for any child who is considered different.

If you want to prevent violence and abuse, either have no children or eight or nine. This was the somewhat common sense outcome of our research on family factors related to violence toward children. It is rather obvious that more children create more stress. Why then did we find no violence in the families with eight or nine children? Perhaps people who have the largest families are the kindest, most loving parents. Perhaps they are simply exhausted. A more realistic explanation is that, at a certain point, children become resources that insulate a family from stress. A family with eight or nine children probably did not have them all at once. With a two- or three-year gap between children, a family with eight or more children has older children at home to help care for and raise the infants, babies, and toddlers. If there is a truly extended family form in our society, it is the large family with children ranging from newborn to twenty living in the home.

A final characteristic of violent parents is that they are almost always cut off from the community they live in. Our survey of family violence found that the most violent parents have lived in their community for less than two years. They tend to belong to few, if any, community organizations, and have little contact with friends and relatives. This social isolation cuts them off from any possible source of help to deal with the stresses of intimate living or economic adversity. These parents are not only more vulnerable to stress, their lack of social involvement also means that they are less likely to abandon their violent behavior and conform to community values and standards. Not only are they particularly vulnerable to responding violently to stress, they tend not to see this behavior as inappropriate.

Abusive Violence Between Partners

Dale, wife of a Fortune 500 executive, wrote us so that we would know that wife beating is not confined to only poor households. Her husband beats her regularly. He has hurled dishes at her, thrown her down stairs, and blackened her eyes. When her husband drinks, she often spends the night huddled in the backseat of their Lincoln Continental. Marion lives so far on the other side of the tracks, she might as well be on another planet. She and her husband live five stories up in a run-down tenement. Heat is a luxury that they often cannot afford, and when they can afford it, the heat rarely works. Marion's husband has broken her jaw and ribs, and has shot at her on two occasions. The range of homes where wife beating occurs seems to defy categorization. One can pick up a newspaper and read of wife beating in a lower-class neighborhood and then turn the page and read that the wife of a famous rock musician has filed for divorce claiming she was beaten.

If there is a typical wife beater, he is not a rock musician, actor, football player, or business executive. The typical beater is employed part-time or not at all. His total income is poverty level. He worries about economic security, and he is very dissatisfied with his standard of living. He is young, between the ages of eighteen and twenty-four —the prime age for violent behavior in and out of the home—and has been married for less than ten years. While he tries to dominate the family and hold down what he sees as the husband's position of power, he has few of the economic or social resources that allow for such dominance; not only does his neighbor have a better job and earn more money than he does, but often so does his wife.

Researchers have found that status inconsistency is an important component of the profile of the battering husband. An example of status inconsistency occurs when a man's educational background is much higher than his occupational attainment—a Ph.D. who drives a taxicab for a living. Status inconsistency can also result when a husband does not have as much occupational or educational status as his wife. Researchers Carton Hornung, Claire McCullough, and Taichi Sugimoto report that, contrary to what is generally believed, violence is less common when the wife is at home then when she works. They suggest that status inconsistency explains this finding.

Husbands, they note, can be more threatened when their wives work and have an independent source of income and prestige than when they are home and dependent. Conflict and verbal aggression are frequent occurrences in the wife beater's home. Verbal violence and mental abuse are also directed at his spouse. Perhaps the most telling of all attributes of the battering man is that he feels inadequate and sees violence as a culturally acceptable way to be both dominant and powerful.

There is a great tendency to blame the victim in cases of family violence. Battered women have frequently been described as masochistic. The debate over such presumed masochism has raged to the point where a substantial group of psychologists have called for elimination of the diagnostic category "masochist" from the revision of DSM-III, the official description of psychological diagnostic groupings.

There is not much evidence that battered women as a group are more macochistic than other women. There are, however, some distinct psychological attributes found among battered women. Victims of wife beating are often found to be dependent, having low self-esteem, and feeling inadequate or helpless. On the other hand, battered wives have been found to be aggressive, masculine, and frigid. In all likelihood these contradictory findings are the result of the fact that there is precious little research on the consequence of being battered, and the research that has been conducted frequently uses small samples, without comparison groups. This makes generalizing from such research difficult and contradictory findings inevitable.

Another problem with assessing the psychological traits of battered women is the difficulty in determining whether the personalities were present before the battering or were the result of the victimization. We will look at the question of the psychological and social aftermath of wife beating in greater detail in part 2.

Pregnant women often report being beaten. Pregnancy, however, does not make women vulnerable to violence and battering. When we analyzed the results of the Second National Family Violence Survey we found that age, not pregnancy, is the best predictor of risk of wife beating. Women between the ages of eighteen and twenty-four are more likely to be beaten, whether they are pregnant or not. Women older than twenty-four years of age are less likely to be beaten.

Although pregnant women are not more vulnerable to violence, the nature of the violent attack does appear to change when a

woman is pregnant. One of the first interviews we ever conducted
still stands out in our minds. The subject was a thirty-year-old
woman who had been beaten severely throughout her marriage. The
beatings were more severe, and took on a different tone, when she
was pregnant: "Oh yeah, he hit me when I was pregnant. It was
weird. Usually he just hit me in the face with his fist, but when I was
pregnant he used to hit me in the belly."

Perhaps the most controversial finding from our 1975 National
Family Violence Survey was the report that a substantial number of
women hit and beat their husbands. Since 1975 at least ten additional investigations have confirmed the fact that women hit and
beat their husbands. Unfortunately, the data on wife-to-husband
violence have been misreported, misinterpreted, and misunderstood.
Research uniformly shows that about as many women hit men as
men hit women. However, those who report that husband abuse is
as common as wife abuse overlook two important facts. First, the
greater average size and strength of men and their greater aggressiveness means that a man's punch will probably produce more pain,
injury, and harm than a punch by a woman. Second, nearly three-
fourths of the violence committed by women is done in self-defense.
While violence by women should not be dismissed, neither should it
be overlooked or hidden. On occasion, legislators and spokespersons
like Phyllis Schlafly have used the data on violence by wives to minimize the need for services for battered women. Such arguments do
a great injustice to the victimization of women.

As we said, more often than not a wife who beats her husband has
herself been beaten. Her violence is the violence of self-defense. On
some occasions she will strike back to protect herself; on others she
will strike first, believing that if she does not, she will be badly
beaten. Sally, a forty-four-year-old woman married for twenty-five
years, recounted how she used violence to protect herself:

> When he hits me, I retaliate. Maybe I don't have the same strength as
> he does, but I know how to hold my own. I could get hurt, but I am
> going to go down trying. You know, it's not like there is anyone else
> here who is going to help me. So . . . I hit him back . . . I pick some-
> thing up and I hit him.

Marianne does not wait until she is hit. She says she has learned the
cues that her husband is about to hit her:

> I know that look he gets when he gets ready to hit me. We've been
> married for ten years, and I've seen that look of his. So he gets that

look, and I get something to hit him with. Once I hit him with a lamp. Another time I stabbed him. Usually I don't get so bad, but I was real fearful that time.

The violence in Marianne's home is not just one way. She has been hospitalized four times as a result of her husband's beatings. Her fears are very real.

The profile of those who engage in violence with their partners is quite similar to the profile of the parents who are abusive toward their children. The greater the stress, the lower the income, the more violence. Also, there is a direct relationship between violence in childhood and the likelihood of becoming a violent adult. Again, we add the caution that although there is a relationship, this does not predetermine that all those who experience violence will grow up to be abusers.

One of the more interesting aspects of the relationship between childhood and adult violence is that *observing* your parents hit one another is a more powerful contributor to the probability of becoming a violent adult than being a victim of violence. The learning experience of seeing your mother and father strike one another is more significant than being hit yourself. Experiencing, and more importantly observing, violence as a child teaches three lessons:

1. Those who love you are also those who hit you, and those you love are people you can hit.
2. Seeing and experiencing violence in your home establishes the moral rightness of hitting those you love.
3. If other means of getting your way, dealing with stress, or expressing yourself do not work, violence is permissible.

The latter lesson ties in well with our finding that stress also leads to an increased risk of violence in the home. One theory holds that people learn to use violence to cope with stress. If this is correct, then stress would be a necessary, but not sufficient, precondition for family violence. In oither words, stress alone does not cause violence unless the family members have learned that being violent is both appropriate and also will not meet with negative sanctions. Another theory is that learning to be violent and stress are two independent contributors to intimate violence and abuse.

The sociologists Debra Kalmuss and Judith Seltzer tested these two theories using the data collected for the First National Family Violence Survey. They found that stress and learning are independent contributions to the risk of abusive violence. Moreoever, observing and experiencing violence while growing up was a more powerful contributor to the later risk of intimate violence than was life stress.

Lurking beneath the surface of all intimate violence are confrontations and controversies over power. Our statistical evidence shows that the risk of intimate violence is the greatest when all the decision making in a home is concentrated in the hands of one of the partners. Couples who report the most sharing of decisions report the lowest rates of violence. Our evidence goes beyond the statistics. Over and over again, case after case, interview after interview, we hear batterers and victims discuss how power and control were at the core of the events that led up to the use of violence. Violent husbands report that they "need to" hit their wives to show them who is in charge. Some of the victimized wives struggle against domination and precipitate further violence. Other wives tell us that they will actually provoke their husband to violence because they want him to be more dominant. This is not so much a case of the wife being a masochist as it is another example of the conflicts and struggles that occur as couples confront the traditional cultural expectation that the male should be the dominant person in the household. Some couples fight against this prescription, while others fight to preserve it.

NO PLACE TO RUN, NO PLACE TO HIDE

Eleanor began to prepare dinner for her two children and her husband. It was evening on a Saturday night in January. While she grilled hamburgers, her husband Albert walked in. An argument began over whether Eleanor had taken Albert's shirts to the cleaners. Eleanor protested she had. Albert said she was lying. Eleanor protested, yelled, and finally said that Albert was drunk so often he never remembered whether his shirts were clean or dirty. Albert lunged at his wife. He pushed her against the stove, grabbed the sizzling burgers, and threw them across the room. He stalked out, slamming the front door behind him. Quiet tension reigned in the house through a dinner of tuna fish sandwiches and some television, and then the children were put to bed. Eleanor went to bed at 11:00 P.M., but could not fall asleep. At around 1:00 A.M. Albert returned home. He was quiet as he removed his clothes and got into bed. Eleanor turned over, her back to Albert. This signaled that she was awake, and another argument began to brew. This time it was over sex. Eleanor resisted. She always resisted when Albert was drunk. Tonight she resisted because she was still angry over the dinnertime argument. Albert lay his heavy arms around Eleanor and she struggled to get free. The quiet, almost silent struggle began to build. Angry whispers, angry gestures, and finally yelling ensued. Eleanor knew that Albert kept a gun in his night table drawer. Once, after a fight, Albert had gone to bed by putting the bullets on Eleanor's nightstand and the gun under his pillow. As the midnight fight escalated, Albert made a gesture toward the night table. For whatever reason, Eleanor thought that this would be the time that Albert would try to shoot her. She dove across the bed, pulled the drawer out of the night table, clawed for the gun as it rattled to the floor, and came to her feet with the gun in her hand. The first shot tore through Albert's right arm, the second slammed into the wall, the third tore away the top of his head. Eleanor stopped firing only after she heard three or four clicks as the hammer struck the now empty cylinders.

This could be a story out of a soap opera or a supermarket news-stand magazine. It is, unfortunately, a story repeated two thousand times a year. We have focused on the family structure and the individual and family characteristics that increase the risk of violence in specific households. Eleanor's and Albert's story illustrates the situational structure of intimate violence.

It goes without saying that intimate violence is most likely to occur in intimate settings. Occasionally couples will strike one another in the car. Husbands sometimes grab their wives at a party or on the street. Husbands or wives rarely slap their partners in public. The majority of domestic combat takes place in private, behind closed doors. We have known men and women to stifle their anger and seethe while guests are in the home. As the last guest leaves and the door closes, the fight and the violence erupt.

Eleanor and Albert began their path to their lethal confrontation in the kitchen. When we interviewed couples about the location of violence between partners and toward children, more than half said that the violence occurs in the kitchen. The living room and bedroom were the next most likely scenes. Only the bathroom seemed free from conflict and violence—perhaps because most bathrooms are small, have locks, or most likely because bathrooms are places of individual privacy.

Students of domestic homicide report that the bedroom is the most lethal room in the home. The criminologist Marvin Wolfgang reported that 20 percent of *all* victims of criminal homicide are killed in the bedroom. The kitchen and dining room are the other frequent scenes of lethal violence between family members.

After 8:00 P.M. the risk for family violence increases. This is almost self-evident, since this is also the time when family members are most likely to be together in the home. We found that four out of ten cases of domestic violence occur between 8:00 P.M. and midnight. Eight out of ten domestic fights take place between 5:00 P.M. and 7:00 A.M. Early evening fights occur in the kitchen. The living room becomes the likely setting for evening disputes, and the most violent and most lethal altercations break out in the bedroom, late at night.

The temporal and spatial patterns of intimate violence support our notion that privacy is a key underlying factor that leads to violence. Time and space constrain the options of both the offender and the victim. As the evening wears on, there are fewer places to run to, fewer places to hide. When the first fight broke out between Eleanor and Albert, it was about 5:00 P.M. Albert rushed out of the house in a huff—most likely heading for the neighborhood bar. The bar closed at 1:00 A.M., and that was when Albert went home to his final conflict.

A fight that erupts in the bedroom, in the early morning, constrains both parties. It is too late to stalk out of the home to a bar and too late to run to a friend or family member. The bed and the bedroom offer no protection and precious few places to flee or take cover. It is not surprising that so many of the most violent family fights end there.

Common sense would argue that weekends are the most violent time of the week for families. Common sense would not lead one to assume that the most violent times of the year are Christmas and Easter. When we looked at which day of the week violence was most likely to occur, we found that the empirical evidence was in full support of common sense. Weekends are when families spent the most time together and when the potential for conflicts and conflicts of interest is greatest. Not surprisingly, seven out of ten violent episodes we talked about with family members took place on either Saturday or Sunday. Weekends after a payday can be especially violent. Janice, the mother of an infant daughter, told us about the typical weekend fight:

> It starts over money. He gets paid on Friday. So he comes home on
> Fridays and I ask him for money. I am usually at the stove cooking

when he comes home. And, I have no money left. So I asks. This last Friday he said he didn't have no money. I got real mad. I mean, its payday and he has no money? He said he borrowed money and had to pay it back. I said he just must be lyin'. He spends it on booze or gambles it. Other times we fights because he gives me only fifty dollars. I can't feed him and the baby with just fifty dollars. So I got mad and started to yell.

Thus, the days of the week that are the most violent are those that combine the most conflict and violence-producing structural components of family life—time together, privacy, and stress.

Common sense would not suggest that violence is most likely to erupt at times of the year when families celebrate holidays and the spirit of family togetherness. Yet, contrary to common sense, it is the time from Thanksgiving to New Year's Day and again at Easter that violence in the home peaks.

As we conducted our interviews with members of violent homes we heard again and again about violence that occurred around the Christmas tree. Even the Christmas tree became a weapon in some homes:

> I remember one particularly violent time. When we were first married. He was out drinking and he came home stinking drunk. I suppose I must have said something. Well, he took a fit. He started putting his fist threw the walls. Finally, he just picked up the Christmas tree and threw it at me.

Another woman recalled her most violent experience:

> He hit me just before New Year's Day. I don't really recall what went on. We argue a lot. This time it might have been about money, or maybe the kids. Anyway, he got fierce. He punched me again and again. I was bleeding real bad. He had to take me to the hospital. It was the worst time of the year I ever had.

Perhaps people have a clearer memory of a violent event if it happens around a holiday. While this is a plausible explanation for our findings, it is not the complete answer. We have examined weekly reports of hospital admissions for child abuse and neglect, and found that the peak times of year for admissions were the period from Christmas to New Year's Day, and again in the spring around Easter Sunday.

A number of factors may contribute to the likelihood of domestic violence and abuse during the Christmas season. This is a time when families can assume tremendous financial burdens. Purchasing Christmas gifts can either take a toll on a family's resources or plunge a family into debt. Stress can also come from *not* buying gifts and presents. If a family cannot afford gifts expected by children, loved ones, and others, this can be extremely frustrating. The holiday season offers a stark contrast between what is expected and what a family can afford.

Holidays also create nonfinancial stress. Christmas and Easter holidays project images of family harmony, love, and togetherness. Songs, advertisements, and television specials all play up the image of the caring, loving, and even affluent family. A family with deep conflict and trouble may see these images in sad and frustrating contrast with their own lives. We know that prison riots are more likely to occur during holiday seasons, as prisoners apparently become stressed about being separated from family and friends during times of the year when such closeness is expected. Clearly, being with family and friends, but having unmet expectations for love and warmth, can also be extremely frustrating.

Time of day and time of year analysis supports the notion that privacy and stress are important structural contributors to domestic violence. Conflict frequently erupts over a stressful event, during a stressful time of the day, or around a stressful time of year. If the eruption takes place in a private setting, and at a time and place where it is difficult to flee or back down, the conflict can escalate into violence. The more privacy, the greater the power difference, and the fewer options the victim has in terms of getting help or finding protection, the more the violence can escalate.

The saddest and most frustrating aspect of our analysis of the structural, personal, familial, temporal, and spatial dynamics of intimate violence is that our results seem to say that violence in the home is inevitable. Lessons learned as a child set the stage for using violence as an adult. The structural makeup of the modern family is like a pressure cooker containing and escalating stress and conflict. If violence breaks out late at night, on a weekend, or a holiday, victims often have no place too run, no place to hide.

Our profile of violent families is not quite as bleak as it might seem. First, no one structural factor, personal experience, or situation predetermines that all or any family will be violent. Second, families do not live in a vacuum. Family members and people outside of the home can intervene to turn down the heat under the pressure cooker. We have found that friends, relatives, and neighbors can successfully intervene and reduce the pressure that could lead to violence. We will have more to say about this in part 2 when we examine the aftermath of intimate violence and the methods that can be used to reduce or prevent violence.

5.

How Violent

Are American

Families?

Consider a glass with but a thin layer of liquid on the bottom. This is not a case of the glass being half full or half empty; the glass is most assuredly nearly empty. Consider the glass again. Suppose the thin layer of liquid on the bottom is poison. Ninety-six percent of the volume of the glass is perfectly safe, but the 4 percent is deadly. How much poison would have to be on the bottom of the glass for people to think that drinking from the glass would be a problem? Not very much. Consider the glass again. How much liquid would we have to add for an observer to believe that there had been a significant increase in the glass? How much would we have to pour out to create a noticeable decrease? Small changes in small amounts may be hardly noticeable. Yet, depending on what the liquid is, an increase may be enough to make the dose deadly; a decrease may change the dose to safe. Just like those who think that just a small amount of poison in a glass is too much, most informed people would consider a single abused child as one too many. An increase from one to two abused children is considered unacceptable. A decrease from three to two is not enough.

Although we would like to believe that one abused child is too many, the practical reality is that social problems like child abuse, wife abuse, and elder abuse bid for a place on the public agenda on the basis of the nature of the problem and how widespread it is. It is not enough for something to be harmful, it has to harm a significant number of people in order to attract public attention and funds for the solutions. Thus, a great deal of effort has been devoted to attempting to measure the extent of violence in the home and demonstrating that there is enough "poison in the glass" to evoke public outcry and social action. This chapter addresses two of the most debated questions in the study of intimate violence: "How violent are American families?" and "Is family violence increasing?"

GUESSTIMATES AND ESTIMATES

"One million children are abused each year," is the sad headline of the National Committee for Prevention of Child Abuse public awareness campaigns.

"A woman is battered by her husband every 18 seconds," the Federal Bureau of Investigation reports.

Lois Haight Herrington, assistant attorney general of the United States, the driving force behind the Attorney General's Task Force on Family Violence, was quoted in *The New York Times* (May 20, 1984) as saying that she did not believe we knew *anything* about the incidence of family violence. Herrington did not come to this conclusion lightly. She had just completed six months of hearings on family violence all across the country, listening to numerous experts and victims of child abuse, sexual abuse, and elder abuse.

One has to wonder which is correct. The estimates repeated almost daily on television and in the public press? The published results of scientific surveys on the incidence and extent of family violence? Or Lois Herrington's conclusion that we really do not know anything about how much violence exists in the American family?

Contrary to Herrington's view, we do know a great deal about the incidence of family violence. However, because there have been nearly as many estimates as there have been estimators, it should not be surprising that an assistant attorney general would become confused when confronted with scores of studies, guesstimates, and estimates, and conclude that they were so variable that they meant nothing. Debates over whether the rate of family violence is increasing, decreasing, or staying the same are equally vocal and contradictory. On the one side are those who argue that we are in the midst of an epidemic of family violence. On the other side are those who see no evidence to support a massive increase in cases that would fit the definition of an epidemic.

When child abuse first began receiving public attention there were few solid statistics that experts could use to make the case that abuse was a common problem in American society. Faced with no hard data, the experts simply guesstimated the extent of physical child abuse. The guesstimates ranged from thousands of cases to millions.

The National Center on Child Abuse and Neglect (NCCAN) settled on an annual figure of one million abused children. Some of the more sardonic in the field of child abuse assumed that this figure was chosen because the director of a federal agency could not get a reserved parking space unless he or she was in charge of a social problem that affected a million people. In reality, this number was not entirely picked out of thin air. Douglas Besharov, the first director of NCCAN, had moved to Washington from New York State where he had been active in studying the legal aspects of child abuse. Besharov had reviewed official report data for New York City and extrapolated them to the national population of children. The extrapolation led him to conclude that one million cases of child maltreatment could be reported each year. When Besharov took over NCCAN the guesstimate stuck as the official government statistic.

There was so little concern with wife abuse in the 1960s and 1970s that the field lacked even guesstimates of the extent of the problem. When we were interviewed for an NBC documentary on violence in America the only segment of the taped interview that was aired was our guesstimate that one million women were abused by their partners each year. The logic behind this figure was that our preliminary studies had found that violence toward wives was about as common as violence toward children. Thus, we borrowed Besharov's one million figure and applied it to battered wives.

As the study of child abuse and family violence matured, the guesstimates were replaced with statistical estimates. Again, the range of estimates was from thousands to millions.

One of the most widely reported estimates was a national opinion survey carried out by David Gil with the assistance of the National Opinion Research Center. Gil asked a nationally representative sample of 1,520 adults if they had personal knowledge of families where incidents of child abuse occurred in the previous year. Forty-five, or 3 percent of the sample, reported knowledge of at least one event.

Extrapolating this number to a national population of 110 million adults, Gil estimated that between two and four million children are abused annually. Gil's estimate was high, and higher than it should have been. Gil extrapolated to each adult in each household. He overlooked the fact that all members of a single household might have personal knowledge of the same case of abuse. In fact, more than one household might know about the same case. The statistician Richard Light corrected Gil's estimate to account for the overlap of knowledge and produced a figure of 500,000 cases of physical child abuse each year. Despite Light's correction, Gil's two to four million estimate was regularly reported in the child abuse literature throughout the 1970s.

Gradually there were fewer and fewer estimates and guesstimates of the extent of child abuse. For one thing, more and more attention was being focused on the causes, treatments, and prevention of abuse. Another reason for the diminished number of guesses was that the counting of child abuse became institutionalized. The American Humane Association has conducted yearly surveys of child neglect and abuse reporting since 1974. The most recent report indicated that in 1984, 1,726,649 children were reported for child abuse and neglect to child protective agencies, one-third of which were reported for physical and sexual abuse. Another one-sixth were reported for both abuse and neglect.

A better estimate of physical abuse is the number of children reported for major or minor physical injury. About one-fifth of the reports (362,000 children) in 1984 were of children who had a major or minor physical injury. A similar number of physically assaulted children was found in the 1979 national survey of recognition and reporting of child maltreatment conducted by the National Center on Child Abuse and Neglect.

In addition to national surveys on physical abuse, the U.S. Justice Department has published two reports on what it calls "intimate victims." The first report, published in 1980, presented the results of interviews conducted between 1973 and 1976. Approximately 136,000 occupants of a representative sample of 60,000 housing units in the United States were interviewed. The major findings from these interviews were:

- There were about 3.8 million incidents of violence among intimates during the four-year period covered by the study. A third of these assaults were between relatives.

- More than half of the violent incidents were between spouses or ex-spouses.

The second study, titled *Family Violence,* was published in 1984. This report stated that:

- The yearly incidence rate of domestic violence among those twelve years of age or older was 1.5 per one thousand people in the population.

The First National Survey of Family Violence

Official report data like those collected by the American Humane Association, the National Center on Child Abuse and Neglect, and the Justice Department reveal only the tip of the iceberg of intimate violence. In order to assess more accurately the full extent of the problem, we need to collect data directly from family members. We conducted the First National Family Violence Survey in 1976 (see Appendix A for a complete discussion of the survey methods).

We had been warned for years that we could not expect the people we surveyed to tell us the truth. We had also committed to memory all the estimates and guesstimates available on domestic violence. We set out in 1976 to interview 2,146 families. If there was a flaw in our survey, it was probably that we interviewed too few people. We feared that we would locate too few cases of violence to allow for meaningful statistical analysis.

The computer spewed out the first printout of our data in the winter of 1977. We hurriedly flipped through the tables with mixed reactions. When we saw the statistics we were more than satisfied. There were enough cases of violence to allow for analysis. Indeed, the incidence was quite a bit higher than we had expected. We had not, after all, wasted a quarter of a million dollars of the taxpayers' money. Finding enough cases to conduct a proper statistical analysis was small compensation for discovering so much human pain and suffering. We were saddened to find the suffering so pervasive, and embarrassed that its existence was necessary to justify our own research.

Finally, we reacted to the data with worry. Would anyone believe our figures? Our estimates of the incidence of violence were so much higher than previous estimates that there was a good chance that no one would believe us. With computer printouts before us, we called around the country to our colleagues and other experts. Did these figures make sense? we asked. To our relief, most clinicians said they did. Thus, with mixed feelings of accomplishment and relief coupled with sadness for the scope of the problem, we presented the results of the First National Family Violence Survey in our book, *Behind Closed Doors: Violence in the American Family.*

Violence Toward Children. Nearly two-thirds (63 percent) of the parents we questioned mentioned at least one violent episode during the survey year. Three out of four parents said they struck their child as least once during the course of the child's lifetime. The milder forms of violence toward children are, of course, the most common. More than half of the parents spank or slap their children each year; nearly half push, grab, or shove their children. The rates of severe violence were, surprisingly and sadly, quite high:

- Three percent of the parents reported that they kick, bite, or punch their child each year, while nearly 8 percent of those surveyed said they have done these acts at least once while the child was growing up.
- A little more than ten parents in one thousand said they beat their child at least once a year, while slightly more than forty in one thousand said they had ever beaten their child.
- One child in one thousand each year faces a parent with a weapon.
- Nearly thirty children in one thousand were threatened with a weapon while growing up.

When we combined all the violent items that could produce an injury into what we call the "Child Abuse Index" we found that:

- Nearly forty parents in one thousand (3.6 percent) reported that they committed an abusive act of violence during the survey year.

What is the meaning of forty children in one thousand being victims of abusive violence? Taking the larger view this means that in 1975, the year about which we questioned parents, 1.4 million children aged three to seventeen years were victims of physical abuse. In more human terms, this means that nearly one child in twenty-two, or one school-aged child in each classroom in the United States was a victim of physical abuse.

There was much to ponder in our results. First, and most alarming to us, was the fact that we produced an estimate of physical abuse that was *higher by 50 percent* then the estimates presented by the National Center on Child Abuse and Neglect. More importantly, we arrived at this staggering figure by using a measure and a methodology that was limited to providing us with a bottom-line estimate of abuse. The real rate of violence and abuse, if all the subjects had infallable memories and told all, and if we had measured all possible forms of abusive violence, would undoubtedly have been two or three times higher than the numbers we reported.

Violence Between Partners. One out of every six wives we interviewed in 1975 reported that she was struck by a husband during the course of her marriage. Considering violence toward husbands as well as toward wives, we found that someone getting married runs greater than a one in four chance of being involved in marital violence at some time in the relationship.

As with violence toward children, the milder forms of physical violence are the most common. Yet, when we examine violence that has the potential of producing an injury, we again find an unacceptably high level of violence.

- About one woman in twenty-two (3.8 percent) is the victim of physically abusive violence each year.
- The average battered wife is attacked three times each year.
- Six wives in one thousand are beaten up by their husbands each year.
- Two wives in one thousand have husbands or partners who have used guns or knives against them.

The results of the First National Family Violence Survey included data on violence toward husbands. A little more than forty husbands in one thousand (4.6 percent) were recorded as victims of severe violence. Violence toward husbands, or so-called husband abuse has been a controversial area in the study of domestic violence. There has been heated rhetoric on this topic but precious little rational discussion.

In 1978 our colleague (and collaborator on the First National Family Violence Survey) Suzanne K. Steinmetz published an article, "The Battered Husband Syndrome." The article was intended to demonstrate that husbands as well as wives were the victims of intimate violence. Steinmetz reviewed numerous investigations of family violence and found, contrary to some feminist and scholarly claims, that women were not the only victims of family violence. Steinmetz went on to claim that it was husband abuse and not wife abuse that was the most underreported form of family violence. She was immediately attacked by feminists, social scientists, and a few journalists for misreading, misinterpreting, and misrepresenting her findings.

Unlike most debates among scholars, this one spilled over into the public media. United Press International headlined a wire service report on Steinmetz's article: STUDY BACKS UP SUSPICIONS HUSBAND IS MORE BATTERED SPOUSE. An Ann Landers column on husband abuse included a letter from Susan Schechter, then director of women's services at the Chicago Loop Center, YMCA. Schechter attacked the validity of the Steinmetz article. She said that Steinmetz's data on husbands as the most likely victims of abuse were being used against women's groups seeking funding for shelters. Steinmetz debated the meaning and interpretation of her data with journalists Roger Langley and Richard Levy on "The Today Show." *Time* magazine devoted a full-page story to husband abuse in March 1978. Dr. Joyce Brothers mentioned the husband abuse data in her newspaper column. With each telling of the story, the estimates of abused men were inflated. Our survey found that about two million men were victims of violence that could cause injury. When journalist Langley wrote an article for the *New York Daily News,* he pushed the figure up to twelve million men. Woozles, it seems, tend to multiply in direct proportion to the degree of controversy associated with a story.

There was no resolution to the public debate over battered husbands. The debate was fought over numbers—how many husbands were hit or abused—and it missed the mark. The real issues are initiation of violence, outcomes, and consequences. The same study that found forty-six men in one thousand being hit also found that the vast majority of these men were hit because they had initiated the violence and abuse. By and large, women used violence to protect themselves. Victimized women are literally between the proverbial rock and the hard place. If they leave, they stand a good chance of joining the millions of other women who have feminized poverty in America. If they stay, they are either beaten again or forced to use extreme physical violence to protect themselves.

Perhaps the most unfortunate outcome of the wrangle over battered men is that since the debate in the late 1970s, there has been virtually no additional research carried out on the topic. The furor among social scientists and in the public media has contaminated the entire topic. Consequently, we have refused every request for an interview or to appear on any talk show on this topic for fear of yet again being misquoted, miscast, or misrepresented. Other social scientists who witnessed the abuse heaped on our research group—especially on Suzanne Steinmetz—have given the topic of battered men a wide berth.

The Meaning of the Incidence of Family Violence

Some people who consider the statistics on family violence believe that glass is near empty. Critics of the statistics are quick to point out that if 4 percent of families are abusive to their children, 96 percent are not. If 4 percent of women are abused, 96 percent are not. The critics point out that such percentages hardly seem to warrant calling the family a "cradle of violence," claiming that violence in the family is "as common as is love," or saying that there is an epidemic of family violence. In fact, the percentages seem to support the notion that the basic structure of the modern family is one of peace and tranquillity.

Let us take a less metaphorical approach than our glass of liquid. Consider the risks of family violence—on average one wife or child in twenty-one has a chance of being physically abused from three to four times per year. If you interviewed for a job and were told that you faced those odds in the workplace, would you accept the position? If these were the odds of being assaulted on a trip to Disney World, how many people would fill the park, designed to hold 100,000 each day? The American public fears violent crime in the streets—and those odds are measured in terms of one per 100,000 people. Family violence is measured in terms of one per one thousand families. The family is hardly a haven—even if 96 percent of homes are not abusive.

IS FAMILY VIOLENCE INCREASING?

Ten years ago only one in ten Americans thought that child abuse was a serious social problem. By 1982, nine out of ten people surveyed by Louis Harris and Associates thought that child abuse was a serious problem. Has the problem increased ninefold, or have Americans just become more aware of the dimensions of intimate violence?

To listen to the talk shows and to read the popular magazines one would be convinced that we are in the midst of an epidemic of domestic assault. Those who believe that there has been an explosion of domestic disturbance in America have ample evidence to support their claim. They point correctly to greater stress in our society, unemployment, economic problems, and the rising numbers of single parent households. They point incorrectly to the supposed rise in the divorce rate—actually the divorce rate increased consistently from 1965 to 1979, but has remained stable since 1979.

Lost among the clamor about the deterioration and near collapse of the family and the daily reports of new and more chilling cases of child or wife abuse is the fact that violence between intimates is not new. Harming those you love and are related to goes back to Cain killing Abel in Genesis. The historical record is full of evidence of the killing, maiming, and beating of children by parents and wives by husbands. Lloyd DeMause examined the history of childhood and graphically noted that in 1526 the latrines of Rome were said to "resound with the cries of children who had been plunged into them." Women, Russell and Rebecca Dobash note, have traditionally been the "appropriate victims" of family violence.

The available historical and cross-cultural evidence might support the claim the violence in the home today is no worse than it has been in the past. Perhaps the chances of violence occurring in the home today are less than chances decades or centuries ago. Current population data could be used to argue that today's families are actually less likely to be violent than families ten or twenty years ago. Couples in the 1980s are marrying later, having fewer children, and are having fewer unwanted children. These factors are all related to reduced chances of violence occurring in the home. In point of fact, these data can also be used to argue that the family is not deteriorating but remaining a strong, viable institution, despite the preachings of conservative politicians and religious zealots.

Those who argue that there is an epidemic of child abuse and family violence are not without compelling statistical evidence. The American Association for Protecting Children, a division of the American Humane Association, claims that abuse and neglect reports are on the rise. They state that "documented reports" of abused and neglected children reached 1,726,649 in 1984—an increase of 17 percent from 1983 and 158 percent above 1976, the first year these data were collected. The American Humane Association data are the *only* hard data available that speak to whether a form of family violence has risen, fallen, or stayed the same. We have no data for years prior to 1976, and with the exception of data on homicide, no data on any other form of family violence. The drawback of the American Humane Association data is obvious. Child abuse reports are not the same as incidents of child abuse. Given that so much attention has been focused on child abuse and neglect in the last two decades, and that there has been a considerable increase in state and local efforts (and funding) to improve reporting, it would be amazing if the number of reports had not increased since 1976.

THE SECOND NATIONAL FAMILY VIOLENCE SURVEY

Our First National Family Violence Survey was the first and only national survey of family violence that was not based on tabulating official report data. We designed the Second National Family Violence Survey to assess whether intimate violence had increased, decreased, or stayed the same since 1975. A nationally representative sample of 6,002 households was interviewed over the telephone for the Second National Family Violence Survey. Telephone interviews were conducted by trained interviewers employed by Louis Harris and Associates.

Quite frankly, even before we designed the Second National Family Violence Survey and applied to the National Institute of Mental Health for the more than $600,000 we needed to conduct the study, we expected to find no change in the rates of domestic violence. Our first survey found the rates of abuse to be around 4 percent. For there to be a statistically significant decrease or increase, we would have had to find a change of plus or minus nearly one or two percentage points. This would represent a change of between 20 and 50 percent. Such a massive change seemed highly unlikely.

We were surprised in 1976 when our computers and calculators told us that the rates of family abuse were as high as they were. We were shocked in 1985 to find that, contrary to our expectations, the rates of abusive violence toward children and women had declined far more than we could have ever expected (see fig. 1, 2, and 3 in Appendix C.)

Our results were the following:

- While thirty-six parents of children three to seventeen years of age per one thousand reported using abusive violence toward their children in 1975, only nineteen parents per one thousand in 1985 reported using such forms of violence. This is a *decline of 47 percent in ten years*.
- Reports of severe wife beating *declined 27 percent* from thirty-eight incidents per one thousand women in 1975 to thirty per one thousand women in 1985.
- Reports of severe violence toward husbands remained essentially unchanged in the ten-year period (forty-six per one thousand in 1975 versus forty-four per one thousand in 1985).

These changes are more important when we estimate how many children and women are being abused each year. The change in the rate of severe violence toward children means that there were more than 700,000 fewer children victimized in 1985 than in 1975. Nearly 375,000 fewer women were victims of severe violence in 1985 than in 1975.

The shock we felt when we first examined our data was echoed when we presented the results at professional meetings. The data on violence toward children were presented at the Seventh National Conference on Child Abuse and Neglect, which was sponsored by the National Center on Child Abuse and Neglect and the National Committee for Prevention of Child Abuse. In preparing for the conference, the National Committee had set an almost unprecedented goal by calling for the reduction of child abuse by 20 percent by 1990. Hundreds of conferees wore buttons which said 20% BY 1990, while we presented data that reported that the rate of severe violence had already dropped by 47 percent! Not surprisingly, our results were received with great skepticism.

Reactions to our report were swift, emotional, and contradictory. Although a *New York Times* editorial called the findings "good news," others were a good deal more skeptical. The *Christian Science Monitor* reported that an unnamed Reagan administration official had "serious doubts" about the accuracy of the surveys. Dr. Frederick Green, vice president of Children's Hospital National Medical Center in Washington, DC, disputed the findings, noting that his caseload of child abuse had not declined, but had risen. The sociologist Richard Berk summed up the skeptics when he was interviewed by the *Christian Science Monitor* and said, "Given all we know about the pattern of crime statistics, a 47 percent drop is so unprecedented as to be unbelievable. Never before has there been a drop of that magnitude, that rapidly."

The strongest argument against the claim that family violence has decreased is that the changes we found may have been artificial—due to what researchers refer to as methodological artifacts. One methodological artifact is that we used different methods to collect our data. We collected the data in 1975 using in-person interviews. The interviews in 1985 were conducted over the telephone. Perhaps the difference in data collection produced the changed rates of violence. Rigorous research methodologists objected to our changing data collection techniques. They pointed out that by choosing to collect data for the second survey by telephone, we were unable to interview families who do not have phones. This amounts to about 5 percent of households. More importantly, these are likely to be low-income households who are at high risk of being violent and abusive.

A second plausible explanation for the decline in the rates of reported child and wife beating is that respondents may have been more reluctant to report severe violence in 1985 than in 1975. There has been a massive amount of public and media attention paid to child and wife abuse in the last decade. There have been numerous national media campaigns, new child abuse and neglect laws have been passed, hot lines for reporting have been instituted, and there has been almost daily media attention paid to the problems of intimate violence. The decrease in reporting may be due to what the sociologist Joseph Gusfield calls a "moral passage." As family violence becomes less acceptable, fewer parents and husbands become willing to admit participating in violence.

Richard Berk claims that a 47 percent decline in the rate of child abuse is unprecedented and nearly unbelievable. Yet, had Berk consulted the Uniform Crime Reports tabulation of homicide rates he would have found that the rate increased by 100 percent between 1963 and 1973, and then dropped by 29 percent between 1980 and 1984. If the same rate of decline is maintained for six more years, the ten-year decline would be greater than our 47 percent change. Thus, there is precedent for our findings. The homicide statistics parallel our own findings.

It is unlikely that our use of telephone interviewing produced an artificial decline in the reported rates of violence. Indeed, if anything, using the telephone would have increased reporting. For one thing, using the telephone produced a higher completion rate. Only two out of three persons contacted by our interviewers in 1975 completed the interview. Using the telephone, we completed 84 percent of interviews with eligible respondents. Assuming that a higher completion rate means a more representative sample, and assuming that people who do not participate are more violent, the better completion rate in 1985 would have produced higher, not lower, violence reporting.

The argument that we failed to interview people without telephones, who may be more violent than those with phones, is valid. However, our colleagues at Louis Harris and Associates point out the coverage difference between in-person and telephone interviews is only theoretical. They have found that households without telephones are nearly impossible to reach in person. For all practical purposes, coverage by the telephone and in-person interviewing are the same.

The anonymity provided by telephone as opposed to in-person interviewing would also lead to more, rather than less, reporting. When we interviewed people in their homes in 1975, we handed them a card with the response categories for the questions on violence. The card included all the possible answers, including "never." Handing a card to a respondent in a telephone interview is obviously impossible. By convention, the interviewer reads a list of possible responses, but "never" or "I don't know" has to be volunteered by the respondents. Experience with sensitive subjects, such as our research on violence or Kinsey's studies of sexual behavior, has determined that rates of reported sensitive behavior are higher when the subject has to volunteer the "no" or "never" answer.

The second proposed flaw in our findings is that the decline may be due to reluctance to report. This is certainly plausible for those parents and husbands talking about their own violent behavior. But it makes no sense to assume that battered wives are less likely to report being hit today than ten years ago. If anything, the increase in public attention should have made women more likely to say they had been beaten. This makes finding a drop in the rates of reported wife abuse all the more remarkable.

Despite our critics, we do believe that there has been a decline in the rates of violence toward children and, to a lesser extent, women. Such a finding is consistent with changes that have occurred in the family and society over the last decade that probably have served to reduce violence in the home. Changes have occurred in five broad areas: (1) family structure, (2) the economy, (3) more alternatives for battered women, (4) treatment programs, and (5) deterrence.

There have been dramatic changes in the structure of the American family over the last decade. The average age a man and a woman first get married has increased, as has the average age for having a first child. Later marriage and later onset of childbearing has led to a decline in the average number of children per family. There has also been a decline in the number of unwanted children born. Parents in 1985 are one of the first generations in history to be able to choose from a full range of options (including abortion) for planning family size. All these factors are related to lower rates of child abuse, and could be related to lower rates of wife abuse by reducing the level of stress in families. In addition to demographic changes, the American family is becoming, bit by bit, more egalitarian. This, too, has important implications for domestic violence, since we know that egalitarian marriages have the lowest risk of intimate violence.

We know that both child abuse and wife abuse are associated with unemployment and economic stress. Our comparison of rates of child abuse was confined to couples with a child between three and seventeen years of age at home (this was due to the sampling procedure used in our 1975 survey). For intact families, the economic climate of the country was dramatically better in 1985 than in 1975. The rates of unemployment and inflation were lower in 1985 compared to ten years earlier. By coincidence, the one-year reference period of our second survey—1985—coincided with one of the most prosperous years of the decade.

There is one caution we should introduce. The year 1985 was not especially prosperous for single-parent, poor, or minority families. Their lot in life has actually declined in the past ten years. Unfortunately, our surveys, because of the sampling rules and the size of the minority-population samples, could not measure changes in the rates of child abuse for poor single mothers. One skeptical reader of our study, Frederick Green, noted that he was seeing more child abuse now than ten years ago. Since he also reported that he sees a largely minority, single-parent, and poor population, this is not surprising.

Ten years ago there were perhaps four shelters for battered women in the United States. Today, there may be more than one thousand. Shelters and other programs for both victims and offenders provide alternatives for protection and services for battered women that did not exist a decade ago. It is rather obvious that even one thousand shelters cannot accommodate more than a million battered wives. Yet, the very existence of shelters can serve to embolden women to tell their partners that violence is unacceptable. With a real alternative to which to flee, women have more than idle threats to make in 1985.

The economic resources that come with paid employment represent a second alternative for battered women. There has been tremendous growth in paid employment of married women between 1975 and 1985. Our own research has found that paid employment of married women helps rectify the imbalance of power between spouses, and provides women with the economic resources they need to terminate a violent marriage. An increased acceptance of divorce also provides battered wives with an alternative they may not have used ten years ago.

A fourth major change in the last ten years has been the development and implementation of new and innovative treatment programs for child and wife abuse. Each state enacted mandatory reporting legislation for child abuse and neglect in the late 1960s. Public and private social services have also been developed to prevent and treat child abuse. These programs are still sadly understaffed and underfunded, but their size and scope are far greater now than in 1975. States have increased their staffs of protective service workers by 20 to 100 percent in the last few years. Programs have also been developed for marital violence. Where there were no programs for battering men ten years ago, now there are a growing number of programs such as Emerge in Boston, Massachusetts, or Brother to Brother in Providence, Rhode Island. Finally, there has been an expansive growth of family therapists and family therapy approaches to family violence. Membership in the American Association of Marital and Family Therapists has tripled since 1975. Perhaps the increase in therapists and therapy approaches has helped to reduce intrafamily violence.

Deterrence of a crime such as child abuse or wife abuse depends on the potential offender's perception that there is a high probability of being caught and punished. Many of the programs that have developed and expanded over the past decade were intended to change people's internal norms about the appropriateness of family violence, and to increase the public punishments for violating those norms. Child abuse reporting is not only victim identification, it is the public stigmatic labeling of offenders. Battered wife shelters and the entire shelter movement are not simply designed to provide refuge for battered women, they also send the message that such behavior by men is inappropriate.

Legal sanctions, nearly absent or not applied ten years ago, have been developed and beefed up. At the time of our 1975 study the training manual prepared by the International Association of Chiefs of Police recommended separating the warring parties and leaving. Today, the manual recommends dealing with domestic assault in the same manner that all assaults are dealt with. A growing number of police departments have implemented a mandatory arrest policy as a means of deterring wife beating. We will have more to say about legal deterrence in chapter 8.

Many people do not want to believe our study, and are quick to criticize it without actually reading our research reports. What could be the possible reason for such skepticism? One key may be the fear that our reported decline in the rate of family violence may be used by state and federal legislators to cut back on funding for domestic violence programs. The fear is real—such funding has been cut at the federal level despite the fact that those in the federal government with responsibility for domestic violence believe the problem is growing. Shortly after we published our results, we learned that a state legislator in Maine had cited the study as part of an argument to cut back on funding for child abuse programs.

Using our research to argue for cuts in programming defies logic. There are still more than a million and a half battered women and another million and a half battered children. A more logical argument is that our study shows that the millions of dollars spent on prevention and treatment programs have worked, and that continued and increased funding is called for. Our findings actually support the claim that an increased national public awareness effort, as well as increased funding for prevention and treatment, will bear more dividends in the decades to come.

The rate of decline of the various forms of intimate violence has been in proportion to the amount of public attention the form of intimate violence has received. Child abuse, which has been on the public agenda for more than two decades, showed the greatest rate of decline. Wife beating, identified more than a decade after the "discovery" of child abuse, has declined, but less so than child abuse. Finally, husband abuse, a form of intimate violence for which there has been no research, no sincere publicity, and no public or private funds invested in the problem, has remained unchanged for the last ten years.

We must, however, remain cautious in our optimism. The reductions we report appear to be large—certainly larger than we expected and larger than some observers want to believe. Yet, even with these reductions, our data still indicate that there remain millions of battered women and children. The next section of the book examines the aftermath of violence, and what life holds for these three million yearly victims of intimate abuse.

PART II

THE AFTERMATH:

OUT FROM

THE SHADOWS

TO SEEK HELP

6.

The Impact

of Intimate Violence

Bill was hardly a model husband or father. Indeed, if he promised his wife Allison and daughter Cindy a rose garden, you may be certain that they got not the roses but the thorns—and worse. His violent outbursts were sporadic, but they could be intensely cruel. He began to hit and batter his wife during her first pregnancy. At first he pushed or slapped Allison when he was angry. After a while, he escalated the violence to kicks and punches. In Allison's eyes there seemed to be no rhyme or reason behind the outbursts. One day it happened because Bill could not find his new shirt. Another day he exploded when he was served fish and not the fried chicken he expected. On this occasion he hurled his plate at Allison and then picked up the kitchen table and threw it across the room. Soon he began to purchase guns—first a shotgun, then a rifle, then two handguns. He would often threaten Allison with one or another of the weapons. She never did know whether they were loaded or not.

Cindy remembers seeing her father hit her mother on many occasions. Bill rarely spanked Cindy. When he did, it was rather mild. But his other punishments were extraordinarily cruel. Cindy's clearest childhood memory was of her father shooting her pet cat. The cat had tracked mud onto Bill's easy chair. In a rage, Bill carried the cat to his closet, took out a rifle, and stomped outside—all the while yelling to Cindy what he planned to do. He threw the cat into the corner of the fenced-in front yard, and shot the trapped animal in full view of Cindy and Allison. When finished, Bill picked up the carcass and ceremoniously dumped it into the garbage can.

Allison suffered the most from Bill's violent outbursts. She was often depressed and had a series of minor health problems. Her depression caused her to miss work frequently, and she had lost two jobs as a result. At one point Allison was so depressed, and felt that her situation was so hopeless, that she tried to take her life. She swallowed a dozen sleeping pills, but then called a neighbor to ask for help. After a brief stay in a psychiatric hospital, Allison returned home. Bill's violence let up for three months, but it returned and so did her depression and headaches.

One afternoon, when Cindy was seventeen years old, her father arrived home drunk. He began to make sexual advances toward her. He wrapped her in a giant hug, and when she tore free, he began to grab and tear at her clothes. With his attention totally focused on Cindy, he did not hear Allison open the hall closet door and remove a shotgun. Allison stood quietly in the hall as the tumult in the living room went on. Finally, Cindy tumbled into the hall. Bill staggered out after her. Allison calmly emptied both barrels of the shotgun into her husband's chest. She put down the shotgun and called the police. "I've just killed my husband," she reported.

No brief written description, television drama, or full-length book can do justice to the experience of living in an abusive household. We can describe the shape and form the physical and mental abuse take, but words are not adequate to capture what life must be like for the victims of domestic abuse. What went on in the mind of six-year-old Cindy as she watched her father shoot her pet cat? How did Allison cope with the violence she experienced, her own psychological distress, and the aftermath of her attempted suicide? More importantly, how did she cope with the uncertainty of not knowing when or why the next violent outburst would take place? Most people would assume that Cindy and Allison could never be normal after enduring the violence and cruelty they experienced. It is generally assumed by professionals and laymen alike that abuse victims sustain lifelong scars.

GROWING UP AMIDST VIOLENCE:
THE IMPACT ON CHILDREN

The belief that battered and abused children grow up to become abusive parents is widely shared and accepted by professionals and the general public. Yet, among students of child maltreatment there is heated controversy over the validity of the claim that abuse leads to abuse. On the one side of the debate are those who see childhood experiences with abuse as a major and direct cause of later violent behavior. Henry Kempe and Barton Schmitt claimed that "untreated abused children frequently grow up to be delinquents, murderers, and batterers of the next generation of children." On the other side is the child development expert Edward Zigler of Yale University who, after a review of the major research studies on the link between abuse experienced as a child and abusive behavior as an adult, concluded that "the majority of abused children do not become abusive parents" and ". . . the time has come for the intergenerational myth to be placed aside."

The most careful review of research on the intergenerational link finds that between 18 and 70 percent of those individuals who grew up in violence will re-create that behavior as adults. Zigler and his colleague Joan Kaufman believe that the most accurate estimate within this wide range is that the rate of intergenerational transmission is about 30 percent. They conclude that this means that the link between being maltreated and becoming abusive is far from inevitable; thus they advocate abandoning the notion of abused children growing up to be abusive.

Kaufman and Zigler's dismissal of the intergenerational link may be as misleading as the zealots who claim that all abused children grow up to be abusive. Kaufman and Zigler are correct on two counts. First, the best available evidence indicates that *most* battered children do not become abusive. Second, it would be incorrect and unfair for individuals who experienced violence as children to see themselves as walking time bombs. Worse, such an incorrect self-image might lead to a self-fulfilling prophecy in which the self-concept, and not the experiences, may induce violent outbursts. Yet, to totally dismiss the experiences of violence as one of the causes of later violence is also misleading and wrong. While a rate of intergenerational transmission of 30 percent is not even a majority, it is far greater than the average rate of abusive violence which is less than 3 percent for the general population. In short, while one could not always predict future violence based on knowing past history, past history is important enough as a causal factor to warrant explanation and clinical intervention.

Since all battered children do not grow up to become abusers, Kaufman and Zigler believe that the most important question to answer is not, "Do abused children become abusive parents?" but rather, "Under what circumstances is the transmission of abuse most likely to occur?"

The researchers Rosemary Hunter and Nancy Kilstrom reported that the parents who did not repeat the cycle of abuse shared a number of characteristics. These nonabusive parents had more extensive social supports and fewer ambivalent feelings about their pregnancies. Their babies were healthier. The parents also displayed more open anger about their own abusive experiences and were able to describe these traumas more freely. If they had been abused, it was by one parent, while the other parent served as a supportive life raft in a sea of trouble and pain.

The psychologist Byron Egeland has also examined factors that enhance or reduce the chances that a violent childhood will lead to adult violence. He cautions that his conclusions are suggestive, since he has not yet subjected his data to rigorous analysis.

One finding is obvious. The more severe the maltreatment experienced by a mother, the more likely it is she will re-create it when she becomes a parent. Those mothers who were severely abused but who did not abuse their children had a number of characteristics in common. First, despite the abuse they had grown up with, they had at least one parent or foster parent who provided some love and support. As adults, their home situation was more stable than that of the abusing mothers. They had supportive husbands and a regular source of income.

The conclusion that we can draw from both studies is that the re-creation of past abuse seems avoidable if present support is available. One of the subjects in Egeland's research appropriately demonstrates this point. The mother came from one of the most abusive backgrounds in the study. She was one of ten children. Her mother beat her often, using a belt one time, a book another, and once a hot iron. She had been emotionally battered as well as deprived of proper medical or dental attention until the time she was placed in a foster home. Despite her background, the woman in the study has not re-created the physical or emotional environment she experienced. She has married, and both she and her husband are regularly employed. In addition to the support she receives from her husband, the woman was also open and articulate about her past, unlike mothers who grew up to be abusive and who spoke of their violent experiences with little emotion or detail. Egeland concluded his case discussion by noting: "With the support she receives from her husband and the help he provides in child care, she is able to provide adequate care to her children."

While much of the research, and most of the public attention, has focused on the question of whether or not abuse experienced as a child leads to violent behavior later in life, less attention has been given to the more subtle developmental consequences of violence. Victims of child maltreatment are thought of as innocent and defenseless. Those who are harmed by the abuse do not remain innocent and defenseless for long. The image of the cute and cuddly battered baby is a myth. Therapists and foster parents have found these children to suffer from numerous deficits which often make them extremely difficult children to raise and nurture.

An example is the case of Frank, Jane, and their son Ben. Frank and Jane already had a son, Danny, who was eight years old when they adopted Ben, who was four. He had been placed in foster care after being removed from the care of his mother. Ben's mother was seventeen years old when Ben was born. She had routinely used severe and harsh punishment. At the time he was adopted, Ben's back was still marked by the scars of numerous cigarette burns and beatings inflicted by his mother. Ben was initially aloof and withdrawn when adopted. He gradually opened up, but remained quiet and wary of strangers. As is common with children who grow up in unpredictable and deprived homes, Ben hid food, even though Frank and Jane's refrigerator was always well stocked. Ben's first eight years in the home were relatively calm, marked by the normal parent/ child conflicts and a handful of violent outbursts, but the situation deteriorated markedly when Ben entered adolescence. His withdrawal increased, as did his aggression. When challenged by Jane or Frank, Ben responded with a torrent of obscenities. Once, he confronted Jane with Frank's hunting rifle. He ran away from home often, experimented with drugs, and was truant from school. Frank and Jane's vision of providing a healthy and warm home for a needy child was shattered by the reality of the many and varied demands made by a child whose first six years of life were marked by emotional and physical damage.

Our knowledge about the long-term effects of abuse during the early years of life is quite limited. In almost no case has an investigator followed abused infants and children from early childhood through adolescence and into adult life. Most of what we know comes from studies that obtain retrospective histories from older children, teenagers, and adults who speak of past abuse and present troubles.

Despite the methodological limitations, a number of investigators have collected data that suggest that growing up in a violent home compromises the intellectual development of abused children. Children who have experienced violence and neglect are reported to have achieved lower scores on formal intelligence tests than peers from nonabusive homes. In addition, other researchers have found that abused and maltreated children exhibit learning problems. There is some evidence that maltreatment experiences translate into poorer school performance and lower grades. Research conducted by Roy and Ellen Herrenkohl of Lehigh University found that children from families in which a child welfare agency had found indications of physical abuse were more likely to have experienced academic failure, to have attended special classes, and to have learning disabilities.

Among the most obvious personality traits of children from violent homes is aggressiveness. It has been our experience, and the experience of many clinicians, that children from violent homes are not only aggressive and oppositional, they are also extremely wary. A social worker who treats battered children described a first session with a battering victim.

We did not exactly start off on the proper foot. I was just finishing my lunch when I took the elevator up to the outpatient clinic where I was to meet the family. My cotherapist had already introduced herself to the state welfare worker and the child. I walked up to all three of them. I had a doughnut on a plate that was to be my dessert. The child (a ten-year-old boy) grabbed the doughnut off my plate and stuffed it into his mouth. Things went downhill from here. I did manage to get him to come with me to the office where we were to meet for therapy. Once in the office he was all over the place. He moved sporadically from one chair to the next, from one toy to another. He would glance or glare at me from time to time, but never directly responded to my attempts to start a conversation. Nor was he interested in any nonverbal interaction—such as a game or playing with a toy. After about fifteen minutes of frenetic behavior, he discovered the window and the fact that we were on the tenth floor. He jumped up onto the inside windowsill and stood flush against the window—first facing me, then facing out. The window was sealed, the building is air-conditioned, but it did not give me a secure feeling to see him pressed against the window staring down. When our fifty-minute session was over I was hungry, exhausted, and frustrated. I had failed to make any real contact with him at all.

Researchers and clinicians list several characteristics that have been found among abused children, including symptoms such as bed-wetting, poor self-concept, a tendency to withdraw and become isolated, and a pattern of hyperactivity and tantrums. E. Milling Kinard reviewed much of the literature on the psychological consequences of abuse and found other traits such as an inability to trust others, difficulties relating to both peers and adults, and a generalized unhappiness. The psychiatrist Brandt Steele notes that many abused children see themselves as ugly, stupid, inept, clumsy, or somehow defective.

Our own experiences with battered children reflect much of what we read in the scholarly literature. The most vivid and sad presentations were the pictures drawn by battered children. Many of the self-portraits drawn by abused children portray them as minute specks, apart from the other members of the family. Abused children frequently draw themselves without arms and hands, a clinical manifestation of their fear of their own anger and aggression. The pictures present sad images of withdrawn children with shattered self-concepts and, in other pictures, aggressive children with violent fantasies and fears.

In short, growing up in an abusive house can dramatically compromise the developmental and personal competence of the children. Many, if not most, maltreated children enter adolescence with severe personal deficits. It should be no great surprise that many of these children are prone to juvenile delinquency.

A variety of data points to the fact that abused children, especially boys, have a much greater chance of becoming involved in juvenile crime than children from nonabusive homes. A number of social scientists point to the fact that what we call juvenile delinquency, including acts such as running away, is a logical form of expression for the maltreated child who has a damaged self-concept and a persistent need to belong to something or do something that will improve the shattered ego. Running away serves the important function of fleeing maltreatment, even though technically it is a status

offense and a delinquent act. Delinquent groups and gangs can provide approval. Delinquent and antisocial acts are a form of direct
and indirect revenge against maltreating caretakers or a society that
is powerless to protect the injured child.

One investigation in New York State tracked children who had
contact with official agencies for child maltreatment in the 1950s.
The investigators examined records of juvenile justice agencies to see
if the maltreated children had later contact for delinquency. A second group of juveniles who had contact for delinquency in 1970
were traced backward in time to determine if they had prior contact
for child maltreatment. Overall, the records of more than four thousand children were examined, tracked, and traced. The investigators
found that one in five children with contact for maltreatment had
later reported instances of delinquency. Similarly, one in five delinquents had prior contact for maltreatment. More importantly, the
kind of maltreatment related to the form of delinquency. If the maltreatment was physical abuse, the delinquency tended toward violent
crime rather than status offenses such as running away or truancy.

The most unusual events are often the most sensational. The rarest
form of intimate violence is children killing parents or siblings. Of
the more that two thousand family homicides recorded by the Federal Bureau of Investigation in 1984, 504 (11.4 percent) involved a
child killing a parent—fathers were the most likely victim; 403 cases
(9.1 percent) involved a child killing a sibling—81 percent of the
victims were brothers. The official statistics overestimate the actual
number of children who kill, since the FBI uses the term "child" to
refer to a family relationship, not an age group. Thus, a forty-year-
old son who kills his father is categorized along with ten-year-olds
or teenagers.

Two of the more sensational recent instances of children killing
parents support the claim that growing up in a violent home increases the risk of fatal violence. Yet these cases have been sensational and controversial because of a darker aspect of the killings. In
both cases the children claimed they killed to protect themselves or
a sibling from an abusive parent.

Late in 1982 Richard Jahnke, a thirty-eight-old Internal Revenue
Service agent, stepped out of his car and opened his garage door. As
he opened the door, he was ambushed by a shotgun-wielding assailant. Jahnke died instantly in his driveway. The killing was the first
homicide in six months in Jahnke's hometown of Cheyenne, Wyoming. Twelve hours after the murder, Jahnke's son Richard, sixteen,

and daughter Deborah, seventeen, were arrested and charged with murder.

Sixteen-year-old Richard Jahnke held his father's twelve-gauge shotgun and waited for his father to open the garage door. Deborah waited in the living room, backing up her brother with a thirty-caliber automatic carbine. The children's defense for their acts was that they were protecting themselves from a brutal and abusive father. The elder Jahnke was known by his neighbors to be a severe and harsh disciplinarian. The children, speaking before and during the trial, told of their futile attempts to enlist local child protection agencies to protect them from their abusive father.

Three and one-half years after Richard Jahnke was murdered, James Pierson, a forty-two-year-old electrician, was about to leave his Long Island home for work when he was shot to death in the doorway to his kitchen. The killer was the seventeen-year-old son of a former New York City policeman. The killer had been paid $400 by Pierson's sixteen-year-old daughter's boyfriend. The daughter, Cheryl, claimed that she had been sexually abused by her father for some time. She had paid to have her father killed because she feared that he was about to begin molesting her eight-year-old sister. Cheryl Pierson was found guilty and sentenced to six months in jail and five years probation.

Did violence beget violence? Was violence used as the ultimate form of self-defense by the desperate victims of private violence who could find no help and no escape from their brutalization? Or did the children use a convenient excuse for their own brutality? The evidence from these cases in unclear. Cheryl Pierson's aunt denies the scenario painted by her niece, and suggests that the killing may have been motivated by Pierson's half-million-dollar estate.

Irrespective of the legal issues involved in the Jahnke and Pierson cases, both cases underscore the deadly and tragic impact of children growing up amidst violence. Richard Jahnke was slain by his own gun. The isolation in which the Jahnke and Pierson families lived insulated them from outside control, and cut off their children from protection and intervention. Faced with no outside help and having grown up in a violent home, fatal violence may be the tragic solution opted for by desperate children. As one of Richard Jahnke's neighbors said to a *Time* magazine reporter, "What those children did, it made terrible sense."

We attempted to add to our knowledge about the impact of growing up in a violent home in our Second National Family Violence

Survey. We interviewed 3,206 parents of children under seventeen years of age who were living at home. After asking parents about their use of violence toward children in the past year and over the course of the child's lifetime, we asked whether there were any "special difficultites" with the child in the past twelve months. We presented the following list of difficulties:

1. Trouble making friends
2. Temper tantrums
3. Failing grades in school
4. Disciplinary problems
5. Misbehavior and disobedience at home
6. Physical fights with kids who live in your house
7. Physical fights with kids who do not live in your house
8. Physical fights with adults who live in your house
9. Physical fights with adults who do not live in your house
10. Deliberately damaging or destroying property
11. Stealing money or something else
12. Drinking
13. Using drugs
14. Got arrested for something

We found consistent relationships between experiencing severe or abusive violence and all of the difficulties. More importantly, the risk of troubles for children who grew up in violent homes was nearly twice that of those children whose childhoods were free of violence. Overall, more than four out of ten children from violent homes had some trouble at school, were aggressive, and/or had troubles with drugs or alcohol in the past year. This compares with 22.9 percent of the children from nonviolent homes (see fig. 4 in Appendix C).

Assessing the more than three thousand children slightly *underestimates* the difficulties they experienced, since the group includes infants, toddlers, and preschool children. Confining our analysis to only school-aged children from violent homes, we find that 44 percent experienced one or more problems in the past year. For children thirteen years of age or older, this figure rises to more than half (50.7 percent).

Across the board, children from violent homes are more likely to have personal troubles—temper tantrums, trouble making friends, school problems—failing grades, discipline problems, and aggressive and violent flare-ups with family members and people outside the home. These children are three to four times more likely than children from nonviolent homes to engage in illegal acts—vandalism, stealing, alcohol, and drugs—and to be arrested.

The research approach we used cannot tell us whether the violence actually *causes* the personal, school, aggression, and delinquency problems. Our survey only studied families at one point in time, and asked about both the troubles and violence. We cannot know from this survey, for instance, whether it was the trouble that led to the severe violence—as when a child is severely beaten because he steals, uses drugs, is failing at school, or fights with a sibling—or whether the violence led to the trouble.

A plausible interpretation of our results, along with the findings from other research on the impact of growing up amidst violence, is that a cycle of violence, troubles, and violence is created in many homes. Violent experiences set the stage for the individual and social traits that lead to trouble. The trouble is responded to with more violence.

One of the least discussed and most surprising aspects of an examination of the impact of growing up amidst violence is that not all children who experience severe physical and emotional abuse go on to have difficult lives. Cindy, the teenager described in this chapter's introduction, seems to have escaped the lifelong scars that many would predict for her. In spite of growing up in a tense, explosive environment, being sexually molested by her father, and witnessing her father's murder, Cindy seems to be headed for a relatively normal adult life. She endured her mother's trial and ultimate acquittal for murder, enrolled in college, and graduated with honor grades and a major in psychology. She is a vivacious, articulate, poised, lovely young adult who survived a family holocaust.

History is full of "survivors" of unhappy childhoods. Brandt Steele notes that many famous figures in the world had bad experiences with maltreatment early in their lives and yet amounted to something very important. The list includes French philosopher Jean Jacques Rousseau who grew up in a foster home with a punitive aunt during his youth in the 1700s. Mary Wollstonecraft was badly beaten and maltreated by her father, and went on to write "A Vindication of the Rights of Woman" in 1792, a manuscript that marked the beginning of the women's rights movement. Steele lists Rudyard Kipling, Richard Nixon, Eleanor Roosevelt, and George Orwell among the other familiar names who became successful despite significantly unhappy childhoods.

What insulates the survivors? What makes them invulnerable children? We can only speculate. Based on the results of work such as the research conducted by Byron Egeland, we suspect that one major factor in the lives of survivors is the presence of a nurturing adult. For Cindy, this was clearly her mother. For others it may be a relative, foster family, or friend. The nurturance can be personal and economic. Survivors not only need to have their personal and psychological needs met, they need to grow up in an environment that meets their needs for consistent shelter, food, and medical care. Timely, appropriate, and effective intervention also can change the equation for these children from a bleak cycle of violence and abuse to a more hopeful and productive life.

LIVING ON THE EDGE: THE IMPACT ON WOMEN

The physical consequences of wife battering are often obvious—blackened eyes, bruises, and fractures. Many battered women try to hide these physical scars with dark glasses, makeup, or by staying out of sight until the bruises and scars fade. Psychic scars are not visible. They are hidden deep within the battered spirit of the victims of domestic assault.

The actual physical assaults are only one cause of the psychic damage experienced by women. Many battered women explain that waiting and wondering what will set off the next incident is even more damaging than being hit. Joyce, a thirty-five-year-old secondary-school teacher, explained that many times being hit was a "relief" after walking on eggshells for weeks at a time.

> I did not, and even today, do not think of my husband Lou as a violent man. He wouldn't always be violent when he was upset. I guess that's what unsettled me the most. I could never exactly figure what it was that would set him off. He hit me for the first time shortly after we were married. He couldn't find his cuff links. Since I unpacked everything, he tore into me. He hit me with the back of his hand and sent me across the room. He was full of apologies the next day, and more than a year went by before he hit me again. I don't really remember what set him off that time. But soon the time between the hitting was down to months, then weeks. I did everything I could to please him. But I just couldn't think of everything. I remember once when I yelled at him, he came back at me and said, "I guess things are getting too easy around here." Then he slapped and punched me.

> I started to go a little crazy. I just couldn't think of everything. All the
> time he was around I felt like I was walking on a tightrope. Just one
> little slip and I knew I might get it. When he did hit me, I was relieved.
> At least I didn't have to be so tense anymore.

The psychologist Lenore Walker explains that women are neither
constantly abused nor is abuse inflicted at totally random times. She
describes her theory of the "Cycle of Violence." The first stage is the
"tension building stage." Verbal abuse, threats, and minor battering
incidents occur at this time. Women attempt to calm the batterer
during this phase. They may become nurturant or compliant. They
try to anticipate every need, wish, and whim. Their goal is to keep
the minor incidents from escalating. Yet the battering does escalate
to stage two, "the acute battering incident." Walker describes this
stage as characterized by the "uncontrollable discharge of tension."
Uncontrolled battering is usually brief and followed by the third
stage of "kindness and contrite loving behavior." The abusive husband knows he has gone too far and tries to compensate by being
kind and loving to his victim. Eventually, the calm is followed by a
slow buildup of tension. As Joyce explained, a husband begins to
think that his victim is getting a little too free. Minor battering is
used to bring the victim "back into line." John, a twenty-four-year-
old blue-collar worker, described how he used minor violence to try
to keep his wife "in line":

> She was being a pain. I mean dinner was never ready. The kids were
> running around wild. I think she was seeing other guys when she went
> out . . . you get tired of this. I mean, the man's supposed to be the
> boss. One night she came home and I just was fed up with nothing
> being done around here. She just kept denying . . . so I threw her
> down on the lawn and I kicked her.

It is the full cycle of violence and not just the battering incidents that
inflict the psychic and physical damage on battered wives.
    Clinicians who have worked with and studied battered women
report consistent patterns among their patients and clients. Battered
women are generally reported as having poor self-concepts. Battering
leaves them feeling worthless, powerless, helpless, and humiliated.
Shame and self-blame are two of the most common feelings expressed by battered wives. Many of the women we interviewed in
small towns explained that they were so ashamed of being beaten

that they would not even call the police for help. They feared that the incident would be reported in the newspapers. Shelley, a forty-year-old homemaker who had been beaten for most of her marriage, reported:

> I was so ashamed. I didn't want any of my friends or neighbors to know. I didn't want anyone around when Henry was behaving that way . . . that's why I didn't have any neighbors. I didn't even call the police because I was afraid they would put it in the papers.

Also common among battered wives is the feeling that they deserve the beating because they provoke their partners. Sylvia, a forty-three-year-old beautician, reflected the views of many wives:

> Well, I am the first to admit that none of the wars would have started if I didn't provoke them. I just never can keep my big mouth shut and go and let well enough alone. I just keep after him until he reaches his breaking point.

Some women go to great lengths to take responsibility for a husband's violence. June, a nineteen-year-old woman who had been beaten for most of her short marriage, took responsibility for her husband's jealousy.

> Tim [her husband] is really jealous. I remember once when we were at my girlfriend's house. I had to use the bathroom. The bathroom is upstairs. Well, my girlfriend's brother's room is next to the bathroom. I stood in front of his door and talked to him for a minute on my way back downstairs. When I got to the stairs Tim was waiting for me. He called me a whore and a tease and slugged me 'side of my head. I fell down the stairs. I can't blame Tim, though. I guess I shouldn't have talked to my girlfriend's brother. I mean, I know Tim's real jealous.

Not surprisingly, fear is one of the most common characteristics of battered women. For many women the fear is so great that it all but immobilizes them. Joyce, whom we described earlier, said that the fear and anxiety built up so much that: " . . . at the end I became a lump. I couldn't do anything. I was numb. Sometimes I would just let him hit me. I don't even think I felt much by then."

Clinicians note that battered women tend to resemble other patients characterized by agitated depression. Victims of battering tend to report physical problems such as backaches, headaches, and gastrointestinal problems. Fatigue, restlessness, loss of appetite, and sleep problems are also common.

One of the saddest and most striking portraits we have come away with after interviewing thousands of battered women is that they all appear to have aged prematurely. Virtually every battered woman with whom we have talked appears ten or even twenty years older than she is. Puffy facial features and a generally aged and fatigued look are the most visible of the scars women carry.

All battered wives do not become depressed, withdrawn hostility sponges. Just as parental violence can beget violence in offspring, so too marital violence can beget violence—sometimes lethal violence. If a woman is going to kill someone, chances are it will be her husband or partner. In 1984, 806 women killed their husbands— this constitutes more than a third of all marital homicides. If a woman does kill her partner, it will likely be in self-defense—experts estimate that three out of four women who kill their partners do so in self-defense.

On the evening of March 9, 1977, Francine Hughes carried a can of gasoline into the bedroom of her Dansville, Michigan, home. She poured the contents around the bed where her husband James "Mickey" Hughes lay sleeping. Francine backed up to the door of the room, dropped a lighted match, and fled the house as flames engulfed her sleeping husband. She packed her children into the car and drove to the Ingham County Sheriff's Office, where she sat trembling in the car as her daughter told a police officer that her father had been beating Francine for years. The sobbing Francine forced out a confession of "I did it! I did it! I did it!" When asked what she did, she choked out, "He was sleeping and I set the bedroom on fire."

Francine's lawyer, Aryon Greydanus, defended her by, in effect, putting her battering husband on trial. The nature of the crime made a plea of self-defense problematic. Francine had slain her husband while he slept, not while he was in the act of trying to assault or kill her. She had not used deadly force to counter deadly force. In 1977 there were no legal precedents for the argument that killing a battering husband under any condition could be self-defense. So, Francine's attorney chose to plead her innocent by reason of temporary insanity. Greydanus argued that Francine Hughes was temporarily insane as a consequence of Mickey Hughes's beatings. Greydanus was allowed to introduce evidence that Francine was beaten, and, in the end, she was acquitted by a jury on grounds of temporary insanity.

The sensational nature of the case, the unusual tactic of seeking acquittal by reason of battering, and the timing (the Francine Hughes case unfolded just as feminists across the country were striving to define wife battering as a major social problem) led to Francine's story being reported in the news across the country. She appeared twice on "The Phil Donahue Show." Ultimately her story was told in the book, *The Burning Bed*. *The Burning Bed* was turned into a "made-for-television" movie starring Farrah Fawcett. The movie was widely watched and received critical acclaim.

Other battered wives also turned their internal anguish on their husbands. Some of the episodes were as grisly and sensational as the case of Francine Hughes.

Early in the morning of January 28, 1977, Joyce Hawthorne killed her jusband, Aubrey Hawthorne, in the bedroom of their Pensacola, Florida, home. A fight that had festered all day erupted again. Aubrey had his hands around Joyce's throat, and in Joyce's words: "I remember him grabbing me. . . . I thought, this is it. . . . I remember his reaching for the gun beside the bed. . . . I thought, this is it . . . he is going to kill me." Although Joyce reported that she does not remember much of what happened next, Aubrey was found dead in the bedroom, shot seven times with a total of five different guns.

Joyce Hawthorne was tried three separate times by the state of Florida. Each time her attorney attempted to introduce evidence that Joyce was a victim of the battered wife syndrome, and therefore her act was one of self-defense. Each time the trial judge refused to allow such expert testimony. Each time the state court of appeals threw out the conviction based on procedural errors. Ultimately, the state of Florida refused to prosecute Joyce Hawthorne a fourth time and dropped all charges.

A third case that captured some national attention involved Roxanne Gay, a small black woman who had slit the throat of her sleeping husband, the 225-pound defensive lineman for the Philadelphia Eagles, Blenda Gay. Supporters of Roxanne Gay attempted to show that she had been the victim of battering over the course of her marriage to Blenda. The efforts failed, because a psychiatric examination revealed no evidence of batterings. Ultimately the charges were dropped, and Roxanne Gay was admitted to a psychiatric hospital.

There are other cases, some as sensational as those of Francine Hughes or Joyce Hawthorne, or even more so; some involved men and women as well known, or better known, than professional actors or sports figures. Today, in many cases of husband murder it is routine for defendants to claim that a killing was done in self-defense or as a result of the psychological damage inflicted by years of beating and battering. Prior to the case of Francine Hughes, it was unheard of for a woman to be acquitted for murdering her husband if she argued that the murder grew out of abuse. By contrast, today such acquittals are somewhat commonplace. It should be noted that a number of jurisdictions, such as Florida, still refuse to allow expert testimony on the clinical condition of the battered woman syndrome as part of a self-defense or insanity defense. However, this is becoming the exception rather than the rule.

The current controversy is whether or not all claims of self-defense are legitimate. As we pointed out when we discussed children who kill, there are doubters who feel that some murderers who kill family members are simply adopting a trendy and socially accepted defense when they choose to defend their actions on the grounds that they were beaten. The private nature of the family again make such a defense difficult to prove. One should not, however, lose sight of the fact that the private nature of the family often deprives an abused wife or child of any form of effective defense other than murder.

Virtually everything we know about the impact of spousal violence has been learned from those battered women who have come forward to seek help, shelter, or refuge. Our information comes from observing women in battered wife shelters, clinical interviews, or case studies of women who volunteered to be interviewed or to complete our questionnaires.

Those who seek help, flee batterers, or volunteer to participate in social research are not representative of the large population of battered women. One obvious difference is that women who come forward may have endured more severe or frequent violence than women who do not seek help. Another plausible difference is that women who are willing to seek help or talk about their lives may have actually suffered *less* psychic damage than women who keep their victimization private. If battering induces fear and shatters self-esteem, severe battering must leave many women unable even to seek shelter or help. Last, women who keep their victimization private may come from different social and economic backgrounds than women who seek counseling, shelter, or agree to be interviewed by social scientists.

Our Second National Family Violence Survey offered us the unique opportunity to ask a large national sample questions about physical/mental health and emotional conditions. Here, for the first time, we could compare women who lived in violence-free homes with women who endured a wide range of violence at the hands of their partners or mates.

Sadly, the results of our national survey confirmed what we had already expected. The pain and suffering endured by battered women are substantial. Our statistical data bear out the expectation that women who live amidst violence are compromised in nearly every area of their physical and mental health. Moreover, the greater the severity of violence, the greater the chances that a woman's well-being will suffer.

We looked at a variety of possible consequences—a woman's perceptions of her health, stress, depression, and drinking or drug problems; mental health consequences, including thinking about or attempting suicide; and some of the behavioral consequences of living in a violent environment.

We asked women who live in violent homes to compare their health and personal problems at the time of the interview with the same issues before they started having physical fights with their husbands or partners. Women who had experienced violence, especially severe violence, reported that their health, the amount of stress they were experiencing, the chances of their feeling bad or depressed, and their own drinking and alcohol problems were now much worse than before the violence began (see fig. 5 in Appendix C). Some of the differences were staggering:

- Compared with women who had hit their husbands but had never been hit, women who experienced severe violence were nearly *500 percent* more likely to report that their feelings of depression had gotten much worse since the violence began.
- Drinking or drug problems were reportedly much worse in thirteen of one hundred homes of severely battered women, compared with four homes in one hundred of women experiencing minor violence and slightly more than three homes in one hundred of women who were not hit by their husbands at all.

We asked each of the more than three thousand women in our survey to give us a general evaluation of her health. The greater the violence experienced, the less likely it was that a woman would report excellent health, and the more likely she would tell us her health was fair or poor (see fig. 6 in Appendix C). Abused women stay in bed due to illness one day each month, twice as often as women from peaceful homes (see fig. 7 in Appendix C).

The psychic scars that clinicians have reported among their abused patients are readily evident in our examination of women's mental health. We adapted a "Psychiatric System Check List" from a variety of measures that had been used by psychologists to assess mental health status. In order to measure the level of depression and demoralization experienced by victims of violence, we asked women how often they experienced each of the following eleven psychological symptoms in the past year:

1. Had headaches or pains in the head.
2. Been bothered by cold sweats.
3. Felt nervous or depressed.
4. Bothered by feelings of sadness or depression.
5. Felt difficulties were piling up so high that you could not overcome them.
6. Felt very bad or worthless.
7. Found that you could not cope with all the things you had to do.
8. Have you had times when you couldn't help wondering if anything was worthwhile anymore?
9. Have you felt completely hopeless about everything?
10. Thought about taking your life.
11. Have you actually tried to take your life?

In only one case (women bothered by cold sweats) were women from nonviolent homes more likely to report a psychological symptom than were women in violent homes. Furthermore, abused wives were more likely to report symptoms occurring fairly or very often than women whose victimization was limited to pushes, shoves, or slaps (see fig. 8 in Appendix C).

The collection of statistics, the comparison of each symptom, the assessment of each bar graph, all bear out the same message—violence, and most especially severe and abusive violence, leaves victims depressed, demoralized, despondent, and in despair. More than a third of battered women frequently feel sad or depressed. More than one in five often feels bad or worthless. About the same number often wonder if life is worthwile anyone. The fact that thirteen battered women in one hundred feel completely hopeless fairly or very often is of great concern. An individual who feels that life is completely hopeless is unlikely to attempt escaping from a violent home or to seek help. Our data mean that hundreds of thousands of battered wives have been so beaten down they have been reduced to hopelessness and helplessness. Unable to protect themselves, trapped behind closed doors, many battered wives think about and attempt to end their lives.

Whereas but two women in one thousand thought about taking their own life fairly or very often in the last twelve months, forty-six abused women in one thousand contemplated suicide frequently. Furthermore thirty-four in one thousand women who contemplate suicide actually attempt to take their lives. This is the sad silent toll of wife abuse.

Victims of violence do not simply internalize their experiences. Just as violence toward a child appears to increase the children's anger and aggressiveness, so, too, victims of spousal violence are more likely to become angry and lash out verbally and physically (see fig. 9 in Appendix C). Victims of violence, and especially victims of abusive violence, told us that they were more likely to get angry and yell or shout at a nonfamily member, or to express aggression by kicking or smashing something, punching a door, wall, or other object. Remarkably, nearly three women in one hundred who experienced violence told us that they got into a fight with a nonfamily member and hit the person. This is remarkable since women rarely if ever physically fight with nonfamily members. Here again, we see how intimate violence has the potential for spilling over into the street and becoming part of the public violence problem.

We assume that violence causes physical and mental health problems, feelings of worthlessness, depression, and anger. This is both logical and consistent with evidence from other studies of wife battering. Nevertheless, we must point out that we cannot tell from our survey whether, in fact, the violence came before the problems or whether the problems produced the violence. It is certainly plausible that health or psychological problems create stress in a home. This can lead to violence. However, as with our look at children, we think that this is the least plausible order of events. If the problems come first, the violence most certainly makes these problems worse over time.

Not every woman who experienced violence reported negative health, psychological functioning, or angry and violent reactions. Actually, as with battered children, the majority of wives who experience violence do not report intense psychological suffering. The suffering and pain we uncovered are high in comparison with the general levels of such problems and symptoms among all married women.

Many battered women, including those who flee the most violent environments, are not permanently damaged victims of their husbands' brutality. Women who arrive at shelters seeking refuge have already demonstrated self-sufficiency and an ability to take control of their lives. Battered wives have demonstrated their resourcefulness, bravery, creativity, and perseverance in remaining with their abusive husbands, in taking steps to stop the violence, and in seeking to protect themselves and their children. Although she may have killed her husband in a desperate act of self-protection, Joyce Hawthorne also demonstrated her strength and capability as a mother of five children. She continued to raise her children during the abuse, after the killing, and through three long and painful trials. At the time of the last trial, her older daughter was enrolled in college, and Joyce continued to be a loving and caring mother for her family.

There is a bleak side as well as a somewhat brighter side to our investigation of the impact of living amidst violence. The bleak side is our finding that women and children who live with violence are much more likely to suffer psychologically than those living in violence-free homes. More bleak is the fact that these victims carry their pain and suffering beyond the walls of their homes. Battered children can become behavior problems at school and are at risk for violent delinquent behavior in the streets. Victimized women and children express their anger outwardly in acts of violence against parents and partners in the home, and against friends, neighbors, and strangers in the streets. Anger can also be turned inward as victims reach a stage of demoralization and hoplessness, and attempt to take their own lives.

The brighter side is that the deepest pain and suffering are experienced by less than half of all victims. Compassionate friends, supportive family, available community resources, and social and personal resources buffer many victims from the psychic pains of violence. In some cases, rare individual women and children turn their experiernces into strengths and rise above their bleak backgrounds to make major contributions to society.

There is one remaining dark side to the impact of intimate violence. This is the double whammy that victims, especially women, experience as a result of being beaten and brutalized. Where violence does lead to depression, demoralization, anger, and frustration, these outcomes are often turned back on the victim and used to justify the beatings received. To a lesser extent battered children find that their reactions to their beatings are used to justify why they were beaten in the first place. Victim blaming is always out of place in the arena of human relations and especially in families. We believe that no one, regardless of psychological state, degree of anger, or aggressiveness, ever deserves to be hit.

7.

Coping

with Violence

At the conclusion of her third trial, Joyce Hawthorne was found guilty of manslaughter. A reporter waiting in the counthouse hallway overheard a juror's comment as she filed out of the building. The juror looked curiously at her companion and said: "I know her husband beat her. I know she feared for her life. I guess what I still don't understand is why she just didn't leave him after the violence got so bad." Given the toll that intimate violence takes on women—both physically and psychologically—one of the more frequently asked questions is, "Why do they stay?" We noted in chapter 2 that common sense would seem to argue that battered wives should just pack up and leave if they want to prevent future abuse.

Waiting along with the reporter in the courthouse lobby was the psychologist, Lenore Walker. Walker had traveled to Florida for the trial, just as she had come for Joyce Hawthorne's first two trials, to serve as an expert witness. Walker, had she testified, would have offered an answer to the juror's question about why a physically and psychologically battered woman would choose to remain with her abuser. But the trial judge ruled that Walker's testimony would not be allowed. Among the reasons was his opinion that research on family violence had not developed to the point where it could sustain expert testimony. Later, an appeals court in Florida would rule that the judge did have the discretion to disallow expert testimony. The appeals court, however, overturned Joyce Hawthorne's conviction on other grounds. She was freed when the state of Florida declined to prosecute her a fourth time.

Had Walker testified, she would have described the results of her interviews with Joyce and with hundreds of other battered women. Walker would have described how Joyce Hawthorne was the victim of the battered wife syndrome and also a victim of "learned helplessness." Walker observes that women who experience repeated physical assaults at the hands of their husbands have much lower self-concepts than women whose marriages are free from violence; she postulates that the repeated beatings and lower self-concepts leave women with the feeling that they cannot control what will happen to them. They feel unable to protect themselves from further assaults and feel incapable of controlling the events occurring around them.

Walker's theory of learned helplessness has its roots in the research of the experimental psychologist, Martin Seligman. Seligman and his associates placed dogs in cages and administered electrical shocks at random and varied intervals. The dogs learned quickly that no matter how they responded, they could not control the shocks. At the beginning, the dogs tried to escape. When they found that they could not stop the shocks, they stopped searching for an escape and became passive and submissive. At this point the researchers altered the experiment. They first tried to teach the dogs to cross to the other side of the cage and escape. The dogs remained passive. The researchers then left the cage doors open and showed the dogs the way out. The dogs were still passive, made no attempt to get out, and made no attempt to avoid the shocks. Only by repeated attempts to physically drag the dogs out of the cage were the dogs motivated to overcome their learned helplessness and attempt to escape. Seligman's group and other experimental psychologists have repeated these experiments with cats, fish, rats, birds, primates, and even humans with the same results.

Walker and others conclude that learned helplessness occurs when a person either does not have control, or believes that he or she has no control, over the outcome of events. Thus, even if it is objectively possible for a battered wife to flee her husband, her long-term inability either to predict or control his violent outbursts will result in her believing that she cannot escape. Walker proposes that once people think that they cannot control what happens to them, it is difficult for them to believe they can ever influence events. Battered women, says Walker, become like Seligman's shocked dogs, cats, and rats.

There is indeed some evidence to support Walker's theory of learned helplessness. As we saw in the previous chapter, a number of victims of severe violence—13 percent—feel that things are completely hopeless. Yet, to cast all battered women as being compliant, passive, and submissive is unfair and unjust. Violence does indeed take a significant toll of the victims' sense of self-worth and undermines their belief that they can control their destiny. Some women become so desperate that they feel the only escape is either suicide or killing the attacker. Yet, a substantial number of women do not fall into the depths of learned helplessness. They search for avenues of reconciliation, therapy, and escape.

STAYING OR LEAVING: FACTORS AFFECTING THE CHOICE

Students of family violence have long tried to study the process of battered wives staying or leaving abusive relationships. One of the first essays on the subject was by the legal writer, Elizabeth Truninger. Truninger identified seven factors that help explain why women do not break off relationships with abusive men. The reasons are: (1) the women have poor self-concepts; (2) they believe their husbands will reform; (3) economic hardship; (4) they have children who need a father's support; (5) they doubt they can get along alone; (6) they believe divorcées are stigmatized; and (7) it is difficult for women with children to get work.

In our own research we found a number of factors that distinguish women who stay from those who leave. First, women who leave seemed to have experienced more severe violence. Second, women who grew up in violent homes were more likely to stay with abusive husbands. Apparently the experience with, and exposure to, violence either made these women more tolerant of domestic violence or more lacking in hope of really escaping. Perhaps their helplessness was learned as children when they saw their mothers hit and fail to prevent future violent attacks.

Women who stayed in violent marriages were less educated, had fewer job skills, and were more likely to be unemployed than women who sought help, called the police, or left their violent partners. One explanation for this finding is that women who have few resources

are more entrapped in violent homes. Another explanation was offered by a woman who remained with a violent husband until she
began working.

> Until I started going out in public I didn't realize what was going on
> around me. I was so darned stupid and ignorant. I didn't know how
> the other half of the world lived. And when I started being a waitress
> —I used to love to sit there when I wasn't busy and watch the people.
> The mother and the father with their children—and see how they
> acted. And I started to feel like I was cheated . . . and it started to
> trouble me and I started to envy those people. So I said, "You know
> . . . am I supposed to live the way I'm living?"

Last, we found that women with young children were more likely
to stay. As the children got older, the likelihood of their involvement
in marital conflict and strife increased. Many women left immediately after their teenage children had been hurt trying to protect
them. Sandy was forty-three years old when she fled a violent home
for a shelter:

> I guess I took his violence for too many years. I never liked getting
> hit, but I guess I could write it off because he only was really violent
> a few times. When the kids were little our fights wouldn't start until
> they were put to bed. But I think as the kids got older they kind of
> knew we were fighting and he was hitting me. This really began to
> bother my son Ricky. He got sadder and sadder. Finally, my husband
> and I had a fight at the dinner table—I think Ricky was about twelve
> years old. Ricky threw something—I guess a plate—at my husband
> and said that he wasn't going to let his mom get hit anymore. My
> husband was really enraged. He gave Ricky a backhand and knocked
> him off his chair. I made up my mind then I couldn't stay any longer.
> I packed and left for the shelter when my husband went to work the
> next morning.

Other investigators have focused on the factors that influence
whether women remain with their batterers, seek help, or leave. The
sociologist Mildred Pagelow administered questionnaires to 350
women who sought temporary residence in shelters. Pagelow also
found that limited educational resources and occupational skills appear to inhibit women from leaving violent relationships. The sociologists Michael Strube and Linda Barbour talked with ninety-eight
battered wives and also confirmed that economically dependent

women were more likely to remain with abusive husbands. They also found that wives who stayed reported that they were more "committed" to the marital relationship.

In contrast to studies that focus only on women who leave violent marriages, the sociologist Lee Bowker examined the stories and situations of women who chose to stay with their husbands *and* reported that they were successful in having their husbands stop the violence. Bowker used newspaper advertisements, personal contacts, and television appearances to recruit 126 women who said they they had been beaten but who also reported that their husbands had stopped being violent.

The techniques used by women to get their husbands to stop the violence clustered into three categories: (1) personal strategies which included talking, promising, threatening, hiding, passive defense, aggressive defense, and avoidance; (2) use of informal help sources including family members, in-laws, neighbors, friends, and shelters; and (3) formal help sources, including police, social service agencies, lawyers, and district attorneys.

The most common personal strategy was passive defense—covering one's body with arms, hands, or feet. However, although nine out of ten battered wives tried this approach, few reported it had positive effects on their partners. The most common informal strategy was seeking the help of friends. Bowker described the case of one wife—a woman married to a man in the military. Her husband, a hard-driven career soldier, frequently took out the frustrations of the workday at home. The woman feared that if she told anyone on the base it would quickly get back to her husband and further enrage him. Finally, she chose to talk about her problem with friends. As they talked about what she would do, the woman came to realize that she was not to blame and did not have to put up with her husband's violence. At one point, she borrowed money from her friends and visited her sister. Her husband was frantic—not enraged. After a week, the woman spoke with him and demanded that he seek psychiatric help. The most commonly used formal strategy was seeking counseling from a social service agency.

Bowker's study, and the resulting book, offered the promise of finding out which particular strategy used by battered women worked best to eliminate the violence in their lives. When we read the book, we quickly turned to the last chapter to discover which specific approach was best. We, probably like many other readers of the book, *Beating Wife Beating,* were disappointed. We had assumed that there was a simple answer to a complex problem. There was not. Bowker reports that no one strategy worked best. Women in different situations clearly found different strategies to be most effective in ending the violence. In the end, Bowker concluded that almost any strategy or help source can ultimately work. The critical factor was not a specific technique, but the woman's conviction and determination that the violence *must stop now*. As one of Bowker's respondents said:

> Don't tolerate abuse. When you say stop it, mean it. Leave the situation if it gets close to violence. Recognize that you don't need to be dependent. Put yourself as number one. Don't assume blame for the abuse.

The research on the factors that determine whether women stay or leave violent relationships effectively explodes the myth that wives who remain with violent men are masochistic. The weight of the collected evidence points more to social factors entrapping women in violent marriages. Research such as that conducted by Lee Bowker convincingly shows that even the women who remain in violent homes are far from passive, submissive, or compliant hostility sponges. The notion of "learned helplessness" rings true for a number of battered wives. But the majority of victims appear to struggle every day to find the key personal, informal, or formal strategy which will stem the flood of their husbands' violence and abuse.

We used the opportunity of our Second National Family Violence Survey to extend the research carried out by Lee Bowker. Whereas he advertised for a small sample of women in Milwaukee, we had access to more than three thousand women representative of the entire population of married women, women living with men, or women recently divorced.

AFTER THE VIOLENT EPISODE

Our first concern was with women's actions immediately after the violent episode. The Conflict Tactics Scales asked women to tell us about whether they had experienced any of a number of violent acts and how often. When we finished administering the scales, we asked those women who had experienced violence to think back to the most recent occurrence of the most violent behavior. Then we asked which of the following described what they did as a result:

1. Hit back or threw something
2. Cried
3. Yelled or cursed at him
4. Ran to another room
5. Ran out of the house
6. Called a friend or relative
7. Called the police
8. Other

Shock, surprise, and the stunning realization that a woman has been assaulted by someone she loves probably explains why crying was the immediate response to violence most frequently reported (see fig. 10 in Appendix C). More than half of the victims of violence (54.9 percent) reacted immediately by crying.

Patty, a nineteen-year-old who was already the mother of a three-year-old daughter when we interviewed her, explained why crying was her reaction to being hit:

> I was stunned . . . shocked. I mean, this was the man I loved . . . the man I was going to live my life with. Now, don't get me wrong, I never thought that he was any kind of Prince Charming. But he had never even touched me during the time we were dating. The baby was two years old when we were married . . . so I didn't have to marry him. I married him because I loved him. All of a sudden, he hauls off and punches me. I just couldn't believe it. I started to cry right away. I just didn't know what else to do.

In all likelihood, the percentages *underestimate* how common a reaction crying is to being hit. We would guess that most of the 209 women with whom we talked reacted to the first violent incident with tears. By the time we interviewed many of the women, violence had become an all-too-common part of their lives. Fully one-third of the women we interviewed had been hit four or more times in the previous twelve months alone. Typically, the violence had gone on for at least two years before the interview. However, even for the women who endured years of violence, crying was a common reaction. Jane, forty years old and divorced, explained why she cried when her ex-husband abused her:

My ex used to beat on me all the time. Once he pushed me down the stairs. I would just sit alone and cry when he beat me up—and he did it quite often. I never called the cops or hit him because if I did that he would just have beat the shit out of me.

Many women reacted more actively. The second most common immediate response was yelling and cursing at a violent spouse. Nearly one in four victims (24 percent) hit their attacker back—despite the obvious risks of escalating the violence. Not surprisingly, those women who were victims of severe violence were somewhat more reluctant to hit their husbands back than were victims of minor violence.

There are various reasons women hit back. First, there is self-defense. Many battered wives strike back because it is the only immediate way they can protect themselves.

When he hit me I would hit back. Maybe a woman doesn't have the strength to hold her own, but I sure want to go down trying. . . . I mean, you know, he hits me late at night when we are alone. I'm not just going to stand there and let him hurt me. So I hit him back. . . . I am more liable to pick something up than hit him with my fist.

After he hit me and I was hurt, I was afraid he would hurt me again, so I went after him with a kitchen knife and put him in the hospital.

When women do hit back, they often tend to compensate for their lack of physical size and strength by choosing to hit their husbands with objects. The stereotypical image of the wife chasing her husband with a rolling pin is not far from the truth—what is missing in the stereotype is the fact that the woman has been beaten and is trying to protect herself, or punish her abuser.

Running to another room was the third most common reaction, while fleeing the home altogether was a bit more unusual—13.5 percent of victims responded in this manner. The private and intimate nature of the family, and perhaps the fact that domestic violence typically occurs later in the evening, seems to limit the likelihood that battered wives will flee their homes or seek help from a friend or relative. Obviously, another possibility is that husbands prevent their wives from leaving. A number of husbands frequently rip and tear the woman's clothes. There appears to be no sexual motive in this behavior; rather, it seems that the husbands are attempting to prevent their victims from fleeing the home or seeking outside help. Husbands use other tactics to immobilize their victims. One wife told us that her husband routinely disconnected her car's distributor cap before every beating. Another husband took his wife's car battery out of her car every night. A third man actually locked his family in the house each night with a double-lock dead bolt.

Immediately seeking help from the police was the least likely response, especially for victims of minor violence. Less than 3 percent of the victims of minor violence immediately called the police after they were attacked, while five times that percentage (14 percent) of the victims of beatings, choking, and other forms of severe violence immediately called the police. Although an unusual example, one interview with a battered wife stands out in our mind. When we asked this particular woman whether she called the police, she responded quietly and politely, "Honey, in this town my husband is the police."

Overall, nearly every woman we talked with (95.6 percent) identified one or more immediate reactions to being hit. The victims of abusive violence were even more likely than victims of slaps, pushes, or shoves to take immediate steps to defend or protect themselves immediately after being hit. Our interviews do not support Walker's theory of learned helplessness. Many of the women we interviewed were hit many times before the instance we discussed. Yet, even after years of repeated slaps, pushes, and beatings, most women react vigorously each time they are hit.

A Note on Men

As we remarked in an earlier chapter, controversy over the issue of battered men and whether battered men even exist has produced a complete research and perceptual blackout of the issues of men who are hit by their wives. We did talk to 177 men who had been hit by their wives. The larger number of these men had also struck their wives, while a smaller percentage told us they had been hit by a spouse or partner but had never behaved violently themselves.

As with women, most men reacted immediately when hit. More than eight out of ten men (85.5 percent) identified one or more actions they took after being hit. Victims of slaps, pushes, and other forms of minor violence were actually more likely to respond than victims of abusive violence (91.4 percent versus 84 percent). The response pattern of men who were hit was quite different from that of women. A man's most likely immediate reaction to being hit is to yell and curse at his wife. Fleeing the room or house is the next most common reaction. Surprisingly, given the assumption that men react violently if hit, fewer than fifteen in one hundred men said they hit back when struck. A small, but not totally insignificant, number of men told us they cried immediately after being hit (4.8 percent for victims of minor violence; 6.8 percent of victims of severe violence). Men are least likely to call a friend, neighbor, or the police. It is clear that being hit by your wife or partner is not perceived as masculine, and thus, however a man reacts, he typically reacts in private.

LONGER-TERM STRATEGIES

After we talked with victims of intimate violence about their immediate reactions to being hit, we turned our attention to the more deliberate and long-term steps taken by assaulted women to get their husbands or partners to stop hurting or threatening them. The single most common strategy that victims used to prevent future violence was avoiding their spouses and staying away from certain topics of conversation (see fig. 11 in Appendix C). More than half of the victims of minor violence and seven out of ten victims of severe forms of violence reported using this strategy. Pam was first hit by her husband shortly after they were married. Pam told us that she initiated a conversation about her day, and asked how her husband's day had gone.

> He was quiet at first. I just kind of talked and talked about my day. Then I asked him about his day. He got real upset. I really have no idea why he was so angry. Anyway, first he started to yell, then all of a sudden he just slapped me across the face and said he wasn't going to talk about work. Well, I figured if he was going to be so touchy, I would just not ask him about what went on at work again.

Pam's reaction understates the ways women who are hit go about avoiding their husbands and certain topics of conversation. Ellen, forty-five-year-old elementary-school teacher, explained her strategy for minimizing fights and violence.

> Alan has hit me a number of times. I think the first time he hit me was shortly after we were married. He couldn't find where I put his socks.

The next time I think it was because I served him leftovers. He said he never ate leftovers—his mother never served his father leftovers. I guess I just have learned what things and what issues make him upset and I try to avoid making him upset.

Alice, another victim of sporadic violence, framed her account somewhat differently:

I have learned what gets him mad. I also know, just by looking at him, when he gets that kind of weird, screwed-up expression on his face, that he is getting ready to be mad. So I just get extra careful about what I do and what I say. I sure try to stay away from him during the times he looks weird and everything. Most of the time I figure I just have to walk on eggshells.

Avoidance is an active and often exhausting strategy. The women with whom we talked admitted that they were not always able to predict what topic, issue, or event would lead to violence. Many women invested their entire time at home trying to anticipate what they should avoid to prevent angering their husbands. Was walking on eggshells effective? According to the women whose husbands' violence was restricted to pushing, slapping, shoving, or throwing things, the answer is generally yes. Nearly seven out of ten victims (68 percent) of acts we labeled "minor violence" told us that simply keeping our of their husband's way was usually effective. Unfortunately, those women married to men whose violence ranged up to choking, beating, punching, and kicking found that avoiding their husbands was not especially effective; less than a third of these women said they were able to limit violence.

The second most common long-range prevention strategy was trying to talk husbands out of being violent. The women who use the talking strategy generally try to use logic, rational discussion, and argument to persuade husbands to stop being violent. Karen was a thirty-eight-year-old wife with two daughters. Her husband, a veterinarian, sometimes got enraged and beat Karen. Karen conceded that once the violence began, she had no hope of getting her husband to stop. But between incidents, she tried to reason with him and get him to admit that his violence was wrong:

I could never really predict when Howard [her husband] would lose his temper and get mad at me. There didn't seem to be a pattern to when or why he would get crazy and beat me. While he beat me he was like insane—you couldn't talk with him or reason with him at all. So I tried to reason with him when he wasn't violent. I would talk to him about why he would get so mad. I also tried to get him to see that it was wrong to beat his wife. He would tell me that he loved me and that he hated to hit me, but he couldn't stand my nagging him all the time. He said he was tired at the end of the day, and he couldn't stand any more nagging. I got him to agree that I would stop nagging him if he would stop hitting me.

We found that the next most widely used mechanism for attempting to limit violence was hiding or leaving. For years researchers and the public alike have asked the question, "Why do they stay?" The answer to the question is, "They don't." In just the last year before we interviewed them, nearly all of the battered wives (seven out of ten) had left their assaultive spouses. Keeping in mind that these are women who have been battered for a number of years, it is reasonable to assume that every one of them left for some period of time during the course of the battering.

Battered wives are not masochistic and they do not remain with their violent partners because they somehow like being hit. Sadly, our results explode the commonsense notion that leaving is a solution. About half of those who have left violent partners rated this strategy as "very effective." Obviously, this means that for the other half of battered women, even the drastic step of leaving a batterer is not too effective. A more sobering finding was the discovery that leaving made things even worse for one out of eight of the battered wives. How can it be that leaving is not an effective solution? The answer is that even though women left, they still faced considerable pressure to return, and returning is what made the strategy less effective or caused things to become worse.

There are a number of pushes and pulls that bring women who have fled violence back to the violent home. Economic factors are a major push. Women who flee to a hotel or motel simply cannot afford to remain there indefinitely. Only a few women actually go to motels and hotels; the remainder find shelter with parents, siblings, relatives, or friends. While they find help and hospitality at first, there is a limit to how long battered women feel they can impose or feel welcome. Having worn out their welcome, battered women must choose between returning home or setting out to find a place of their own. For women with dependent children, the latter option is often not open to them. One mother told us of the choices she faced after she left her husband:

I left and went to my mother's the last time he hit me. I was hurt and my mother was willing to take care of me and watch my kids. But, you know, I mean I got better and didn't need to have my mother take care of me. And the kids . . . well, when you have four kids you really need a place of your own. What was I going to find? I didn't have a job, money, or nothin'. I could get welfare, but I couldn't even afford a rat's nest on that. I was pretty depressed, and I guess I figured I really had no place to go but home.

A second push comes from social expectations that women are supposed to keep their families together. The women who fled to the homes of friends or relatives generally found help and support. Frequently, they also were confronted with pressure to return home and "work things out."

I was staying with my friend. She was real nice. But she also kept telling me that I should try to go home and work things out with Paul. She said that it was a woman's job to keep her family together. That's what my mother said too. So, I went back.

There are also a number of pulls to return home. The primary pull comes from the batterer himself. Many battered wives who have left report that their husbands beg and promise anything if the wives return. Julie, a twenty-three-year-old battered mother of an infant son, said her husband pleaded for her to return:

Oh, I went back because he begged me. He would come to my mother's house every day to talk with me. At first I wouldn't talk to him at all. He sent me notes and flowers, and even candy. He called every night to talk to me. He apologized and promised that it would never happen again. I mean, he made so many promises. . . . I felt he learned his lesson, so I went home . . . he hit me two weeks later.

For other women, the pull is for the sake of their children.

My kids should have a father. I figured I could deal with him, and at worst, I could suffer through his spells. But I thought my kids, especially my son, should have a father. Kids shouldn't grow up with just a mother, they need a father. I didn't want my kids to have the kinds of troubles the kids from broken homes have.

The final pull is the love and attachment that are part of marriage, even a violent one. Beyond the concern for children and concern for the reaction of friends and relatives to the breakup of a violent marriage, there are the love, shared interests, and companionship found in the marriage. Balancing three or four violent incidents a year against the loss of love, home, companionship, and economic security, many women return home, even aware of the obvious risks of doing so.

> I went home because I love him—I still had feelings for him even after what he did to me.

> My mother and my friends want me to stay away from him, to get a divorce, to get him locked up. But I love him . . .

> When he came to my mother's to see me, I felt sorry for him. I remember how things were and thought that if he felt this bad, well, he would change and we could be happy like we used to.

> All the times he hit me still didn't destroy the feelings I have for him.

Our interviews and statistical data all add up to a simple conclusion: Ending a marriage is very difficult. It is perhaps even more difficult if the marriage is a violent one, because the victim has had her sense of self-worth and self-confidence systematically eroded by the violence.

Thus, although battered wives typically leave, they also typically return. Those who have carefully and forcefully negotiated for a fundamental change in the relationship have a chance of reducing the risk of future violence. For those who do not, or cannot, negotiate such a change, there is likely to be more violence since their husbands know that they can behave as they wish with impunity.

Thirty percent of the victims of minor violence and half of the victims of abuse fought back as a means to both protecting themselves and trying to prevent future violence. This is not an altogether unreasonable approach since inflicting costs on an offender may be an effective means of reducing the use of violence in the home.

We find that intimate violence tends to start out with slaps, pushes, shoves, and other less dangerous acts. With the passage of time, some husbands appear to learn that they can "get away" with hitting their wives. On the one hand, their wives may either be unwilling or unable to put a stop to the violence. On the other hand, outside agents of social control are rarely called in to intervene and break up the more minor of violent attacks. With few costs to pay, violent men may become more aggressive and more violent. The longer a man can inflict severe pain without cost, the less success his wife has in protecting herself and stopping the violence.

When we talked with battered women about which personal strategies they used to attempt to stop or reduce violence, we discovered a bitter irony in our findings. Victims of abusive violence are much more likely to take steps to try to stop future violence. Yet, despite their efforts, victims of the most severe forms of violence are the *least successful* in preventing their husbands from hurting or threatening them.

The key to preventing severe violence is taking action against the first and more minor acts of physical aggression. What should a woman do? Just as Lee Bowker discovered that the most effective strategy for stopping wife beating was a woman's conviction and determination that the violence must stop now, so, too, we found that the single most effective strategy used by our national sample of victims was persuading husbands to promise not to be violent again. We base this conclusion on a cost-benefit ratio, which we calculated for each of the eight strategies used by victims of violence. The ratio was computed by dividing the percent of women who said a strategy was effective by the percent who said the approach made things worse (see fig. 12 in Appendix C).

Getting a husband to promise to refrain from violent behavior was between five and six times more effective than leaving him for two days or threatening a divorce. The least effective strategy was hitting back. Not only did the fewest number of wives view fighting back as "very effective," but 16 percent of the victims of minor violence and one in four victims of abuse told us that fighting back actually made the situation much worse. As one woman put it: "He hit me when I was nice and tried to reason. I shouldn't have been too surprised that he hit me when I hit him back."

There are profound implications that can be gained from our cost-benefit ratio. First and foremost, we know that fighting fire with fire is unlikely to help battered women. An intervention program built around self-defense instruction and techniques for fighting back is unlikely to pay any kind of dividend for either individual women or society. Fortunately, virtually no responsible spokespersons on the issue of preventing and treating family violence advocate that women protect themselves by striking back.

An important and beneficial way to help battered women is empowering them to engage in negotiation with their husbands to end the violence. Among the intervention services that would help women to get their husbands to cease the violence would be educa-

tion in mediation or conflict resolution techniques, and family therapy for couples engaging in acts of minor violence.

SEEKING HELP

The majority of victims of violence attempt to use some kind of
personal strategy to protect themselves and prevent future violence.
In this section we look at whether women try to cope with violence
by seeking help outside of their homes, what factors influence
whether or not a woman seeks help, which sources of help are used,
and which are most effective.

We asked each of the nearly three thousand women we interviewed to tell us what they did when they had a family or personal
problem in the past year. Thus, we are now able to compare not
only victims of minor and severe violence, we also have a comparison
sample of the help-seeking behavior of women whose problems did
not include family violence. We found a stark measure of the impact
of domestic violence in our comparison. Overall, only one in four
(23.6 percent) women who had experienced no violence in the last
year sought any kind of help outside their families for personal or
family problems. Victims of minor violence were twice as likely (46.2
percent) to go outside of their home for help and guidance, while
almost seven out of ten victims of severe violence (69.8 percent) told
us they turned to someone for help (see fig. 13 in Appendix C). Here
again, we found little evidence of battered women suffering from
learned helplessness. Overall, the greater the violence, the more active women are in seeking help.

Clearly, the data from our national survey support our earlier notion that the key factor that influences whether a woman would take
action and seek help was the severity of the violence experienced.
Women who are punched, kicked, bitten, choked, hit with an object,
beaten, or threatened with weapons responded more to the most recent attack and tried to get more help from more different sources
than women who were victims of less severe forms of violence.

Additional factors that influenced whether victims would seek
help included:

- *Previous Marriage.* Women who had been married previously
  were more likely to seek help. Perhaps they had learned from a
  previous marriage that things would not work out unless they
  actively tried to bring about a change. Julie, a battered wife in

her third marriage, told us why she left her husband for a shelter: "You know, I really do feel like a failure. Here I have left my third marriage and I'm not even thirty-five years old. But I just couldn't stay and let him hit me. I can't let than happen again."

- *The Possibility of Divorce.* Those women who told us that they thought a lot about whether they should end their relationship tried more strategies to end violence. It would appear that a critical factor was being willing to end a violent relationship permanently.
- *Conflict.* The greater the conflict in a marriage, the more issues causing disagreement and argument, the *less* likely a woman was to seek actively to end the violence.
- *Health.* Women whose health was poor did less. Poor health tends to have a demoralizing effect and to sap one's ability to deal with serious problems effectively.
- *Verbal Abuse.* Women who were verbally battered as well as physically abused did more. This is surprising, since we might assume that the verbal battering would break down a woman's self-concept and render her less likely to seek help actively.
- *Psychological Problems.* Another counterintuitive finding was that women who reported being stressed or depressed tried a lot more strategies to end violence and made a lot more use of various sources of help.

Social factors played little or no role in determining whether a woman sought help. For instance, better-educated women reacted about the same as those with less education. Family income made no difference, nor did the size of the town or city in which the victim resided. Last, those women who grew up in violent homes made just as great an effort to end the violence as women who did not.

When women have family or personal troubles, whether they are victims of violence or not, they are most likely to turn to relatives, friends, and neighbors for help (see fig. 13 in Appendix C). The next most likely source of help is human-service professionals and agencies, including psychotherapists, family therapists, doctors and nurses, and the clergy. Least likely to be used are legal resources, such as lawyers, police, and district attorneys. The findings from our national survey confirm the pattern discovered by Lee Bowker that informal sources of help are the most commonly used and that legal resources are the least likely avenues of assistance for women with family problems.

It comes as no surprise that victims of violence seeking help from a human-service resource are most likely to seek psychotherapy and/or family therapy. As we have noted again and again, the public perception of wife abuse is that it is caused by the mental illness of the offender—that men who abuse their wives are truly psychotic. Less obvious in the pattern of help-seeking behavior is that women turn to therapists or counselors because they feel they may have psychological problems. Diane was thirty-seven and the mother of two children when she made her first appointment with a therapist.

> I couldn't do anything to get him to stop hitting me. I tried and tried. I wouldn't disturb him when he got home. I didn't complain when he was drunk. I kept the house clean. Nothing mattered. Finally, I made an appointment with a counselor. Frank [her husband] was absolutely charming. He said he didn't mind seeing the counselor because he wanted to help me work out my problems. He cooperated with everything, but he refused to admit that he had ever hit me. You know, after a while I thought there really was something wrong with me. So I asked Frank to stop coming and I went alone. I spent some time on a psych ward. I was sure there was something wrong with me. It wasn't until I was in a support group that I began to realize that the problem wasn't mine.

More important than knowing which sources of help and services victims of violence seek is knowing which are the most effective. Yet in this case, effectiveness is a subjective matter, since it is based on women telling us that the resources or services they sought were either very effective, somewhat effective, slightly effective, not effective, or made it worse. Among those resources or services viewed as the most effective by battered women (rated "very effective" by more than half of the women who used the service) were the batterers' relatives, mental health centers, alcohol/drug therapists, family therapists, psychotherapists, doctors and nurses, and other social agencies. Victims of minor violence gave the clergy high ratings, along with alcohol/drug therapists, family therapists, psychotherapists, women's groups, social agencies, and lawyers. However, some of the same services and help sources were also reported as making things worse. A significant percentage of battered wives said that seeking help from the batterer's relatives and the clergy made things worse. Many victims of minor violence also told us that the partner's relatives also made things worse.

A complicated, but useful, picture emerges from our look at how victims of intimate violence cope. First and foremost, our results explode the theory that all, or even most, battered wives react to abuse in the same manner that caged dogs react to repeated shocks. There is no evidence that the majority of battered women suffer from learned helplessness. The more severe the violence, the more likely women are to try to protect themselves and to seek outside help.

If there is a message in our analysis of the steps taken by women to cope with violence and the relative usefulness of those steps, it is that they are much more effective if they are taken after the first incident of the most minor violence. Delaying until the violence escalates to a frequency or severity that would generally be considered abusive is too late. A firm, emphatic, and rational approach appears to be the most effective personal strategy a woman can use to prevent future violence. Ours was the second research project to find that a woman who firmly negotiated an end to the violence and indicates that she will not tolerate being hit has the greatest chance of ending her partner's violent behavior. Last, we note that friends, neighbors, social agencies, the clergy, and to a lesser extent, lawyers and the police are called upon by victims to provide help and counseling.

Our analysis of how victims of intimate violence cope leaves us with a paradox. In discovering that battered women do not generally suffer from learned helplessness, and by uncovering the many personal and formal strategies used by victims to protect themselves and prevent violence, we seemed to have failed to answer the question posed by the juror at the beginning of the chapter. To rephrase the question, "If battered women can and do leave, if they try many and varied techniques to protect themselves and get help, why would such a woman be forced to kill her husband to protect herself?" The answer is simple. All sources of help are not available to all battered women, and those that are available may not always be effective. There was no shelter for battered wives in Joyce Hawthorne's community. She had turned to the police, but they had been of little help. The other techniques and services she sought failed her. With her back to the wall, no place to go, and fearing for her life and the welfare of her children, killing her husband was her last desperate hope. The next chapter continues our examination of the aftermath of violence by examining the structure and effectiveness of legal, social, and medical services that are designed to help and protect victims of family violence.

8.

Compassion or Control:

Legal, Social,

and Medical Services

On June 10, 1983, Charles Thurman, Sr., went to the home of Judy Bentley and Richard St. Hilliare in Torrington, Connecticut, a small city about thirty miles west of Hartford. Thurman demanded to speak to his twenty-one-year-old wife Tracy, who, along with her son Charles, Jr., had been staying with Bentley and St. Hilliare. Tracy called the police—just as she had done numerous times before when Charles, Sr., had either threatened or attacked her in the Bentley/St. Hilliare residence. After a few minutes Tracy went outside to speak with her husband and attempt to calm him down, thus hoping to prevent another episode of violence toward her or her son.

When a police officer arrived about twenty-five minutes later, he found Tracy on the ground. She had been stabbed thirteen times in the chest, neck, and throat. Charles, Sr., dropped a bloody knife, kicked his estranged wife in the head, and dashed into the house. He came out of the house carrying his son, dropped the boy on his unconscious mother, and yelled that he had killed the boy's "fucking mother." Again he kicked the prostrate Tracy in the head. Three more officers arrived, and Charles continued to wander around the yard yelling and screaming before he was finally arrested. Tracy Thurman was in a coma for eight days, hospitalized for several months, and remains scarred and partially paralyzed. Charles, Sr., was convicted of assault and is currently serving a fifteen-year prison term.

As brutal as the assault was on Tracy Thurman, it was only one of hundreds of thousands of brutal and injurious assaults on women by their husbands each year. Her call to the police was but one of hundreds of thousands of such calls each year. Her story would have only made news in Torrington and some of the surrounding communities had she not brought a civil suit in district court against the city of Torrington, twenty-nine police officers, and three police chiefs. Thurman argued that the police failed to provide her with equal protection of the law as guaranteed by the Fourteenth Amendment of the U.S. Constitution. She maintained that the police treated her numerous requests for help (dating back to October 1982 when Charles, Sr., first attacked her in the Bentley/St. Hilliare home) differently because her assailant was her husband. She reasoned that had she been threatened or attacked by a stranger, she would have been given more protection. Her second argument was that the police had been negligent in failing to protect her from assault by her estranged husband.

On June 25, 1985, a jury, sitting for the U.S. District Court for the District of Connecticut, awarded Tracy Thurman $2.3 million in compensatory damages against twenty-four police officers. Charles, Jr., was awarded $300,000 against sixteen police officers. The jury held that the police officers in Torrington had acted negligently in failing to protect Tracy and Charles Thurman, Jr., from the violent acts of Charles Thurman, Sr. The case was appealed, and Tracy Thurman later settled out of court for $1.9 million.

Three years to the day after Tracy Thurman was stabbed and kicked into unconsciousness, Connecticut Governor William A. O'Neill signed into law a family violence bill that, among other provisions, requires police officers to arrest offenders in cases of probable domestic assault, regardless of whether the victim is willing to sign a complaint. Thus, Connecticut joined with seven other states that had initiated what is commonly referred to as "mandatory arrest" for domestic violence. Other states and municipalities are sure to follow this trend, no doubt alarmed by the implications of the Thurman case.

The case of Tracy Thurman and her successful suit against police officers and the city of Torrington is the latest in a series of events that illustrate how the treatment of choice in cases of wife assault and domestic violence has moved from a pattern of "selective inattention" to a strategy of control. The increasing tendency to recommend the arrest of abusers has been met with enthusiasm by a variety of groups from feminists to the U.S. attorney general and the U.S. surgeon general.

While arrest and incarceration of offenders are currently the preferred approach for police intervention in cases of wife abuse, controlling the offender is not the only means of dealing with wife or child battering. Along with the mandatory arrest statute, Connecticut also appropriated $2.7 million for training programs, social services, and shelters for battered women. Compassion for both the victim and the offender is another approach to treating and preventing family violence.

In this chapter our analysis of the aftermath of domestic violence continues, and we examine the structure and effectiveness of the three major service systems for treating domestic violence: the criminal justice system, the social service system—in this chapter we focus on shelters for battered women—and the services provided by the medical system—doctors, nurses, and hospitals. The underlying theme of our investigation is the tension between compassion and control—the desire to help victims and even view offenders as victims—versus the pressure to treat all offenders as criminals and punish them as any violent offender would be punished.

INDIFFERENCE, COMPASSION, OR CONTROL

There are three philosophies that have been applied to providing services in cases of domestic violence. The first is indifference. Perhaps indifference is too strong a word, but it accurately captures one approach (or nonapproach) to intimate violence. Indifference arises out of either ignorance that family violence occurs, or the conviction that if there is violence between family members it is a private matter that ought to be resolved within the confines of the home. Many of Tracy Thurman's calls for help to the Torrington police were met with apparent indifference. When Charles, Sr., used physical force to remove his son from the home of Judy Bentley and Richard St. Hilliare, the police refused to accept a complaint from Tracy or Richard St. Hilliare against Charles for trespassing. When Charles violated a court-imposed "stay away" order, the Torrington police made no attempt to locate or arrest him, even after Tracy made numerous calls to the police. Again and again Tracy Thurman asked for enforcement of court orders, and again and again no action took place until she lay unconscious on the front lawn of the Bentley/St. Hilliare house.

Specialists in the field of child abuse note that one of the major obstacles that prevents adequate protection of children is the failure of mandated reporters to report suspected abuse cases. Some nonreporting is due to a lack of faith in child protective services, fear that reporting will make things worse for the child, or the belief that the mandated reporter can do a better job than child protective services. However, a considerable amount of nonreporting is the result of individuals failing to recognize a case as abuse or failing to understand that the abuse requires intervention. An example of indifference due to ignorance occurred in a hospital specializing in the care of children. The social worker who headed the hospital child abuse team was horrified to learn that a six-month-old girl had been treated in the emergency room for a lacerated vagina. The girl had been admitted to the hospital without the admitting physician calling the child abuse team for a consultation. When the social worker confronted the physician and asked why he had not thought of calling in the child abuse team for advice and consultation, he replied that he did not see any reason to bother the team for a such a routine case. "How," the social worker asked, "can you view a six-month-old with a lacerated vagina as routine?" The physician responded that kids stick things in themselves all the time.

Indifference also occurs when the observer, a physician, social worker, police officer, or judge, actually approves of the use of violence toward a victim. In one case a presiding judge refused to sentence an alleged sexual abuser to jail because he believed that the six-year-old victim had acted provocatively and enticed the abuser into having sex with her. Those who think that sparing the rod spoils the child are often reluctant to intervene in cases of physical abuse unless grievous damage is inflicted upon the child. Feminists have argued for years that police and court officers fail to protect victims of battering because they condone women being hit. Two judges in Massachusetts have recently volunteered to stop hearing domestic violence cases because their actions and comments on the bench persuaded the state chief justice that the judges were biased in their handling of domestic violence cases—a polite way of saying that the judges were far too approving of the violence inflicted on women.

Compassionate intervention in cases of family violence has its roots in the traditional approach to child abuse. According to the physicians Alvin Rosenfeld and Eli Newberger, child abuse intervention strategies have always been based on an underlying philosophy that was humane and compassionate. Rosenfeld and Newberger explain that the clinician who employs the compassionate philosophy of intervention is expected to approach each case with an abundance of human kindness and a nonpunitive outlook. The goal is not to punish the offender but to strengthen the family system. Abusers are not seen as cold, cruel, inhumane creatures, but as needy, sad, and deprived individuals who are themselves victims.

By and large, compassionate intervention is offered by counselors, medical personnel, and social service workers. During the 1970s, as police departments were pressured by feminists and social activists to be more effective in intervening in cases of domestic assault, they, too, began to employ compassionate interventions. Some police departments created domestic intervention teams that consisted of police officers and social workers who would enter violent homes and attempt to mediate the problem. Other departments trained their own officers in techniques of family mediation.

Compassionate intervention relieves the physician, social worker, or police officer of the need to play the role of the "bad guy." Yet, the compassionate approach may ultimately paralyze and demoralize the clinician or agent of social control. Fear of disrupting the therapeutic relationship, fear of alienating the family, and overidentification with the family may prevent effective and timely intervention. At its worst, compassion may paralyze the clinician into inaction. Rosenfeld and Newberger say that many children's injuries and fatalities are directly traceable to the inability of physicians, nurses, social workers, or judges to act on perceived danger to the child. Clinicians and agents of social control may ultimately burn out and become demoralized as they find an empty promise in the curative powers of love and genuine concern for families. "We had a good talk this week," or "This time I am sure I convinced them not to do that again" are the halfhearted sighs of clinicians whose compassion quota and professional energy have been exhausted.

The injuries and fatalities that arise out of professional inaction and paralysis, the high rate of burnout of professionals, and the desire to "do something" to prevent family violence all point to the need for stronger actions to prevent and treat family violence. A control approach to domestic violence involves the aggressive use of intervention to limit and, if necessary, punish domestic violence.

Control can come in the form of mandatory reporting, arrest, prosecution, and incarceration of child, spouse, or parent abusers.

One push for a control approach came from battered women who collectively felt that their plight was not taken seriously by the agencies they turned to for help. The police are generally perceived as able to provide the quickest and strongest response. Yet, as Tracy Thurman found, the police often fail to meet the expectation of the victims who call for help and protection. Three class-action suits in the mid-1970s set the stage for the effort to increase control approaches to domestic violence—especially wife abuse. In December 1976, wives in New York City filed a class-action suit (*Bruno* v. *Codd*) against the New York City Police Department, probation officers, and family court employees for failing to prosecute abusive husbands. The police settled the case in 1977. In 1974, a class-action suit was filed against the Cleveland district attorneys for denying battered women equal protection under the law by not following through on prosecution of abusive husbands. That suit was settled by a consent decree ordering the prosecutors to change their practices. In Oakland, California, the police department was accused of illegal conduct in its pattern and practice of discouraging arrests in cases of domestic violence. Similar suits and actions in other communities followed these cases into the 1980s, all with the goal of insisting that police treat domestic assault in the same fashion as criminal assault between strangers.

Two key events in 1984 brought about a significant change in public and criminal justice agency attitudes toward wife abuse. The first event was the publication of the results of the Minneapolis Police Experiment conducted by Lawrence Sherman, then of the Police Foundation, and Richard Berk, of the University of California at Santa Barbara. Over the sixteen-and-a-half-month-study period some thirty to thirty-five cooperating officers in the Minneapolis Police Department employed three different tactics to handle cases of misdemeanor, or "moderate" domestic violence (simple assaults that did not cause severe or life-threatening injuries). The three tactics were arrest (the control intervention), advice or mediation (the compassionate intervention), or ordering the violent spouse to leave the house for eight hours.

The most significant aspect of the study was that police were assigned the tactics randomly—prior to arriving at the home. Thus, the investigators eliminated police discretion as a factor that might affect intervention and outcome. They were able, as a result of the design of this field experiment, to assess the impact and effectiveness of each intervention.

Sherman and Berk followed the families for six months. They checked police reports to see if the police had been called back to the homes for cases of domestic violence. They also attempted to conduct follow-up interviews with the family members who had been involved in the three forms of police intervention. After six months only one home in ten in which the violent spouse was arrested had generated a new official report of domestic violence, compared with 16 percent for those given advice or mediation, and 22 percent of those homes in which the offender was ordered to leave the home for eight hours.

Sherman and Berk were appropriately conservative in their interpretation of the findings. Sherman, quoted in *The New York Times,* said that the findings of his research "suggest that police should reverse their current practice of rarely making arrests and frequently separating the parties [involved in domestic violence]." "The findings suggest," Sherman went on to say, "that other things being equal, arrest may be the most effective approach and separation, the least effective approach."

The investigators' conservative interpretation notwithstanding, police departments were quick to adopt Sherman's advice. Ten days after the Sherman and Berk study was reported in *The New York Times,* New York Police Commissioner Benjamin Ward initiated new rules requiring officers to make arrests in most instances of domestic violence. Other municipalities were quick to follow.

The September following the release of the results of the Minneapolis Police Experiment, the United States Attorney General's Task Force on Family Violence released its final report. The first recommendation of the report and the cornerstone of the entire document was the statement, "Family violence should be recognized and responded to as a criminal activity." The report drew heavily on the results of the Minneapolis Police Experiment and strongly recommended creating criminal sanctions for family violence, and supported the call for presumptive arrest in instances of marital violence.

Calls for control approaches have not been limited to cases of marital violence. Prosecution has become an increasingly common intervention in cases of child abuse—especially when the child is perceived to be a victim of sexual abuse.

It should not be overlooked that the advocacy of a control model of intervention flourished in the mid 1980s, a period of political

conservatism and repeated calls for strict and severe controls to punish all forms of crime, not just family violence. In point of fact, the
membership of the United States Attorney General's Task Force on
Family Violence was carefully selected so that the task force would
reflect a control point of view.

In a matter of a decade, public policy in cases of family violence
has swung from indifference to control. Those who first discovered
child abuse were strong advocates of a compassionate approach.
Those who first discovered the problem of wife abuse were among
the strongest voices advocating that the criminal justice system treat
violence against wives as a crime.

Has the pendulum swung too fast? The move from apparent indifference to vigorous control has been swift, with precious little balancing of the advantages and disadvantages of such a change. The
Minneapolis Police Experiment was but a single study. The general-
izability of the research is unknown. We will address this in the next
section as we review the role, function, and effectiveness of the legal
and criminal justice system.

LEGAL AND CRIMINAL JUSTICE REMEDIES

The police are often viewed as the poor's social worker. They are on
call twenty-four hours a day, are capable of making a swift response,
are able to impose certain and severe sanctions, and do not charge
for their services. Thus, it is not surprising that the police and the
criminal justice system are frequently expected to provide effective
and immediate response to violence in the home. Ironically, the expectations and evaluations of the police are quite different depending
on the form of violence with which they are dealing.

Browsing through a collection of books and articles on the topic
of child abuse and neglect, one would find that the police are virtually the missing persons of the child maltreatment literature. Books
and articles that discuss the role of criminal justice agencies have
typically examined reporting laws and the implication of reporting
laws for mandatory reporters (which typically include police officers). By and large, police officers are not discussed in these articles,
except for the occasional notation that the police are more prone to
report cases of neglect than those involving physical violence.

Lately, however, prosecution has become an increasingly prevalent
form of intervention in cases of child abuse, and the criminal justice

system has begun to play a larger role in prevention and treatment of maltreatment. Eli Newberger, a leading voice in the field of child abuse treatment and prevention, has criticized the more aggressive role now played by the criminal justice system, and notes that prosecution itself is an increasingly prevalent form of abuse. For example:

A 12-year-old girl in California became the subject of a mandated child abuse case report when she, her mother, and her stepfather sought help from a therapist for a problem in the family. The details of the report have not been made public, but there apparently was concern on the part of the therapist that the child might be a victim of sexual abuse. The agency receiving the report made the district attorney aware of the complaint. A criminal charge was brought against the stepfather, but at trial the child refused to divulge what may have happened between her stepfather and her. The prosecutor asked the court to find her in contempt if she continued to refuse to testify. The judge ordered her held in solitary confinement until she agreed to tell the court the facts. She was held in solitary for nine days until she was freed by a higher court.

Two brothers, 7 and 12 years old, were ordered a week ago to remain in the custody of a father accused of sexually abusing the younger child. To quote yesterday's article in the *Chicago Sun-Times:* "The boys wanted to be with their mother, but the judge said she could take custody only if she came up with a cash bond she couldn't raise . . . "

Newberger, an ardent supporter of the compassionate approach to child maltreatment, notes with concern that the current punitive approach to deviance in our society has led to a reckless abandonment of social welfare approaches to giving support to families and children under stress. Prosecution of abusers, he notes, serves a number of functions—some helpful, some harmful, and some futile. Prosecution, according to Newberger, can:

1. Punish offenders—its first and most appropriate function
2. Provide public entertainment
3. Provide excellent opportunities for district attorneys to further their political ambitions
4. Provide work and income for defense lawyers
5. Justify the abandonment of social welfare approaches to human troubles

6. Serve as a smokescreen to hide the real causes of abuse (and thus continue to support the myth of abusers as aliens and victims as innocents)
7. Punish the victim

There may be only the slightest hyperbole in Newberger's attack on the criminal justice approach to dealing with abuse. Those who think prosecution of child abuse does not provide good entertainment need only follow the press coverage of abuse cases in print and on television, or examine the ratings of television movies of the subject of abuse and neglect. Newberger represents the prevailing child welfare sentiment that the preferred role for the police and criminal justice agencies in cases of violence toward children should be subordinate to the compassionate roles offered by the medical and social welfare communities.

The expectations of the police in dealing with instances of spouse abuse, especially violence toward women, are exactly the opposite of those for their role in dealing with child abuse. In contrast to the literature on child abuse, which either ignores the police and the criminal justice system or calls for reduced prosecution, nearly every book on wife abuse discusses the police and courts; and each one calls for stepped-up intervention, arrest, and prosecution. While child abuse has been conceptualized as a social welfare problem, wife abuse has been laid on the doorstep of the criminal justice system.

Since the time when wife abuse was placed on the public agenda, the police have been criticized for continued inaction or ineffective intervention. Morton Bard was the pioneer student of police intervention in cases of domestic violence. His first observation in the early 1970s was that little formal training was given to police on methods of intercession in conjugal disputes. Elizabeth Truninger observed that the criminal justice system was mired in mythology about family violence. Police and judges often noted that "being a victim of violence fulfilled a woman's masochistic need." Martha and Henry Field commented in 1973 that the criminal justice system was unable to deal effectively with marital violence. Police were found to apply "stitch rules" whereby they would not seek to arrest an offender unless the victim required a specific number of surgical sutures to close a wound. In the 1970s, unless a victim died, chances were slim that the police or courts would deal seriously with the offender.

As we noted earlier, all this changed in the 1980s. First, there was the pressure exerted by various class-action suits brought by battered women who felt they were not being afforded equal protection under the law. Next was the increasingly punitive attitude toward all crime and deviance in the society. An example of the increasing "control" and punitive attitude in the society was the gradual increase in support for the death penalty in the United States. By the mid-1980s more than two-thirds of those surveyed supported the use of capital punishment; ten years earlier less than half of those surveyed displayed the same support for capital punishment. The battered women's movement deserves considerable credit for both focusing attention on the plight of battered women and forcing a change in police and criminal justice agency attitudes toward appropriate intervention. Last, there was the Minneapolis Police Experiment which provided "hard" scientific evidence to support both the advocates of battered women and those in the criminal justice system who urged swift and severe punishment as a means of controlling crime.

In the course of our Second National Family Violence Survey, we talked with more than eight hundred individuals who had been involved in some form of marital violence in the previous twelve months. Overall, the police were called to a little less than one of twenty houses (4.8 percent) in which there was some kind of marital violence in the previous twelve months. Twenty-four women and seventeen men had called the police. The number of calls made ranged from a single call to ten, with the average being a little less than two calls.

Mediation, in one form or another, was the typical form of intervention used by police officers. The most common form of intervention used by the police when they were called by a woman was to try to calm everyone down (see fig. 14 in Appendix C). Other frequent interventions included taking time to listen to the woman's story, taking information and filing a report, issuing a warning, and breaking up the fight if it was still going on. Stronger steps were somewhat less common. Four out of ten women said that the police ordered the man out of the house. As we noted earlier, arrest (and even its threat) is the least common form of police intervention. Only four women said that the police arrested their husbands or male partners, while one woman was herself arrested. Two women said that the police did nothing. Asked whether they thought the police should have been easier or tougher, most women said that the police officers' response was about right. Overall, the women we talked to seemed satisfied with the actions taken by the police.

Police intervention when called by men is similar to intervention when the caller is female. Mediation is still the most common intervention. Police were most likely to try to calm everyone down, take time to listen to the story, take information, and file a report. Two of the men who called the police were themselves arrested, while the police never arrested the wife or female partner of the man who called. The range of actions and interventions used by the police was much narrower when they were called by men; neither the man or his partner was ordered out of the house, no threats of arrest were made, and there was no hitting or pushing of the parties involved in the marital violence. Two men said that the police did nothing.

Men were a bit less pleased with how the police handled their calls. Less than half said that in general what the police did was all right. Although more than half of the men who called the police reported that they were satisfied with the manner in which the situation was handled.

Even with a survey of more than six thousand individuals, we had too few subjects to conduct some of the more refined analyses of men's and women's evaluations of police response. We wanted to determine if the type of intervention used by the police influenced whether men and women thought the police should be tougher or easier. In addition, we wanted to learn which forms of intervention were preferred by those who called the police. While we cannot look individually at women's versus men's evaluations, we did examine the overall evaluations of men and women.

The perception of whether the police should have been easier or tougher was strongly influenced by the police officers' actions. If the police intervention was to hit or push someone, or to arrest either the respondent or the spouse, subjects reported that the police should have been easier. Police who broke up the fight or ordered the caller out of the home were regarded as being too easy. The highest levels of satisfaction were reported in homes where the police ordered the respondent out of the home, took time to listen to the story, and gave a warning. The lowest levels of satisfaction were registered when the police hit or pushed someone, broke up the fight that was in progress, threatened arrest, or arrested the person who made the call in the first place. (All of the latter respondents were obviously dissatisfied with the police.) Overall, our respondents generally preferred the police to use compassion and mediation, with appropriate control under certain circumstances.

Only a tiny fraction of incidents of marital violence reach a courtroom. Of the more than eight hundred homes that reported some form of marital violence in the last year, five went to court. The few cases of spouse assault that ended up in court resulted in a variety of actions, which included dismissing the charges, warning the abuser, requiring the abuser to enter counseling, fining the abuser, jail, or a suspended sentence.

Respondents indicated a wide range of satisfaction with the results of their appearances in court. The largest percentage said they were not sure.

Mirroring the participants' uncertainty is the uncertainty of experts over the proper role of prosecutors and the courts in cases of spouse assault. There is a tug-of-war involved in explaining why so few cases of domestic assault are adjudicated by the court. On the one hand, police, prosecutors, and judges argue that the small number of cases that are prosecuted is due to the reluctance of victims to press charges. Police, district attorneys, and judges are quick to cite many instances where women dropped charges or failed to prosecute even after sustaining grievous injuries. Court officers are often angry and resentful toward these women if they have invested time in a case that never comes to court. On the other hand, victims respond with anger and frustration that the police, prosecutors, and judges fail to take them seriously, advise them to "kiss and make up," and send them home to their abusers. As one prosecutor noted:

> We created a self-fulfilling prophecy. We would tell women that we would prosecute their husbands if they wanted us to, but all the time we knew that they would probably drop the charges, so we really did not take them seriously. In fact, I know that we often told women that they would probably drop the charges later. From their point of view we did not look like we would be much help, so there was little point to their filing charges.

One response to women's perceived reluctance to follow through on filing charges, and the prosecutor's failure to take the charges seriously, has been the proposal that prosecution of wife assault is mandatory after an arrest has been made. In this way women could not be pressured or coerced by their abusive partners into dropping the charges, and prosecutors would be required to treat each case of spouse assault seriously. The sociologist David Ford, however, argues that mandatory prosecution may work against long-term solutions and may result in continuing abuse. Calls for mandatory prosecution ignore the individual needs, problems, and motives of victims of wife abuse. Ford goes on to note that victims need to be helped to gain control of their lives. Mandatory prosecution deprives women of choice and control over how they want to manage cases of abusive violence.

PROTECTION FOR VICTIMS

An alternative to controlling offenders is to protect victims. Protection has been a traditional intervention in cases of child maltreatment. Physicians and hospitals are able to hospitalize children who are suspected of child abuse for up to seventy-two hours while they complete an examination of the child and an investigation of the circumstances surrounding the suspected abuse. Longer-term strategies for protecting battered and abused children often involve removing the children from their homes and placing them either with relatives or in foster families. Badly abused and psychologically damaged children may be placed in residential treatment facilities. Finally, in instances where maltreating parents are seen as continuing threats to their children, court action may be taken to terminate parental rights.

Removing children from their natural homes, even in cases of maltreatment, continues to be a controversial form of intervention. The protection offered victims is balanced against the disruption and potential destruction of their families. Children may also suffer from the treatment more than the abuse itself. The psychologist James Kent and his colleagues found that children removed from their natural homes and placed in a series of foster homes suffered long-term psychological problems. Ironically, physically abused children who remained with their parents continued to be at-risk for abuse, but did not evidence the same psychological deficits exhibited by the children placed in a series of foster homes. One explanation for why the "protected children" suffered was offered by a clinical social worker:

> I think you have to understand the typical pattern of abuse and neglect. Many children are told that the reason they are being hit or beaten is that they [the children] have done something wrong. If they are punished in other nonphysical ways—say they are locked in a closet—they are also told that they have been bad. From the children's

point of view they suffer because they are bad. Moreover, they really have no way of knowing that what they are going through is different from what other children experience. When we remove an abused child to protect the child, the child may see this as the ultimate punishment for bad behavior. From the child's point of view the explanation for being removed may be, "I must have done something really wrong this time for my parents to give me up or send me away. . . ."

A final risk of protecting battered children is that they may be at greater risk in the foster homes than their own homes. By the time they are removed, battered children have probably suffered consistent and considerable abuse and neglect. As a result, these children may not only be physically harmed, they may be psychologically damaged as well. Needy and demanding, children placed in foster homes may require more care and attention than the foster family is capable of providing. A mismatch between the needs of the child and the capabilities of the foster parents may place the child at greater physical and psychological risk.

Protecting children by removing them from their natural parents and placing them with relatives, foster families, or in institutions has long been considered an undesirable method of treating maltreatment. In the last decade attempts have been made to reduce and limit interventions that require the short- or long-term removal of maltreated children from their parents. Programs that protect women by encouraging them to leave their violent homes, on the other hand, have grown rapidly since the 1970s.

A social movement emerged in the early 1970s that confronted the apathy and antagonism characterizing institutional and individual responses to wife battering. The battered wife movement and the refuge/shelter movement grew side by side. One of the first battered wife shelters was created unintentionally. Early in 1971, a group of women in the Chiswick section of London began meeting to discuss their concern about rising food prices. Out of these meetings a Women's Aid project was established by Erin Pizzey. Soon a house was set up as Chiswick Women's Aid. The house became a center for women with personal problems. Before long, the house filled with women facing a common problem—battering. Within three years Women's Aid of Chiswick became the model for women's shelters around the world. Pizzey authored one of the first books on wife abuse, *Scream Quietly or the Neighbors Will Hear,* and produced a movie of the same name.

The shelter movement grew rapidly in Great Britain. The National

Women's Aid Federation was established in 1974, and held its first meeting in the spring of 1974. According to the sociologists Rebecca and Russell Dobash, by the second meeting of the federation in 1975, eighty-two groups had been established, twenty-five with refuges for battered wives.

There is some controversy about the first shelter for battered women in the United States. Some claim that the first shelter opened in a private home in Pasadena, California, in 1964. Other shelters, such as those started in Minneapolis, Philadelphia, Cambridge, Massachusetts, and Washington, D.C., also claim to be among the first established in the United States. By 1976 there were but six shelters for battered women in the United States. Ten years later this number rose to at least eight hundred, if not one thousand.

Shelters provide a range of services for victims of wife abuse. First —and to many minds, foremost—shelters provide short-term protection and refuge for battered women. They are a place to go and be safe. The shelter, often in a secret location, provides alternative room and board in a safe and secure place. Shelters may also provide more than refuge. Some provide personal, marital, legal, and occupational counseling. A theme of many shelters is that they provide short-term refuge and long-term consciousness-raising for women. Shelters may help women to decipher the puzzle of the welfare and legal systems. A goal of many shelters is to provide the battered woman with sufficient self-confidence that she will choose to leave her violent relationship.

There is no typical shelter with typical services. Although the goal of each shelter is to protect women from violent men, the rules, regulations, and organizational structure of shelters vary considerably. Some are in secret locations. Women who call for help are told they will be met and brought to the shelter. Many shelters prohibit men, including workmen or the police, from entering. Male children are accepted into these shelters, but older male adolescents are not allowed to stay with their battered mothers. Virtually all shelters have rules that prohibit the spanking of children. There are limits on how long women can remain, and limits as to how many times women can return to the shelter after going back to their violent partners.

Despite the fact that shelters offer battered women immediate refuge and protection, they are the least likely human service resource to be used by battered women. Less than two women in one hundred of those we interviewed who had experienced severe violence reported seeking help from a battered women's shelter in the last year. No victims of minor violence sought help from shelters.

Simple arithmetic explains why so few women sought help from shelters. Our data indicate that there are about 600,000 women who are severely and repeatedly (more than four times each year) battered by a partner each year. There are about one thousand shelters in the United States, with the ability to accommodate approximately ten to twenty women at a time. Thus, the total capacity of all available refuges may be as low as 42,000 women and no greater than 150,000. Thus, for all practical purposes there is not enough space for 80 to 90 percent of the severely and repeatedly battered women in America. The actual capacity is even less, since the one thousand shelters are not distributed in all geographic areas. In most communities there are no refuges for any battered women.

The growth in the number of shelters has not been matched by a growth in scientific research on how they function or their potential impact. Beyond the philosophy and ideology of the shelter movement, we have little knowledge of whether shelters actually provide a benefit beyond short-term refuge. The sociologist Jean Giles-Sims studied thirty-one women who sought help from a shelter. She interviewed twenty-four of these women six months after they left the shelter and found that the shelter had beneficial effects by helping to empower the victims. Of course, this is a small sample with no comparison group, so one can neither generalize from this research nor attribute the changes to the shelter. Other studies that examined the impact of shelters suffer from the same methodological problems and cannot be used to determine whether women who return to their husbands after a shelter stay are at greater or lesser risk for abuse.

A recent study by the sociologists Richard Berk, Phyllis Newton, and Sarah Fenstermaker Berk, followed 243 wife battery victims in Santa Barbara, California. At the end of eighteen months they were still in contact with 155 of the victims. Using the records from a shelter, the researchers were able to determine which of the 243 victims had stayed in a shelter between the time of the first and second interviews. Fifty-seven women had used a shelter, staying between one and thirty days. Based on their interviews, the investigators concluded that shelters appear to have a beneficial effect. However, the benefits depend on the attitudes of the women. When a victim can actually take control of her life, a shelter stay can dramatically reduce the likelihood of new violence. More than eight of the ten women who stayed at a shelter experienced no new violence between the time they left the shelter and when they were interviewed (an average of fifty-four days). For women who cannot take control of their lives, shelters either have no impact, or worse, may actually trigger retaliation from an angry partner or husband. Five percent of the women who left the shelter were beaten more than once after returning home.

Berk and his associates caution that theirs is but a single study with some important methodological limitations. It would be premature, the researchers argue, to base major policy changes on this single study. The study does, however, illuminate the fact that the impact of shelters is not uniform for all victims of wife battery.

MEDICAL SERVICES

Researchers, clinicians, and policy makers agree that the medical system is a, if not *the,* key system in the identification, treatment, and prevention of intimate violence. The most severe instances of battering come to the attention of physicians and nurses. More minor instances of violence and abuse may also come to the attention of medical personnel in the course of routine clinical appointments.

Child abuse has been seen as a major social problem by both the public and the medical community since Kempe and his colleagues published their first article on battered children in the *Journal of the American Medical Association.* Kempe, however, noted that although the medical community has had a long-standing concern for child welfare, the medical community ignored the implications of abuse and neglect because of a "process of denial that was unequal to anything . . . previously seen in pediatrics." Eli Newberger and Stephen Bittner note that the denial continues today in spite of the increasing and visible literature on abuse.

Denial takes many forms, from failing to see an injury or condition as abuse, to choosing not to report the condition as suspected abuse, to applying a treatment approach based on an inaccurate or incorrect perception of the causes and consequences of abuse and neglect. Physicians, nurses, and other members of the medical community have been criticized both for denying the existence of a case of abuse, and for intervening improperly by falsely accusing parents.

The medical community is confronted by a stark dilemma when dealing with physical abuse and neglect of children. On the one hand, there is the risk that failure to identify and treat properly a case of abuse will lead to the permanent injury or even death of the child. On the other hand, physicians and nurses run the risk of subjecting families to the stigma of being improperly labeled abusers.

Newberger and Bittner offer seven axioms of child abuse management to help guide physicians, nurses, and other members of medically based child abuse intervention teams:

1. Once diagnosed, abused children (especially infants under one year of age) are at great risk of reinjury or continued neglect.
2. If a child is reinjured, it is likely that the parents will seek help at a different medical facility.
3. There is no real need to establish exactly who injured a child or whether the injury was intentional. The symptom itself should trigger intervention.
4. If the evidence points to significant risk for the child, hospitalization is appropriate to allow time for a more comprehensive assessment.
5. Protection is the principal goal of intervention, but this must go hand in hand with a family-oriented service plan.
6. Traditional social casework alone may not be enough to protect children. Multidisciplinary follow-up is often necessary.
7. Social service agencies frequently are unable to provide a full range of appropriate services. Thus, simply reporting a case to a service agency is not sufficient to properly protect the child or help the family.

Clearly, the medical approach to child abuse is guided primarily by the goal of protection through comprehensive compassion.

Wife abuse has not assumed the same place on the medical system's treatment and policy agenda that is held by child abuse and neglect. For the most part, doctors and psychiatrists are seen as even less helpful to battered women than are the police. The sociologist Evan Stark and his wife, the physician Anne Flitcraft, have conducted the most extensive program of research on medical response to wife battery. Both conclude that the medical profession has been more a part of the cause of battering than of the cure. Physicians often treat the victims as mentally ill. Injuries are overlooked or minimized. The battered woman's distress and disorientation are frequently the only symptoms that are attended to. Stark and Flitcraft note that physicians may often view battered wives as either psychotic or hypochondriac, prescribe tranquilizers, and send the women home. Treated this way, many battered women begin to doubt their own mental health and question if they are victims, or alternatively if they actually did cause their own physical abuse.

The frequent indifference or victim blaming found among physicians who treat battered women may be a cause for considerable concern, primarily because so many women seek help and treatment from the medical community. However, the results of our Second National Family Violence Survey found that while only a fraction of victims of domestic violence sought treatment from physicians, those who did seek help were satisfied with the services they received.

Of the more than eight hundred men and women who had experienced one or more incidents of marital violence in the last year, only eighteen (2 percent) sought help from a physician. Twice as many women as men sought medical attention for their injuries—confirming our notion that although men and women may hit each other with equal frequency, women are much more likely to be hurt in incidents of marital violence. Treatment was typically sought in either a physician's private office or an emergency room. Women who saw physicians were relatively satisfied with the treatment. About one-third of the victims of minor violence and half of the victims of severe violence told us that the services they received were very effective. Not a single woman in either category said going to a doctor or nurse made the situation worse.

COMPASSION OR CONTROL?

The women we spoke with seemed relatively satisfied with the assistance they sought, regardless of whether the help source applied control or compassion. If we step back from the victims' perspectives and consider compassionate versus control interventions from a wider perspective, there are various costs and rewards associated with each.

The single most significant advantage of the control approach is that police and court intervention raises the costs of intimate violence for offenders. Arrest and the possibility of court appearances and jail can inflict a social stigma in addition to monetary fines and deprivation of rights and privileges. Neighbors and friends may stigmatize and ostracize wife and child beaters. In rare instances, an abuser may lose his or her job. An official with the federal Security and Exchange Commission resigned in February 1985 after widespread publicity that he had allegedly beaten his wife. The threat of arrest and public exposure of deviant behavior may ultimately serve to deter potentially violent men.

Legal interventions may have latent advantages for victims of family violence. Wives may decide to take stronger steps to terminate violent relationships if they find that formal arrest and punishment do not deter their violent partners. Michael Strube and Linda Barbour discovered that a number of women left violent relationships when arrest did not reduce or eliminate beatings. Thus, while arrest itself may not deter some men, the fact that the strongest available form of social control does not work may actually force women to end violent relationships or seek shelter.

There are disadvantages to arrest, court action, and jail. Social scientists have found that individuals who have experienced self-devaluating episodes and have poor self-evaluations as a result, are prone to using violence as a means of maintaining mastery and achieving higher self-esteem. If men and parents use violence to control their wives and children because they themselves feel controlled and belittled, a controlling experience that further belittles them may lead to more, not less, violence.

A second limitation of the control approach is that it may actually contribute to the inequitable status of the victims. Mandatory arrest and prosecution laws which are designed to empower and aid battered women may actually serve to disempower them. Rather than returning to battered wives the control of their own destinies, they are still forced to watch their fates being determined by others—typically male police officers, male district attorneys, and male judges.

The sociologist Kathleen Ferraro spent many evenings riding in police cruisers with officers whose community enacted mandatory arrest statutes for wife beating. Ferraro cautions that mandatory arrest is not likely to aid abused women, and is unpopular with street police officers because it reduces their discretion. Thus, many officers either ignore or circumvent mandatory arrest policies. This seriously undermines the intent of mandatory arrest. As one battered woman put it:

What am I supposed to do? I read in our paper that the cops are supposed to arrest men who beat their wives. I told my husband that the next time he beat me I would call the cops and he would be arrested. So he hits me and I call the cops. They came soon enough, but they didn't arrest him. They tried to convince me that it would be best to just cool down and make up. Great. What do I do now? What do I do the next time? How can I keep him from beating me?

Although individuals may be deterred by the threat of severe punishment, such a deterrent works only if punishment is certain. Even the most severe punishment, the death penalty, fails to deter when application of the punishment is not uniform or certain.

Ferraro continues her argument against mandatory arrest by noting that arrest and formal social controls do little to change the underlying power imbalances that she perceives as the generative sources of wife battering. Mandatory arrest policies hide from public view the societal, cultural, and family organizational forces rendering women the "appropriate" victims of men's violent behavior. Similarly, mandatory reporting laws for child abuse may cover up the structural inequities that leave certain children vulnerable to abuse.

The main advantage of compassionate approaches is that they help to develop a positive self-image of the victim and offender. Offenders and their families are viewed not as criminals, but as people in need of help, support, or education. Family systems escape the stigma of being labeled "violent homes." Shelters and medical and social services can be used to change the factors associated with violence. Aiding in stress management and coping, improving the family economic situation, and working with the family system are among the supportive approaches that could reduce the risk of violence.

Family system interventions are a controversial form of compassionate intervention. Family system therapy avoids labeling "victims" and "offenders," and works with the entire family to develop nonviolent interaction patterns. Many feminists strongly argue that such intervention actually places women at greater risk of abuse. Women who bring up the issue of violence in front of their husbands are thought to run a major risk of retaliation after the therapy session.

The most obvious drawback and risk of compassion approaches are that they may unintentionally support the status quo. When violence is not viewed as wrong or criminal, then the same tradition that permits people to hit family members is reinforced. Compassionate intervention may serve to communicate to offenders that society does not view what they have done as wrong. Obviously, had offenders hit strangers, they would not be treated with kindness and understanding. Another risk of compassion is that it may indirectly reduce the status of women and children by not providing them with full protection under the law.

In a matter of a decade, public policy has swung from indifference to a choice between compassion and control. Calls for stronger measures to stop wife abuse have led to the police taking stronger stands with violent men. The results of the Minneapolis Police Experiment, the U.S. attorney general's study of family violence, and the reverberations of the Tracy Thurman case have spurred police to adopt mandatory arrest policies. Yet evidence that demonstrates the effectiveness of such policies is sparse and tentative, and there are some clear disadvantages to mandatory arrest as a control policy. At the same time that calls for more control have been heeded, social and medical services for women and children have been expanded. The greatest expansion has been the creation of shelters for battered women. Again, evidence that demonstrates the effectiveness of such services is far from definitive.

After weighing the advantages and disadvantages of compassion and control, experts tend to call for a mix of the two. Rosenfeld and Newberger advise that effective treatment of family violence requires compassion and control. Richard Berk and his colleagues, who have investigated the effectiveness of both mandatory arrest and shelters for battered women, also argue for a mix of compassion and control. Shelter stays, they explain, could be accompanied by formal complaints leading to the arrest of the batterer, or be coupled with restraining orders.

The debate between compassion and control may be a debate over a false dichotomy. It may also be a debate at the wrong level of analysis. Interventions aimed at the individual level actually do little to change the societal organization that underlies violence in the family and allows an environment in which people can be violent toward loved ones. Our concluding chapter examines steps that could be taken at the individual, family, and societal levels to make it so people can't.

9.

Making It So People Can't:

Treating and Preventing

Family Violence

Working with battered children and battered wives evokes the saddest and strongest emotions. Those who treat intimate violence often need to manage their own anger. Sometimes, the first reaction of a frontline clinician is one of unbridled rage. Sadly some clinicians cope by turning their anger on their clients or colleagues.

One evening we had the unfortunate experience of observing an abused child treated in a hospital emergency room. The two-year-old child had been so severely beaten, she was black and blue. The outline of a hand, including the impression of a wedding band, was visible on the side of her face. The child had clearly been battered before and had some healed bruises on her back. The intern on duty began yelling at the child's mother at the top of his lungs. He screamed that someone who has abused a child was not fit to have a child. He said he would see to it that the mother never saw her child again.

A social worker took the intern aside and said, "You seem upset." The intern was no less pleased with the social worker than he was with the alleged abusive mother, and he turned his wrath on her. The social worker asked the physician to describe the mother. The social worker's first goal was to calm him down. Next, she wanted the intern to focus on providing some sort of clinical description of the family. The intern responded, "I don't know what the hell you're talking about." The social worker persisted, "What does she look like?" "She's short!" he said curtly. The social worker pursued the description and asked him to provide more detail. The intern could barely remember what color clothing the woman was wearing. Finally, the social worker said, "Well, let me ask you a question. Did you ask her why she had no front teeth?" He had not noticed that the mother had no front teeth. The intern looked puzzled and said, "No, I didn't ask her that." "Let's go back and talk to her and forget the child for the moment," the social worker suggested. She found the woman and asked, "Tell me, what happened to your front teeth?" She said, "They were knocked out." The social worker then asked the direct question that so many clinicians are too timid to raise. "When did your husband knock your teeth out?" She said, "He knocked them out three weeks ago; we had a fight in the car." She continued with a rather elaborate discussion of how, in fact, she was a battered woman. At the end of the discussion the social worker turned to the intern and said, "You have two victims here. You had better start figuring out a way to deal with both of them." Clearly the physician's anger had blocked his ability to effectively diagnose and treat the entire situation.

Most clinicians know they should not take out their anger and frustration on either victims or offenders (the intern in the emergency room notwithstanding). Yet, dealing with family violence does produce anger and frustration. Often, the anger is directed at other professionals: physicians get angry with social workers, social workers get angry with physicians, and they both direct fury at the criminal justice system.

The Federal Aviation Administration is frequently criticized for making aviation safety policy over broken bodies. The FAA, it is said, waits for the plane to go down and then identifies safety problems amidst the broken bodies scattered over the field. Public policy for intimate abuse is often generated in the same way. We often wait for the babies and women to die, and then make postmortem policy decisions about how to manage cases of violence and abuse. Making policy to treat the last tragic case of abuse hinders the implementation of long-term policy that can effectively treat a problem as complex as domestic violence.

Humans seek an orderly world. Those who are charged with providing treatment for victims of family violence not only must cope with the anger, frustration, ambiguity, and chaos generated by incidents of domestic assault, they are also frequently overworked, understaffed, and undertrained. Under these conditions, a frequently applied remedy is to develop simple solutions to complex problems, or to base tomorrow's treatment on today's hindsight.

Two cases illustrate the problems of generating policy over broken bodies and the tragic consequences of permitting overworked and understaffed systems to rely on simplistic solutions to order a chaotic world.

Case 1: Keeping the Family Together

For many years, the prevailing approach to child abuse was to protect the child, but to keep the family together. Family courts would allow a child to be removed from the home only when the child was clearly at risk and the parents or caretakers refused to accept ameliorative aid or intervention. Protective workers, without adequate training and poorly supported by the child welfare system, were quick to apply the simple principle of "keeping the family together" in nearly all cases of physical child abuse and neglect.

During this time, when family courts and protective service agencies sought to "keep families together," a young girl named Diane and her brother, Tim, were being treated by a hospital child abuse team and a state department of protective services. Both children had been reported for abuse and neglect. The hospital team believed that the children were at considerable risk and should be removed from the home. The protective service worker and the family court thought that the mother was willing to accept help, and that the children should remain with her.

The protective worker was overwhelmed with child abuse cases. At the time he was following more than thirty separate families; thus, he was only able to telephone Diane and Tim's mother once a week and to make home visits infrequently. Each week the protective worker called and asked, "How are Diane and Tim doing?" The mother always replied, "Great." Six weeks went by, and finally a neighbor called the Department of Social Services to report, "We haven't seen Diane in almost two months. We think something may have happened to her." The protective worker decided to make a home visit. He went to the house, and Diane was not there. First her mother said that Diane was visiting friends. The worker returned the next week, and still Diane was not at home. This time the mother said that Diane was at a neighbor's. Finally, after a few visits, the protective worker realized that Diane was not at any of the places the mother claimed. After being confronted, the mother admitted that her boyfriend had struck Diane two months earlier. Diane had fallen against a table, fractured her skull, and died. The boyfriend had left Diane's body in an unheated back room of the apartment. When spring came, he buried the body in a nearby landfill.

BABY DIES UNDER CARE OF PROTECTIVE SERVICES, the newspaper headlines read. An investigation of the Department of Social Services was initiated. The director resigned, and a new director was appointed. The standard practice for dealing with battered children changed from, "Keep the family together," to "at all costs, protect the child." This mollified the public, and it also restored calm to relations among the police, social services, and the hospital child abuse team—all of whom blamed each other for Diane's death. Eighteen months later, the protective service system experienced another tragedy that swung the pendulum back to the principle of keeping families together.

Case 2: "Protecting" the Victim

Some months after Diane's death, an investigation revealed that a one-year-old child was being neglected by his mother. The mother was a teenage, single parent, who seemed both uninterested and unable to care for the needs of her son. The Department of Social Services chose to remove the young boy from his mother and to place him in a foster home. Within six months the boy was dead, beaten to death by his foster father. Again there were newspaper headlines. Again an investigation was begun—this time it revealed that the overworked Department of Social Services had not carefully investigated the foster family. The foster father, it seems, had previously been reported for physical and sexual abuse. Again the agency director was replaced. Again the medical, social service, and criminal justice agencies pointed hostile fingers of blame at one another. The pendulum swung again. The standard practice of intervention became, "above all, keep the family together."

The complexity of the problem of child abuse and family violence, coupled with the strong feeling aroused by individual cases, invite a search for an orderly world and attract those involved in providing services to simple solutions like moths to a flame.

National social work guidelines recommend that protective service workers be assigned between twenty and twenty-five cases. The protective worker who was following Diane and Tim shared his desk with two other workers in his office. He had no telephone. His training consisted of a master of social work degree and a fourteen-day training course in protective service work. His salary at the time was less than that of a kindergarten teacher, less than an assembly line worker, less than a unionized trash collector in the same city. Under these conditions, he was charged with the responsibility of protecting the lives and welfare of more than thirty children who were deemed to be at the highest risk of harm.

The most obvious constraint against effective intervention and prevention of family violence is insufficient funding to provide adequate services for all victims and families involved in domestic violence. The amount of money allocated to prevent and treat private violence and abuse is so small that it would be considered a rounding error in the Defense Department. Worse, over the past six years even this small amount of funding has been slashed. Within weeks of Ronald Reagan's election in 1980, the federal Office of Domestic Violence was eliminated. The budget of the National Center on Child Abuse and Neglect was cut, and most of the experienced staff in the office had their positions eliminated in a federal "reduction in force" effort. The budget for research on family violence was also severely pared. The burden of providing treatment and prevention services was shifted from federal government to state governments and the private sector.

Inadequate funding creates two nearly intolerable frustrations for frontline workers who deal with victims of child and wife abuse. First, inadequate funding means insufficient staff. Insufficient staff means that agencies and workers must constantly triage—or decide which victims have the highest priority of need. Frequently, child abuse reports are either not attended to or are given the most superficial review. Unless a child suffers grievous injury or harm, protective service agencies are unable to attend to the child's needs. Second, even when attended to, abused children may suffer what Eli Newberger calls "the harm of the helping hand." As we reported in the second case we described above, placing victims of foster care may be the first, rather than last, resort of protective workers charged with protecting the welfare of children. Many children languish for years in the foster care system, shuffled from home to home, physically protected but with their emotional needs unmet or neglected. The investigation of Diane's death revealed that her mother had also been neglected and that she had spent fifteen years moving around the state foster care system. Since she had never had her own emotional needs met, it is not surprising that she failed to meet the needs of her children.

Even the best trained workers encounter roadblocks caused by lack of funding. Having decided who has the greatest need for intervention, workers often find that the crisis day-care center has no room for the abused child, or the visiting nurse cannot make a home visit for a month, or the hospital cannot keep a child any longer because the child needs only social and not medical care, or the battered wife shelter is full, and so on, and so on.

Unfortunately, the scarcity of resources has not led to agencies and institutions banding together to lobby and demand more resources for the prevention and treatment of family violence. Instead, as is often the case when the need is great and the resources are small, there has been fierce competition for the limited resources that are available.

We have spent the better part of our professional careers watching those concerned with child abuse compete against those who wanted to provide services for spouse abuse and vice versa. An example of this kind of competition is the radical feminist argument that there is no such thing as a battered husband. That concept flies in the face of logic and empirical data. Yet, radical feminists believe that if we acknowledge the existence of battered husbands, then the funding designated for programs to assist battered women will be cut further because monies will be directed at programs for battered men. Thus, many radical feminists have fought for years to keep battered husbands closeted so that the small amount of money that was available for wife abuse would not be jeopardized. Battered men have been kept closeted, but the funding has been cut nonetheless.

We have listened to very intelligent physicians claim that spouse abuse is not a major problem, and that the real problem is child abuse. On the other hand, those concerned with wife abuse maintain that wife abuse is the real problem and that if it could be prevented we would not need to spend money on child abuse. The rationale (such as it is) behind these arguments is that the resource pie for domestic violence is only so big, and "we need all of it that we can get."

The sociologist Kai Erikson once said that our systems of preventing deviance operate so poorly that one has to wonder if the systems are organized to encourage and maintain deviance rather than to control and prevent it. There are many government policies that not only fail to help victims of family violence, but actually exacerbate the problem. One example is government policy eliminating funding of abortion services for women receiving welfare. Child abuse researchers are convinced that if an unwanted baby is born to a household with low resources, that child is at the highest risk of being abused. I was called to testify before the U.S. Senate on the reauthorization of the Child Abuse Prevention and Treatment Act of 1978. When asked, "What can we [the government] do to stop child abuse," my answer was, "With all due respect, what the government ought to do is stop passing laws that encourage people to abuse their children. Then we can begin to talk about what you can do to stop it." The senator who posed the question asked what I meant. I replied, "When the government cuts off abortion funds for women who are on welfare, it guarantees an increase in child abuse in this society. When the government fails to enact gun control legislation, it guarantees the maintenance of a certain level of family violence. And, when politicians say they are going to fight inflation and recession by allowing eleven percent or seven percent of the population to remain unemployed, and we know that unemployment is highly correlated with child abuse, do not ask what you can do—you are part of the problem." Government policies that endorse the use of violence to solve problems, and government action and inaction that increase family stress in certain strata of the society serve to encourage and not to prevent family violence.

The impact of the constraints is often tragic. Fewer than one out of three abused children are reported to the proper agency. The deaths of women and children at the hands of partners and parents are preventable—nine out of ten women and children who die have already come to public attention before their deaths. We know many of the victims who need services, and yet we have not organized ourselves in such a way as to help.

TREATING INTIMATE VIOLENCE

"Making it so people can't" does not simply mean that intimate violence can be prevented by vigorous formal social control. When we say we want to "make it so people can't" we are not implying that child and wife abusers should all be arrested, put into dark cells, and the keys thrown away. A society "makes it so people can't" by organizing its culture, norms, and social institutions to support families as well as by creating internal and external controls that constrain people from choosing violence as an acceptable and approved form of resolving marital problems.

That families and family members need support is a primary assumption of a policy that treats intimate violence. The roles of husband, wife, father, and mother are the most demanding roles humans can assume. The hours are long: We said in chapter 2 people spend more time with their families than with any other single social group or institution. The potential compensation for the hours invested is equally great—intimacy, acceptance, social support, nurturance, social approval, warmth, sharing, in short, fulfillment of one's social and emotional needs. Family roles are demanding for reasons other than simply the time and effort required. The standards of performance are unrealistically high. In point of fact, the standard is perfection—nothing less. A mother is expected to be all-nurturing, selfless, a provider of love, comfort, and support, as well as a source of discipline and control for her children. Having given all this, she must somehow magically transform herself into lover, friend, partner, and confidante for her husband. Social norms demand that husbands play the role of provider and task leader for the family. Today's husband is also expected to be a sensitive and compassionate lover and friend for his wife, and her equal as a loving, comforting, supportive parent for their children. Parents and partners are expected to be all these and more—they must be everything their partners, children, and society seek in a husband, wife, father, or mother.

Meeting all the goals and expectations society places on parents and partners is nearly impossible. It becomes absolutely impossible if one does not possess the social, economic, or psychic resources to support his or her efforts to meet the needs of children and spouse. In a society that generally approves the use of violence as a means of expression and problem solving, it should come as no great surprise that individuals whose accomplishments fall short of society's expectations, whose resources simply are not equal to the attainment of goals, will respond to the frustration of dashed expectations and blocked goals by lashing out with violence. What more appropriate victim than the very individual who stands as a reminder of one's inadequacy? Where more appropriate setting for violence than a private environment, hidden from the view of agents and agencies of social control?

Properly funded, an effective treatment system for family violence would be capable of identifying all the victims in need of services, quickly and effectively intervening to protect victims, and providing support for families under stress.

The first step in an effective intervention system is the ability to identify families at risk. Mandatory reporting of child abuse was the first legislative step enacted to prevent and treat abuse and neglect. Today, more than twenty years after every state enacted reporting laws, the promise of those laws is an empty one for many victimized children. Perhaps only a third of all instances of child abuse and neglect are reported, and those that do come to public attention are but a selective sampling of the true population. Eli Newberger and his colleague, Robert Hampton, have found that white and affluent families are underreported for abuse, while poor and minority children are overreported. While middle- and upper-class victims fail to receive proper ameliorative treatment and protection, poor and minority families may be unfairly and improperly singled out. Worse, Newberger and Hampton note, punishment may be meted out to poor families in the guise of help.

It is axiomatic that mandated reporters—including physicians, social service workers, police officers, teachers, counselors, and the general public (in some states)—should be properly trained in identifying and reporting child abuse. The most important first step is that mandated reporters of child abuse and nonmandated reporters of spouse abuse and elder abuse see these problems not as private matters, but as public matters in which the victim requires protection and the family needs support.

Professional schools that prepare individuals to work with families and children should include modules on family violence in their curricula. The curricula should include classroom and clinical experiences that focus on developing diagnostic as well as treatment skills.

Public awareness campaigns ought to educate the public that family violence is a public matter requiring informal as well as formal intervention. At the informal level, the public ought to serve as an agent of social control, as is the case in Sweden. Sweden enacted legislation prohibiting parents from using corporal punishment on their children. We observed a parent swat a child at a bus stop in Stockholm. We then watched a passerby calmly and gently approach the parent and say, "Hitting your child is not permissible in Sweden." At the formal level, the public needs to learn how and to whom to report instances of abuse and neglect that require legal or criminal interventions.

At-risk women, children, and elderly victims require protection.

We can only protect children if our protective service system is capable of quickly investigating reported cases of child abuse and neglect, and bringing protective resources to bear when needed. Appropriate protective placements, including kin, foster, or residential placements, ought to be a last resort, but a resort that is available to all children at risk. Intermediate protection may be provided by crisis nurseries, day-care facilities, or by a variety of support services.

Child protection services are typically the state agencies that are charged with identifying, preventing, and treating child abuse. Ideally, child protection workers must be adequately trained, reasonably supported, and rendered capable of providing both short-term intensive treatments to families in crisis, as well as long-term treatment approaches aimed at supporting families and reducing the use of violence.

Each and every community must have available a shelter or a safe home for victims and their children. Presently, there are no more than one thousand such shelters in the United States. A society that is capable of providing shelter for dogs and cats must be prepared to provide similar protection for humans.

In order to intervene effectively in the full spectrum of family violence, communities and community agencies must stand ready and be capable of fully supporting families under stress. This means that a full range of health, mental health, legal, and social services for victims and abusers should be available in each community. Communities must also provide vital support services to families, including, when needed, home health visitors, day care, homemakers, health care, clothing, shelter, and other resources that ease the burden of child care for parents.

Our listing of services speaks to the issue of treatment in the most general language. The following examples illustrate the various types of intervention that can be implemented on the individual and community level:

Nancy was a single mother who had moved to a Northeast city with her three children. The move and some administrative delays had left Nancy without food stamps, a welfare check, or support for her dependent children. Two months after the move, Nancy's youngest daughter was reported to the state protective service agency as an abused child. The signs of physical abuse were minor—healing cuts and bruises. The distinguishing feature of the child was that she was so thin—painfully thin for a four-year-old. During the course of a complete family evaluation, it was determined that Nancy had a painful abscess on her hip. Nancy was in so much pain she was unable to feed herself, let alone her young children. The youngest daughter had simply not been fed. She had also been the target for Nancy's violence during the pain. A minor surgical procedure solved the medical problem. A homemaker visited the house daily for a month, and a hospital family clinic provided medical care for Nancy and her children. Ten years later there has been no recurrence of either the violence or neglect, and the youngest daughter is a happy and healthy fourteen-year-old student with good grades in junior high school.

Henry Kempe and his colleagues at the University of Colorado Medical Center developed a perinatal screening procedure to identify mothers as high risk for what the researchers termed "abnormal parenting." The hospital team collected information on the parents' upbringing, feelings about this pregnancy, expectations about the unborn child, and other attitudes. The team then observed the parents in the labor and delivery room. Finally, interviews and observations were conducted after the delivery of the baby. Interventions for those parents deemed at high risk consisted of providing pediatric intervention for the newborn. A pediatrician was assigned to the family, who examined the baby, talked with the parents, scheduled the first clinic visit of the newborn, and saw the child on a bimonthly basis. Additional visits were also scheduled by the doctor or the mother. In addition, the pediatrician contacted the mother by telephone a couple of days after discharge and during the weeks when the child had no clinic appointment. Home visits by public health nurses were also made. Whenever necessary, referrals were made to other medical facilities or health care facilities. Kempe and his group found that they were able to correctly assign families to "high-risk status." The observations of the parents' behavior during the labor and delivery were particularly sensitive diagnostic tools. One of the key high-risk predictors was mothers who did not make eye contact with their babies at birth. The data collected by the team seemed to indicate that the modest pediatric and supportive intervention provided to the high-risk parents prevented severe injury to the high-risk mothers' babies.

The late Jolly K., a battered child and a battering parent, formed Parents Anonymous at her kitchen table with another abusive parent and Leonard Lieber, a volunteer professional. Parents Anonymous grew to thousands of chapters around the world. The model is simple; it is a nurturing and teaching group run by the participants with the help of a professional. Meeting weekly, the group provides support and acceptance to abusive parents. Evaluations indicate that lay therapy, such as offered by Parents Anonymous, is cost-effective and clinically effective in reducing the risk of future abuse and neglect.

Brother to Brother is a men's counseling group established in Providence, Rhode Island. The group is operated as a collective and runs counseling sessions for abusive men. The sessions are typically small —five to eleven members and run for twenty-one weeks. Follow-up indicates that about half of the men who have participated in the counseling have remained violence-free for a while after the counseling sessions.

PREVENTING FAMILY VIOLENCE

The treatments we just described are a start in the right direction. But even the most effective treatment program is only a start. Domestic violence has become woven into the fabric of society, and to prevent it we must be prepared to alter fundamentally the core values, norms, and allocation of resources that contribute to the harmful extent of violence in the home.

Prevention policies and programs must be directed at the two factors that make it possible for people to abuse and maltreat those they love. First, we need to eliminate cultural norms and values that accept violence as a means of resolving conflict and problems in families. Second, we must develop programs and policies that support families and reduce internal and external stresses and inequalities.

Eliminating norms and values that support the use of violence in the home will help develop internal controls so that family members will not resort to violence as either a first or last resort in expressing themselves or dealing with conflict and stress. The most important step in preventing intimate violence is cancellation of the hitting license in families.

Establishing the moral value that loved ones are not to be hit begins by banning spanking and corporal punishment. It is here we come up against the most difficult roadblock in our efforts to prevent intimate violence. Corporal punishment is so ingrained as a childrearing concept that parents take it for granted. Children are hit almost automatically, with little forethought or consideration of other possibilities for training, disciplining, or punishing.

How do we develop internal control? We develop a cultural ethic that hitting children is inappropriate. As a country, Sweden represents a pioneer in the Western world in attempting to develop such a cultural norm. Sweden has taken a strong stand against the use of violence as a means of punishment. Capital punishment has long been banned. In 1952 the corporal punishment of children in schools was outlawed. Legislation prohibiting spanking was enacted in 1979, and has since been adopted by all other Scandinavian countries. Sweden has gone beyond simply legislating against using state, school, or parental violence in its effort to develop a nonviolent moral climate. Firearm ownership is rigorously controlled. While at least half of all American households contain guns, mostly handguns, gun ownership in Sweden is controlled, and gun ownership is limited mostly to weapons used for hunting. Television violence offers another important contrast. Violent programming in Sweden is severely restricted. Actually, Swedish television is barely on the air as many hours as the average American child watches television each week. The level of concern for media programming for children can be seen in the decision in Sweden to limit the popular American movie, *ET* to audiences over eleven years of age.

The difference between attitudes and national posture in the United States and that in Sweden can best be illustrated by American reactions to the Swedish antispanking law. The first reaction is typical: The Swedes are going to raise wild and spoiled kids. The second reaction is even more intriguing. When told that Sweden has a law prohibiting spanking, most Americans ask what the punishment is for breaking the law. In point of fact, Sweden changed only its criminal code. The penal code was not changed; thus, there is no punishment for spanking a child (other than disapproval from observers or bystanders). Americans take for granted that a violation requires a formal punishment. Few Americans can begin even to imagine that an antispanking law would be aimed at merely establishing a moral objection to spanking or that this law would be enforced only by informal and internal social controls. The third reaction is that the law is absurd because children should be spanked, and spankings "work." After all, parents tell us, "When I spank my children, they stop doing what it was that I wanted them to stop."

The conventional wisdom that spanking is effective flies in the face of scientific evidence. Psychological research has *never* demonstrated that punishment is an effective training technique. Actually, rewards are much more effective. Moreover, there is no evidence in homes or schools that physical punishment works. Surely, if you hit a child hard enough he or she will stop an offending behavior and recoil in shock or pain. Children might not engage in that specific behavior again, but the slap, spanking, or even the beating does not deter them from other offending behaviors. If corporal punishment "worked," we could spank children in first grade, and the deterrent effect would last for the next eleven years. We do spank in school, from first grade right though high school. Similarly, if spanking in the home was a deterrent, one good spanking would be sufficient. But our research indicates that half of all parents are still hitting their eighteen-year-old children. Clearly, spanking has virtually no deterrent or training value in the home or school.

When spanking and hitting loved ones are part of the social fabric of a society, it is difficult for members of the society to imagine other ways to solve problems, seek goals, express anger, or deal with stress and frustration. One standard response to a call for a ban on spanking is the question, "How will I effectively punish my child if I don't spank him?" Another response is, "I tried to stop spanking, but it didn't work, so I *had* to spank my kids for their own good."

The topic of how to raise children nonviolently is worthy of a complete book, and we do not have adequate space in this chapter to explain fully a nonviolent approach to childrearing. Suffice it to say, parents will *never* find an appropriate nonviolent technique until they give up, forever, the use of violence. As long as spanking remains a "last resort," no workable alternative childrearing approach will be adopted.

What are the alternatives to using spanking at home or corporal punishment at school? In our opinion, there are many. First is talking to children, particularly young children. Parents can effectively train, raise, and discipline children by explaining, suggesting, and generally using the spoken word to identify and solve problems. Obviously, talking works if parents approach children reasonably. The parent who assumes that children are unreasoning and unreasonable will never connect with a child verbally. Yet, children who are treated with reason tend to behave reasonably.

In addition to talk, parents can control their children with appropriate rewards and punishment. It is axiomatic among psychologists that reward is a much more effective means of training children than is punishment. Equally axiomatic is that the most effective way of encouraging a child to stop a particular behavior is to ignore it totally rather than to draw attention to it by expressing anger or outrage in a violent way.

"What do I do," a parent asks, "if my child touches a hot stove, puts his finger into a plug socket, or runs into the street?" Certainly, parents cannot ignore acts that endanger children. Childproofing homes is a simple nonviolent means of protecting children. Poisons should be stored out of the reach of children. Childproof latches should be placed on drawers or doors to protect valuables and to hide dangerous items. Plug covers keep little fingers away from sockets. As for children running into streets, we have found that talking to children about the dangers of running into the streets is far more effective than a slap on the bottom after the youngster's dash into the street.

Another effective means of controlling behaviors and situations is to remove children from the scene of misbehavior. Psychologists call this "time-out." "Time-outs" are not only for children. Overstressed parents who snap at their children for minor things ought to consider sending themselves to their rooms when they are unable to react reasonably due to anger.

After nearly two decades of research on the causes and consequences of family violence, we are convinced that our society must abandon its reliance on spanking children if we are to prevent intimate violence. If we are ever to accomplish this goal, we must reject the belief that spanking is an effective discipline tool and we must abolish corporal punishment for all time. When parents believe they cannot spank children, then and only then will they search for and adopt alternative childrearing techniques.

Banning spanking is but one means of developing internal control. Other means include eliminating cultural messages that violence is an appropriate mechanism for self-expression or problem solving.

Television violence frequently is targeted as a cause of family violence. On the one hand, we think that television violence receives far too much of the blame for violence in the home. After all, families were violent in the United States long before the invention of television. Yet, on the other hand, while not the major causal factor that some think it is, television violence plays a role in creating a social climate that violence is appropriate. The average child watches television for as many as twenty hours each week. Research indicates that these children observe eighteen thousand killings before graduating high school. Other acts of violence are even more common. The National Coalition on Television Violence has conducted a monitoring project on TV violence for a number of years. Among the most violent television programs in the fall of 1986 were: "Sledge Hammer," with fifty-eight violent acts each hour; "The A-Team," which averaged fifty-six violent acts each hour; and "Miami Vice," averaging thirty-five violent acts each hour. The popular show "Moonlighting" presented fourteen violent incidents each hour. Saturday morning cartoon shows, a basic staple of television viewing for young children, presented even more violence. The most violent cartoon in 1986 was "Inhumanoids," which averaged eighty-six violent acts per hour. This was followed closely by "Centurions: Power Xtreme," "G.I. Joe," "Gobots," and "Tranformers," all of which averaged more than sixty violent acts each hour. Bugs Bunny (with the Road Runner and Wile E. Coyote) had forty-eight violent incidents each hour. The lovable Smurfs had seventeen incidents each hour.

Children's toys, like the popular Rambo toys, G.I. Joe, and Lazer Tag, also present a proviolence message to children. According to the National Coalition on Television Violence, the sale of such war toys has risen 700 percent since 1982. G.I. Joe tops the charts as the number one best selling toy in America. According to the National Coalition, the amount of war-related cartoons and advertising seen by the average American child totals up to 1,250 hours each year—the equivalent of twenty-two school days.

Internal control is possible only in a society that does not glorify violence on television, in the movies, and in children's toys and games. Equally important is the forsaking of legalized violence by society. We have continually called for the abolition of capital punishment as an important step in eliminating cultural approval of violence. The handful of executions each year fail to deter anyone from criminal homicide. Each execution sends the message to members of society that violent punishment is appropriate for violent crimes.

There are a number of specific policies and programs that should be implemented to change cultural norms and values and encourage family members to develop internal norms that view people as not for hitting:

1. The first step is to enact legislation such as has been enacted in the Scandinavian countries that bans capital punishment, corporal punishment, and the use of spanking by parents. No punishments need be applied to such legislation—the simple statement of a cultural prohibition of violence is the most important impact of such laws.

2. During the time that it takes to develop a generation of parents who forsake violence at home, specific government policies can by

enacted that support an antiviolence sentiment in society. The federal government can encourage schools to abandon the practice of corporal punishment by denying federal funds for school districts that use corporal punishment—much in the same way that funds are denied to schools that engage in racial or gender discrimination.

3. There is a delicate balance between the need to support the consitutional guarantee of freedom of speech and freedom of the press and the need to limit media programming that may be directly linked to violent behavior. An outright ban of violent television programming might be desirable. However, it would also border on unconstitutional infringement of the right of freedom of speech. A useful middle ground would be to set aside Saturday and Sunday mornings as noncommercial broadcasting hours. Without the pressure to achieve the high ratings that sell valuable commercial time, the major networks might be less inclined to produce violent programming designed to capture young viewer attention. Commercials advertising war- or violent-related toys could be banned, much the same way the Federal Communications Commission banned smoking advertisements. At the very least, advertising to counter the message of violent toys and games should be mandated by the FCC.

4. Supportive policies that enhance internal control include establishing educational programs that teach noncoercive and nonviolent means of raising children. Parent education programs such as PET go part of the way by providing parents with alternatives to hitting. Such programs should also explicitly take a nonphysical punishment stand. We mandate that teenagers take driver's education courses to reduce traffic accidents and fatalities. Similarly, mandated parent education programs are needed to reduce the toll of domestic strife and conflict.

Parents and partners will develop internal systems of control only if the belief that people are not for hitting is shared and supported by other social institutions. Individual internal controls will never be developed if police officers fail to respond to instances of domestic violence in the same manner that violence between strangers is dealt with. We cannot expect husbands to develop internal controls as long as judges and prosecutors see intimate violence as a private matter that does not belong on the public agenda or in the public courtrooms. Internal controls will never be applied while family members hear a member of the United States Senate quip, "If you outlaw wife beating, you take all the fun out of marriage," or a state legislator remark, "If you can't rape your wife, who can you rape?"

Police, prosecutors, and judges must respond to domestic assault just as they would approach violence in the streets. Arrest, prosecution, conviction, and sentencing ought to be consistent irrespective of the relationship between victim and offender. When a woman calls the police only to see her husband walked around the block and returned home, she has been victimized again. Her husband has learned, in essence, that there is no real punishment for domestic violence. In effect, he has been licensed to hit.

Each of the major social institutions must take the position that domestic violence is unacceptable and will be dealt with in the same manner as any other crime.

The majority of family homicides involves guns, mainly handguns. Although a weapon may be purchased to protect family members from armed strangers, the sad truth is that the weapon's most likely victim will be another member of the household, even if only by accident as in the following cases:

John was a rabid gun collector. He owned a number of weapons, mostly handguns. He was meticulous in cleaning, maintaining, and presenting his collection. One afternoon he was cleaning a revolver after having used it on a firing range. He was startled by his four-year-old daughter, who entered his study to ask for help finding her slippers. The weapon fell from John's hands, and discharged—one bullet was inadvertently in the chamber. John's daughter was killed by a shot through her brain.

Twelve-year-old Derek slipped into his father's bedroom with his best friend Michael. He climbed onto a chair so that he could reach into a box on the top shelf of his father's closet. From the box he removed his father's small caliber pistol. He climbed down from the chair, and he and his friend examined the gun. His friend took the gun, aimed it at Derek's head, and pulled the trigger. Derek was killed instantly.

Most other family shootings are far less benign, but no less tragic. A heated argument, a fight, an available weapon, and another family homicide is a much more common scenario than the accidents involving family firearms. An example is the case of a young man who shot his brother to death because the brother had used four of the six rolls of recently purchased toilet paper. As absurd as this may seem, it is alarmingly typical of how a small matter escalates into murder if a lethal weapon is available.

Even though other weapons are available in the home—knives, ice picks, and so on, guns are by far the most lethal and dangerous weapons. One effective means of maintaining external control and reducing the tragic toll of domestic homicide is to disarm the American family. The home should be a haven in a heartless land, not an armory with weapons for any unplanned domestic altercation.

Policies and programs that establish external control of intrafamily violence have been enacted in many states. Child abuse reporting laws were designed, in part, to establish regulatory control over parents. Similarly, laws defining spouse abuse and providing legal avenues of redress for victims and punishment for offenders were enacted to extend external controls for violence into the privacy of the home. Additional legislative steps include the enactment of mandatory arrest statutes to assure that police officers treat domestic violence as a crime. Additional prevention policies should include:

1. Laws that treat marital rape as a crime similar to stranger rape.
2. Legislation similar to spouse abuse prevention laws that define violence toward parents as a crime.
3. Strict local, state, and federal gun control legislation that forbids the manufacture or distribution of inexpensive Saturday night special handguns. Rigorous restriction of manufacture, distribution, and ownership of other firearms, especially handguns, is an absolute necessity.

If individuals are expected to develop and maintain internal control, they must have a reasonable chance to develop these controls. Many individuals and families have no such opportunity. In many homes, energies that might be directed at the development of nonviolent means of raising children or resolving marital conflict are sapped meeting the overwhelming stresses of daily living. Poverty, inequality, racism, and sexism often debilitate the most sincere effort to maintain internal controls. Too many families must devote all their available energies and resources to finding suitable housing, food, and clothing to get through each day. Others face the same battles but are further handicapped by serious or chronic physical or mental health problems that impinge upon their ability to function. Prevention of family violence requires preventing the stresses that overwhelm many families and shatter the individual's coping mechanisms.

Family life is fragile enough without the added burdens of poverty, unemployment, inadequate medical and dental care, and various other external stresses. Eliminating poverty and unemployment and assuring that every member of the society has access to adequate health care, housing, clothing, and food would be a worthy goal even if it had no direct impact on preventing violence. Since each of these factors is directly related to increased risk of family violence, our call for the elimination of poverty, unemployment, and other social stresses become even more compelling.

Reducing and eliminating unemployment is perhaps the most direct and useful prevention approach we should pursue. In the context of a capitalistic and competitive society, people can confront no greater stigma than unemployment or underemployment. Joblessness undermines an individual's sense of self-worth and self-esteem. Moreover, unemployment and poverty directly limit an individual's ability to cope with social or psychological stresses.

A second prevention strategy that is within our grasp is providing adequate medical and dental care to all American families. National health insurance was proposed year in and year out in the U.S. Congress in the 1970s. Each year it was defeated because it was considered too costly. Yet the cost of providing national health insurance pales in comparison with the costs that violence in the home is extracting from our society. Days lost from work, the costs of medical and hospital care, and the other direct and indirect costs of family violence—including the immeasurable costs of years lost from life due to family homicide, far outweigh the costs of assuring that each man, woman, and child has access to adequate and appropriate health care.

A third strategy that would reduce stress and support families is effective planned parenthood. We have noted before that unwanted children are an especially high-risk group for abuse. We hypothesized that one change in the last ten years that may have contributed to a reduction of child abuse is the availability of a full range of planned parenthood services, including abortion. We have consistently called for an expansion of family planning services as a crucial means for reducing stress and supporting American families.

Obviously, reducing stress and supporting families will not completely eliminate violence in all families. We know that even the wealthiest and best supported homes are sometimes the scenes of extreme violence. Nevertheless, the steps we propose are necessary. We cannot continue to expect homes to be warm and secure and parents to be available and nurturing if we systematically deny large segments of our population the basic resources that are prerequisites for adequate performance in the roles of parent and partner.

Our examination of family violence over the years has consistently found that socially structured inequality is a prime contributor to violence in the home. We cannot overemphasize the preventive value of promoting sexual equality and eliminating sexism.

One way that sexism in society supports violence in the home is the economic pressure on women to remain in violent relationships. Women with full-time employment earn $0.70 for every $1.00 earned by men. About half of all married women with children are at home and have no income at all. A battered woman seeking to leave a marriage faces the nearly disastrous consequences of almost immediate poverty.

Four specific policy implications follow from our finding that sexual inequality is a prime cause of family violence and our belief that eliminating sexism can prevent violence in the home:

1. At the treatment level, family therapists should regard inequality in society and in the home as a risk factor for family violence. Therapists need to avoid the temptation to blame the powerless for their victimization. Moreover, therapy can attempt to establish equality in the home.
2. The entire mental health movement must join hands with the women's movement and seek the elimination of our culture of sexism. Feminism is directly beneficial to physical and mental health of all members of our society.
3. Women should be encouraged to pursue their goals in the labor market. They should not be discouraged from seeking work or pursuing careers on the grounds that the pressure of work and careers will be harmful to them and their children. Quite the contrary, research indicates that paid employment *enhances* mental health for mothers and their children. We find that paid employment is related to more equality and less violence in the home.
4. Sexism must be eliminated in the workplace. The disparity in pay between men and women must be eliminated.

Changes at home must also be sought. Gender alone is not a sufficient criteria for assignment of all household and childrearing tasks. The gender-linked allocation to roles and tasks in the home must be broken. Individuals ought to be free to select tasks and responsibility based on available time and energies as well as capabilities or interests. Such a change would not only free women, but men as well. No longer trapped in the worker-provider role, men would be freed from the pressure associated with having to be provider, worker, success in the workplace, husband, father, and nurturer all at the same time.

Another means of supporting families is to provide a means of social support at times of crisis and stress. We have found that individuals without friends or relatives to turn to when they are overwhelmed by stress and strain are likely to cope by striking out at family members. One of the most frequent attributes of violent families is their social isolation.

What can be done to better embed families into supportive networks? What can we do at a time when the birthrate is falling, when families are getting smaller, and when the society is becoming more, not less, mobile?

Awareness of the need to promote kin and community linkages is one place to begin. Many government and corporate policies are actually counterproductive and push families away from networks. Corporate transfer for the middle and upper class as well as job displacement due to the changing nature of the economy for the working and lower class undermine community and kin networks. Corporations build factories where land is inexpensive, not where natural communities exist. Urban renewal in the Northeast has destroyed many ethnic neighborhoods that provided families with sanctuary from the storms of social stress.

Government and corporate policies ought to support families, if not for the social good, for the profit motive as well. Violent families produce higher rates of job absenteeism and reduce productivity. Corporations that provide day care, employee assistance programs, and which concern themselves with the individuals and their families can enhance rather than destroy community networks.

Local communities can also take steps to develop and enhance community support networks. Supporting therapeutic groups such as Parents Anonymous, battered wife shelters, and other crisis centers and hot lines have a direct impact on the reduction of family violence. Youth groups, homemakers clubs, recreational clubs and groups have a more indirect, but important, impact on supporting families.

Communities can also establish educational programs that can support families and prevent violence. A true primary prevention strategy must include courses and workshops in family-problem-solving skills and childrearing. Such programs and workshops can be offered by churches, schools, or other community groups.

Much of what we have discussed and reported in this book is new information, gleaned from our own recently completed Second National Family Violence Survey and from the ongoing research of our colleagues in the field of family violence. Our discussion of prevention and treatment is not new. We have traveled around the world for nearly two decades calling for the same policies and programs that we have just summarized. The research data that have been accumulated over the past two decades support and underscore each of the points we make and programs we propose.

We have encountered two roadblocks in our effort to promote an atmosphere in which people cannot hit family members. The first is the outright opposition we face when we call for controversial changes. Arguing for a ban on spanking or total gun control tends to bring out strong, vocal, and dogmatic opposition from many quarters. Calling for a reduction in the number of unwanted children by making family planning, including abortion services, available has brought some of the stronger attacks against our work. The voices of opposition are just as strong, although the numbers are smaller, among those who object to equality between men and women, public support for battered wife shelters, and many of our other proposals.

The second roadblock is quieter, but significantly more important. It is public indifference. It is easy, perhaps, to arouse the public with examples of outrageous and cruel acts of violence toward defenseless and helpless victims. But even here, the half-life of public interest is amazingly short. Today's hot social problem is tomorrow's old news, less worthy of public attention, public support, and social resources —yet all the while just as common and just as harmful as it was when the public paid attention.

Our dilemma is that capturing and holding public attention often necessitates focusing exclusively on the most sensational cases of domestic violence. Yet such a focus, we feel, is counterproductive. These cases are so sensational that they appear to be rare and the product of mental illness. Unfortunately, the most widespread and insidious intimate violence—the nearly routine pushes, shoves, and punches are not perceived by the public as a clear social evil.

We have, throughout this book, attempted to make the case that each and every violent act involving a loved one is a social evil with short- and long-range costs to individuals, families, and the society. Similarly, we have tried to place intimate violence within the fabric of the society, rather than characterizing it as some sort of bizarre aberration.

Treating and preventing intimate violence require us to change the fabric of the society. Treatment ought not depend on forcing the victim to change. Treatment should be aimed at empowering and protecting victims, deterring and yet supporting offenders, and protecting and supporting families. Prevention should be aimed at creating social institutions that explicitly say, "People are not for hitting." To prevent intimate abuse we must reach the point where we believe as a society that each individual is a valuable human being who is entitled to a healthy physical, social, and psychological development.

We appear to have made clear and convincing progress in reducing some forms of family violence in the last ten years. The amount of reduction is nearly in direct proportion to the amount of public concern and social resources directed at prevention and treatment. It is our hope that the next decade will see an expansion of concern and resources and a similar decline in the extent and harm of intimate violence in families.

Appendix A

How the Studies

Were Done

We began our research on family violence early in 1971 when we passed out questionnaires to hundreds of our students enrolled in introductory sociology classes at the University of New Hampshire. Our initial goal was to learn something about the extent and meaning of violence among family members. Rather than ask our students whether they had been abused or had observed their parents abusing one another, we measured violence using a series of questions which we called the Conflict Tactics Scales (the Conflict Tactics Scales are included in the Interview Schedule in Appendix B).

There are three general means of conflict tactics that the scales measure: (1) The use of rational discussion and agreement (e.g., discussed the issue calmly; got information to back my side up; brought in or tried to bring in someone to help settle things); (2) the use of verbal or nonverbal expressions of anger or hostility (e.g., insulted or swore; sulked or refused to talk; stomped out of the room or house; did something to spite the other person; threatened to hit or throw something; threw, smashed, or hit something); or (3) the use of physical force or violence (e.g., threw something at the other person; pushed, grabbed, or shoved; slapped or spanked; kicked, bit, or hit with a fist; hit or tried to hit with something; beat up; choked, threatened or used a knife or gun).

We defined abusive violence as those acts with a high probability of injuring the victim. Thus, we measured abuse by focusing on the most extreme acts of violence in the scale—kicking, biting, punching, hitting or trying to hit with objects, choking, beating, and using weapons.

Our first studies found that family violence was much more extensive then we had imagined. With the knowledge that family violence was apparently more common than we had previously realized, we set out on two paths. One line of work was to assure that the results of the questionnaires were valid. Thus, we sent questionnaires home to the parents of our students to determine if they would fill out the questionnaires and also to learn whether or not the answers would be consistent with those of their children. The parents participated, and the answers were indeed consistent.

The second line of work was a bit more difficult. We had learned that a captive audience of middle-class college students would fill out questionnaires, and that their less captive parents would also. In order to do larger scale survey research, we needed to determine the general public's willingness to be interviewed about violence in the home.

We received almost no encouragement and precious little support in our endeavor. Friends, social workers, police officers, and other social scientists said we were looking up a blind alley. No one, we were told, would let us into the home, and even if they did, they certainly would refuse to answer questions about violence. At best, we were told, we would find nothing; at worst, we would be found beaten to death.

There was some encouragement and a bit of caution. A social service agency agreed to refer clients to us whom they suspected of having violence problems at home. A police department in southern New Hampshire agreed to let us review its log and to cull names and addresses of families listed for domestic disturbance or assault calls. Our comparison group would be the neighbors of these selected families.

Armed with a clipboard and a tape recorder, and careful enough to call the police and advise them of our itinerary, we set out to interview families. The results were again sadly surprising. Overall, nearly half of those with whom we talked reported violence between the partners. Of the so-called "comparison families"—those in which we had no expectation of violent behavior—more than one-third reported violence between partners at some point in the relationship.

Not only were our respondents willing to talk with us, but many of the interviews went on for as long as three or four hours. Sometimes, after the tape recorder was turned off, a respondent remembered another violent incident and asked us to turn the recorder on again. Never were we physically attacked; however, the sight of a husband walking through the front door at 10:30 A.M. while we interviewed the wife in the kitchen caused us considerable anxiety.

The questionnaires from our students and the interviews we carried out in southern New Hampshire convinced us of the viability of survey research. We were also confident about the reliability and validity of the Conflict Tactics Scales as a means of measuring violence.

THE FIRST NATIONAL FAMILY VIOLENCE SURVEY

In 1976 we embarked on our most ambitious survey, a national survey of violence in the American family. The full results of that survey are reported in our book, *Behind Closed Doors: Violence in the American Family*. Together with the survey research firm, Response Analysis, we interviewed a nationally representative sample of 2,146 individual family members. To be eligible for an interview, a respondent had to be presently married or living with a partner of the opposite sex. We excluded people living alone (including single parents) to assure that we had a sufficient number of couples to conduct analyses of marital violence. In each family in which at least one child between the ages of three and seventeen years of age was living at home, a "referent" child was selected using a random procedure. The lower age limit of three years was selected because one aim of the study was to obtain meaningful data on sibling violence. We measured violence, as we always have done, using the Conflict Tactics Scales. Almost two-thirds of those eligible to participate in the face-to-face interviews completed the interview.

THE SECOND NATIONAL FAMILY VIOLENCE SURVEY

Our most recent survey was conducted in 1985 with Louis Harris and Associates. We changed methodologies and interviewed our subjects over the telephone rather than in person. This time a nationally representative sample of 6,002 individuals was interviewed. The sample comprised three parts. First, 4,032 households were selected in proportion to the distribution of households in the fifty states. Then 958 households were oversampled in twenty-five states. This was done to assure that there would be thirty-six states with at least one hundred completed interviews per state. Finally, two additional oversamples were drawn—508 black and 516 Hispanic households. The data reported in this book have been weighted to account for the three separate oversamples.

Eligibility for inclusion in the study required that a household include adults, nineteen years of age or older, who were:

1. Presently married, or
2. Presently living as a male-female couple, or
3. Divorced or separated within the last two years, or
4. Single parents with a child under eighteen years of age at home.

When more than one eligible adult was in the household, a random procedure was used to select the gender and marital status of the respondent. When more than one child under the age of eighteen was in the household, a random procedure was used to select a "referent child," who would be the focus of the parent-to-child violence questions.

Telephone numbers were selected using a procedure called Random Digit Dialing. This procedure begins by stratifying the United States into four regions (East, South, Midwest, and West) and three types of place (central city with populations greater than 100,000; suburbs or cities with less than 100,000 population; and towns, villages, or hamlets with populations of less than 2,500). Within each region and place a primary sampling unit is selected in proportion to the size of the population in the stratum. In the next stage a telephone number is selected for each primary sampling unit. A working number from a library of telephone directories is chosen, and the last two digits of the number are randomly replaced. Thus, the procedure produces a random sampling of all the possible telephone numbers in the United States.

Sample selection and interviews were carried out by the staff of Louis Harris and Associates, the national opinion research company. When telephones were busy or there was no answer, interviewers called back three times before they substituted for the busy or non-answering number. If a contact was made but the person answering refused to participate, trained "refusal conversion" interviewers were assigned to the household. Interviews lasted on the average of thirty-five minutes. More than eight out of ten (84 percent) eligible persons contacted completed an interview. Again, we measured violence using the Conflict Tactics Scales—this time adding the item "burned or scalded" to the measure of violence toward children, and "choked" to the marital violence scale.

STRENGTHS AND LIMITATIONS OF OUR SURVEYS

While questionnaires and interviews allow us to obtain data rapidly from a large number of people, the amount of information obtainable is small compared with data derived from clinical cases of intimate violence. Each interview in 1976 lasted sixty minutes (the maximum length of time for a structured, in-person interview), and we were able to ask about two hundred questions. Each 1985 telephone survey lasted, on the average, thirty-five minutes. This is at the outer limit for how long an interviewer can expect to keep the respondent on the telephone. We were able to ask about 125 questions over the telephone.

Large national surveys allow us to develop a portrait of behavior that can be generalized to families throughout the United States. But such a portrait is little more than a snapshot of families at a particular point in time. Obtaining more data requires additional interview sessions, which raises the cost of such research into the millions of dollars.

A second limitation of our research is that we learn only what people are willing to reveal. Survey research is not a study of behavior; it provides us information on what people say to us about their behavior. As good as our Conflict Tactics Scales and our other measures are, they are by no means perfect. At no time do we believe that everyone we interview tells us all. The most bizarre and humiliating events experienced by the most victimized individuals are typically not accessible in surveys. For this type of information, clinical studies or in-depth interviews with a limited number of individuals offer the the most detailed and useful data.

There are biases of inclusion and exclusion in surveys. Our surveys of college students included primarily white, middle-class students and excluded blacks, Hispanics, and the poor. Our face-to-face interviewers had the most difficulty conducting interviews in the poorest as well as the most affluent neighborhoods. Our telephone survey missed transients and all those without telephones.

The Conflict Tactics Scales are the most widely used measure of family violence. As of the end of 1986, there were more than one hundred publications, including five books, which used or analyzed the Conflict Tactics Scales. Despite the wide-scale use of this measure of intimate violence, it does have some limitations. The most obvious problem is the limited and restricted list of violent acts included in the scales. There literally hundreds of forms of family violence. Time and cost factors would not allow us to include every possible form of violence. The length of the scales required us to omit a number of violent behaviors that may occur in many families. A second concern raised by our colleagues is that the scales measure behaviors but neither the consequences or context of those behaviors. We may learn that people slap or choke others, but not the reasons, the circumstances, the motivations, or the consequences of such behavior.

CONCLUDING COMMENTS

The explosion of interest in the topic of intimate violence has been accompanied by tremendous growth in research and publication on the various aspects of violence in the home. Unfortunately, although the amount of information collected in the past twenty-five years is impressive—at least compared with the dearth of data collected prior to 1962—the knowledge base is still far from solid. By and large, the reason for the lack of a well-defined and delineated knowledge base is the rather brief period of time the topic of intimate violence has been studied. Much of what we know is based on descriptive or exploratory research.

Surveys of family violence, such as those we have conducted, have yielded estimates of the extent of family violence and the patterns associated with both the onset and aftermath of violence between intimates. A major advantage of surveys on family violence is that they are replicable by others who wish to validate the results of the research. Surveys also overcome the biases of using clinical or official report data to learn about the extent and patterns of family violence. Yet, because the advantages of large social surveys must be weighed against the disadvantages of the small amount and the limited kinds of data obtainable with questionnaires or interviews, both clinical and official report data have been used in preparing this volume. When the results from surveys, clinical records, and official report data are consistent, we have the greatest confidence in the accuracy of the knowledge we report and discuss.

Appendix B

Interview Schedule

for the Second National

Family Violence Survey

LOUIS HARRIS AND ASSOCIATES, INC.
630 Fifth Avenue
New York, New York 10111

FOR OFFICE USE ONLY:

Questionnaire No(QN): _____

Sample Point No. |__|__|__|__|__|__|__|__|

NOTE: Sample Point No. includes:
SOURCE, STATEH, and SIZE.

June 10, 1985
(PLEASE PRINT)

Interviewer's Name: _____ Date: _____

Area Code: _____ Telephone No.: _____

— —

Hello, I'm _____ from Louis Harris and Associates, the national public opinion research firm. We are conducting a study for the National Institutes of Health about family life, American couples, and their children and I'd like to ask you (or someone in your household) who is over 18 some questions. So that I will know which questions apply to you, I need to ask you about the people in your household.

A. First, how many couples, either currently married or just living together, are there in this household?

|__| present couples

None	_____	−0
Eight or more	_____	−8
Not sure	_____	−9

B. How many other people are living in this household who are single parents—by single parents I mean persons who are not currently living with a partner but who have children under 18 in the household.

|__| single parents

None	_____	−0
Eight or more	_____	−8
Not sure	_____	−9

C. Is there anyone else you have not already mentioned in your household who was married or living with a partner of the opposite sex within the past two years? How many?

|__| previously coupled

No	_____	−0
Eight or more	_____	−8
Not sure	_____	−9

IF NONE TO Q.A, Q.B, AND Q.C, THEN SCREEN OUT
THANK YOU VERY MUCH. UNFORTUNATELY WE CANNOT INCLUDE YOU IN OUR STUDY
OF FAMILY LIFE AT THIS TIME.
IF "YES," RANDOM SELECTION FROM ALL ELIGIBLE UNITS

RESPONDENT SELECTION GRID

Number present couples in Q.A   _____ _____ (   )
Number single parents in Q.B   _____ _____ (   )
Number previously coupled in Q.C   _____ _____ (   )

**SELECT FAMILY TYPE MARKED "X" ABOVE. IF NONE IN THAT FAMILY TYPE
THEN SELECT NEXT FAMILY TYPE IN ROTATION PATTERN.**

**T.   IF "PRESENT COUPLE" SELECTED THEN SELECT RESPONDENT WHOSE SEX IS
(MARKED "X" BELOW)**

Male   _____ −1
Female   _____ −2

FTYPE S. According to my instructions, I need to speak to (the/a) person in your
household who is (male/female):

A. Currently married or living together   _____ −1
B. A single parent   _____ −2
C. Previously married or living together   _____ −3

RECORD SELECTED UNIT ABOVE

SAY TO DESIGNATED RESPONDENT:

Hello, my name is _____ from Louis Harris and Asso-
ciates, the national public opinion research firm. We are conducting a national study
about family life for the National Institutes of Health. Your participation in the survey is
completely voluntary. The information you provide will be kept confidential. In order to
protect your anonymity, we have selected your phone number completely at random.
We will not ask your name, so that no one will ever know your answers to these
questions.

---

1. First, a few background questions. How old are you?

   |__|__| Years

   97 or older   _____ −97
   Refused   _____ −99

2. How long have you lived in this community?

   |__|__| If less than 1 year, enter 00.

   Refused   _____ −99

3. Are you currently employed full time, part time, unemployed, retired, a student, keeping house, or something else?

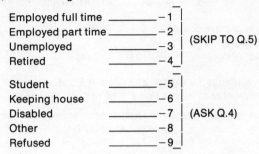

Employed full time _____ −1
Employed part time _____ −2
Unemployed _____ −3   (SKIP TO Q.5)
Retired _____ −4

Student _____ −5
Keeping house _____ −6
Disabled _____ −7   (ASK Q.4)
Other _____ −8
Refused _____ −9

4. Have you ever held a job for pay?

Yes _____ −1   (ASK Q.5)

No _____ −0   (SKIP TO Q.6a)
Not sure _____ −8

5. What kind of work do (did) you do?
NOTE: This verbal description is translated into an occupational code which is recorded on card 7, columns 26–28. Its variable name is Q.5.

INTERVIEWER: ASK FOR JOB TITLE AND MAIN DUTIES—DESCRIBE IN DETAIL:

PAGE 2

NOTE: Question F5 (race/ethnicity) shown on page 26 was asked here for the black and Hispanic oversamples and used to include or exclude respondents.

ASK EVERYONE

6a. Are you currently married, or living as a couple with someone?

Yes, married _____ −1   (ASK Q.6b)
Yes, living as couple _____ −2

No, neither _____ −3
Not sure _____ −8   (SKIP TO Q.10a)
Refused _____ −9

6b. How long have you been (married/living as a couple) to your current (spouse/partner)?

|___|___| Years

Less than one year _____ −00
97 years or longer _____ −97
Refused _____ −99

7. Is your (spouse/partner) currently employed full time, part time, unemployed, retired, a student, keeping house, or something else?

Employed full time _____ −1 ⎤
Employed part time _____ −2 ⎥ (SKIP TO Q.9)
Unemployed _____ −3 ⎥
Retired _____ −4 ⎦

Student _____ −5 ⎤
Keeping house _____ −6 ⎥ (ASK Q.8)
Disabled _____ −7 ⎥
Other _____ −8 ⎥
Refused _____ −9 ⎦

8. Has he/she ever held a job for pay?

Yes _____ −1 (ASK Q.9)

No _____ −0 ⎤ (SKIP TO Q.16a)
Not sure _____ −8 ⎦

9. What kind of work does your (spouse/partner) do?
NOTE: This verbal description is translated into an occupational code which is recorded on card 7, columns 30−32. Its variable name is Q.9.

INTERVIEWER: ASK FOR JOB TITLE AND MAIN DUTIES—DESCRIBE IN DETAIL:

GO TO Q.16a

PAGE 3

10a. **(IF "NO," "NOT SURE," OR "REFUSED"IN Q.6a, ASK:)** Have you ever been married or lived as a couple with someone?

Yes _____ −1 (ASK Q.10b)

No _____ −0 ⎤ (SKIP TO Q.19)
Not sure/refused _____ −9 ⎦

217

*10b. How long ago did that (MOST RECENT) marriage or relationship end?

Q.10b └─┴─┘ years ago

Number of years mentioned	_____ −1	Q.10b2
Less than one month	_____ −2	
One month to six months	_____ −3	
Six months to a year	_____ −4	
Not sure	_____ −8	

* Q.10b and Q.10b2 have been recoded into a single variable named Q10BX. See page 33 for categories and codes.

11a. How long were you married to or living with that person?

└─┴─┘ years

Less than one year	_____ − 00
97 years or longer	_____ − 97
Refused	_____ − 99

11b. Did you and your spouse/partner have any children as a result of this marriage/ relationship?

Yes	_____ −1
No	_____ −0
Not sure/refused	_____ −9

11c. Were you and your spouse/partner expecting at the time your marriage/relationship ended?

Yes	_____ −1
No	_____ −0
Not sure/refused	_____ −9

12. Are you currently widowed, divorced, separated or never been married?

Widowed	_____ −1	
Divorced	_____ −2	(ASK Q.13)
Separated	_____ −3	
Never been married	_____ −4	(SKIP TO INSTRUCTION
Not sure	_____ −8	BEFORE Q.17a)

*13. Was your former (spouse/partner) employed full time, part time, unemployed, retired, a student, keeping house or something else?

Q.13 Employed full time _____ −1
Employed part time _____ −2 (SKIP TO Q.15)
Unemployed _____ −3
Retired _____ −4

Student _____ −5
Keeping house _____ −6 (ASK Q.14)
Disabled _____ −7
Other _____ −8
Refused _____ −9
Q.13b Not sure _____ −9

* Q.13 and Q.13b have been recoded into a single variable named Q13X. See page 33 for categories and codes.

14. Has he/she held a job for pay?

Yes _____ −1 (ASK Q.15)

No _____ −0 (SKIP TO Q.16a)
Not sure _____ −9

15. What kind of work did your former spouse or partner do?
NOTE: This verbal description is translated into an occupational code which is recorded on card 7, columns 34–36. Its variable name is Q.15.

INTERVIEWER: ASK FOR JOB TITLE AND MAIN DUTIES—DESCRIBE IN DETAIL:

16a. Including your current/most recent marriage/relationship how many times have/ had you been married or lived as a couple with someone?

|__|__| times

Eight or more _____ −8
Not sure _____ −98
Refused _____ −99

ASK IF MARRIED OR LIVING AS A COUPLE IN Q.6a ELSE SKIP TO INSTRUCTION BEFORE Q.17a

16b. How many times has/had your spouse been married or lived as a couple?

|__|__| times

Eight or more _____ −8
Not sure _____ −98
Refused _____ −99

IF SINGLE PARENT MALE, SKIP TO Q.19

17a. Are you (is your wife/partner) currently expecting a child?

Yes   ————— −1   (ASK Q.17b)

No   ————— −0 ⌉ (SKIP TO Q.19)

Not sure/refused————— −9 ⌋

17b. How many months pregnant are you/is she?

⌊___⌊___⌋ months

Not sure   ————— −98

ASK EVERYONE

*19. In all, how many children under 18 do you (and your spouse) have living in this household?

Q.19   ⌊___⌊___⌋ number

Q.19b Has children (VALUE GIVEN)   ————— −1

None   ————— −2 ⌉ (SKIP TO Q.29)

Not sure/refused   ————— −9 ⌋

* Q.19 and Q.19b have been recoded into a single variable named Q19X. See page 33 for categories and codes.

20. Would you tell me the age of each of these children, starting with the oldest?

	Q.20A (1 to 8) Age	Q.21 (1 to 8) Sex Boy	Girl	Q.22b1 (1 to 9) Previous Marriage Self	Q.22b2 (1 to 9) Previous Marriage Spouse	Q.22d (1 to 9) Adopted/ Foster	Q.22f (1 to 9) Natural	Q.22h (1 to 9) Not Related
Child 1	⌊__⌊__⌋	——— −1	——— −2	——— −1	——— −1	——— −1	——— −1	——— −1
Child 2	⌊__⌊__⌋	——— −1	——— −2	——— −1	——— −1	——— −1	——— −1	——— −1
Child 3	⌊__⌊__⌋	——— −1	——— −2	——— −1	——— −1	——— −1	——— −1	——— −1
Child 4	⌊__⌊__⌋	——— −1	——— −2	——— −1	——— −1	——— −1	——— −1	——— −1
Child 5	⌊__⌊__⌋	——— −1	——— −2	——— −1	——— −1	——— −1	——— −1	——— −1
Child 6	⌊__⌊__⌋	——— −1	——— −2	——— −1	——— −1	——— −1	——— −1	——— −1
Child 7	⌊__⌊__⌋	——— −1	——— −2	——— −1	——— −1	——— −1	——— −1	——— −1
Child 8	⌊__⌊__⌋	——— −1	——— −2	——— −1	——— −1	——— −1	——— −1	——— −1
Don't know XXXXXXXXXXXXXXXXXXXXXXXXXX		——— −1		——— −1		——— −1	——— −1	——— −1

21. Is the child aged (READ AGE) a boy or a girl? **RECORD ABOVE** IF TWO OR MORE CHILDREN ARE THE SAME AGE (E.G., TWINS) ASK FOR THE OLDEST FIRST.

22a. Are any of these children from a previous marriage/relationship of yours or your (spouse or partner)?

        22a1 Yes, yours ———— −1   (ASK Q.22b)
        22a2 Yes, spouse ———— −1   (ASK Q.22b)
        22a3 No   ———— −1   (SKIP TO Q.22c)

22b. Which ones? **RECORD ABOVE** (Just tell me their age and sex.)

PROBE: OF WHOSE PREVIOUS MARRIAGE/RELATIONSHIP? (RECORD ABOVE)

22c. Are any of these children adopted or foster children?

        Yes   ———— −1   (ASK Q.22d)
        No   ———— −0 | (SKIP TO Q.22e)
        Not sure ———— −8_|

22d. Which ones? **RECORD ABOVE** (Just tell me their age and sex.)

22e. Are any of these children of the relationship between you and (your present spouse or partner)?

        Yes   ———— −1   (ASK Q.22f)
        No   ———— −0 | (SKIP TO Q.22g)
        Not sure ———— −8_|

22f. Which ones? **RECORD ABOVE** (Just tell me their age and sex.)

PAGE 7

22g. Do you care for any other children living in your household who are not related to you or your spouse by birth or marriage?

        Yes   ———— −1   (ASK Q.22h)
        No   ———— −0 | (SKIP TO NEXT
        Not sure ———— −8_| INSTRUCTION)

22h. Which ones? **RECORD ABOVE** (Just tell me their age and sex.)

IF MORE THAN ONE CHILD, USE RANDOM SELECTION TO SELECT CHILD WHO WILL BE ASKED ABOUT.

Variable FCHILD   INDEX NUMBER OF CHILD SELECTED |__|__|

Variable FAGE   RECORD AGE OF CHILD SELECTED |__|__|

Variable FSEX   CIRCLE SEX OF CHILD SELECTED M-1 F-2

*23. We'd like to ask a few questions about one child selected at random in each household. In this household, this would be the (AGE)-year-old (boy/girl).

Within the past year, did (REFERENT CHILD) have any <u>special difficulties</u>, such as (READ LIST)?

a. Trouble making friends   _____ −1
b. Temper tantrums   _____ −1
c. Failing grades in school   _____ −1
d. Disciplinary problems in school   _____ −1
e. Misbehavior and disobedience at home   _____ −1
f. Physical fights with kids who live in your house   _____ −1
g. Physical fights with kids who don't live in your house   _____ −1
h. Physical fights with adults who live in your house   _____ −1
i. Physical fights with adults who don't live in your house   _____ −1
j. Deliberately damaging or destroying property   _____ −1
k. Stealing money or something else   _____ −1
L. Drinking   _____ −1
m. Using drugs   _____ −1
n. Got arrested for something   _____ −1
o. Other (SPECIFY)

_____ _____ −1

p. No problems   _____ −1

* Q.23a to Q.23p have been recoded into variables Q23aR to Q23pR with two response categories, i.e., 0 = NO and 1 = YES.

PAGE 8

---

24. Parents and children use many different ways of trying to settle differences between them. I'm going to read a list of some things that you and your spouse/partner might have done <u>when you had a problem with this child</u>. I would like you to tell me how often you did it with (him/her) in the last year. **READ CATEGORIES**

25. (FOR EACH ITEM "X" ED AS "NEVER" OR "DON'T KNOW" ON Q.24, ASK ACROSS:) When you and (CHILD) have had a disagreement, have you <u>ever</u> (ITEM)? **ASK ACROSS**

RESPONDENT

	Once	Twice	3–5 Times	6–10 Times	11–20 Times	More Than 20 Times	(DO NOT READ) Don't Know	(DO NOT READ) Never	Q.25 Ever Happen		
									Yes	No	Don't Know
a. Discussed an issue calmly	—1	—2	—3	—4	—5	—6	—7	—0	—1	—0	—8
b. Got information to back up your side of things	—1	—2	—3	—4	—5	—6	—7	—0	—1	—0	—8
c. Brought in or tried to bring in someone to help settle things	—1	—2	—3	—4	—5	—6	—7	—0	—1	—0	—8
d. Insulted or swore at him/her	—1	—2	—3	—4	—5	—6	—7	—0	—1	—0	—8
e. Sulked and/or refused to talk about it	—1	—2	—3	—4	—5	—6	—7	—0	—1	—0	—8
f. Stomped out of the room or house (or yard)	—1	—2	—3	—4	—5	—6	—7	—0	—1	—0	—8
g. Cried	—1	—2	—3	—4	—5	—6	—7	—0	—1	—0	—8
h. Did or said something to spite him/her	—1	—2	—3	—4	—5	—6	—7	—0	—1	—0	—8
i. Threatened to hit or throw something at him/her	—1	—2	—3	—4	—5	—6	—7	—0	—1	—0	—8
j. Threw or smashed or hit or kicked something	—1	—2	—3	—4	—5	—6	—7	—0	—1	—0	—8
k. Threw something at him/her	—1	—2	—3	—4	—5	—6	—7	—0	—1	—0	—8
L. Pushed, grabbed, or shoved him/her	—1	—2	—3	—4	—5	—6	—7	—0	—1	—0	—8
m. Slapped or spanked him/her	—1	—2	—3	—4	—5	—6	—7	—0	—1	—0	—8
n. Kicked, bit, or hit with a fist	—1	—2	—3	—4	—5	—6	—7	—0	—1	—0	—8
o. Hit or tried to hit with something	—1	—2	—3	—4	—5	—6	—7	—0	—1	—0	—8
p. Beat him/her up	—1	—2	—3	—4	—5	—6	—7	—0	—1	—0	—8
q. Burned or scalded him/her	—1	—2	—3	—4	—5	—6	—7	—0	—1	—0	—8
r. Threatened with a knife or gun	—1	—2	—3	—4	—5	—6	—7	—0	—1	—0	—8
s. Used a knife or gun	—1	—2	—3	—4	—5	—6	—7	—0	—1	—0	—8

26. When disciplining a child, sometimes an accident happens and the child is hurt. Has this happened in the last twelve months when (you/your spouse) was disciplining (REFERENT CHILD)?

Yes	————–1	(ASK Q.27)
No	————–0	(SKIP TO Q.29)
Can't remember	————–8	(SKIP TO Q.29)

27. Did the child ever need to see a doctor as a result?

Yes	————–1	(ASK Q.28)
No	————–0	(SKIP TO Q.29)
Not sure/refused	————–9	

28. Did the child have to be hospitalized overnight as a result of such an injury?

Yes	————–1
No	————–0
Not sure/refused	————–9

ASK EVERYONE

29. Thinking about when you yourself were a teenager, about how often would you say your mother or stepmother used physical punishment, like slapping or hitting you? Think about the year in which this happened the most.

Never	————–0
Once	————–1
Twice	————–2
3–5 times	————–3
6–10 times	————–4
11–20 times	————–5
More than 20 times	————–6
Did not live with mother/stepmother (vol.)	————–7
Don't know	————–8
Refused	————–9

30. How about your father or stepfather? Again, thinking of the year in which it happened the most, how often would you say he used physical punishment in the course of a year?

Never	————–0
Once	————–1
Twice	————–2
3–5 times	————–3
6–10 times	————–4
11–20 times	————–5
More than 20 times	————–6
Did not live with father/stepfather (vol.)	————–7
Don't know	————–8

224

31a. Now, thinking about the whole time when you were a teenager, were there occasions when your (father/stepfather) hit your (mother/stepmother) or threw something at her?

Yes	———— −1	(ASK Q.31b)
No	———— −0	
Don't know	———— −8	(SKIP TO Q.32a)
Refused	———— −9	

31b. How often did that happen?

Never (vol.)	———— −0
Once	———— −1
Twice	———— −2
3–5 times	———— −3
6–10 times	———— −4
11–20 times	———— −5
More than 20 times	———— −6
Don't know	———— −8
Refused	———— −9

ASK EVERYONE

32a. What about your (mother/stepmother) hitting your (father/stepfather)? Were there occasions when that happened when you were a teenager?

Yes	———— −1	(ASK Q.32b)
No	———— −0	
Don't know	———— −8	(SKIP TO INSTRUCTION
Refused	———— −9	BEFORE Q.33)

32b. How often did that happen?

Never (vol.)	———— −0
Once	———— −1
Twice	———— −2
3–5 times	———— −3
6–10 times	———— −4
11–20 times	———— −5
More than 20 times	———— −6
Don't know	———— −8
Refused	———— −9

ASK Q.33 IF CURRENTLY PARTNERED IN Q.6a, ELSE SKIP TO INSTRUCTION BEFORE Q.34

33. Now, let me ask you a few questions about you and your partner. Every couple has their ups and downs. Surveys like this have shown that at some time or another, most people wonder about whether they should continue their (marriage/relationship). What about in your case? How often in the past year have you wondered whether you should continue your relationship—often, sometimes, rarely, or never?

Often	_____ −3
Sometimes	_____ −2
Rarely	_____ −1
Never	_____ −0
No answer	_____ −9

ASK Q.34 IF FTYPE = 1 OR 3
IF FTYPE = 2 SKIP TO Q.49

34. I am going to read a list of things that couples do not always agree on. Please tell me how often you and your (spouse/partner) agreed <u>during the past year/(during the last year that you were together)</u>. Did you and your (spouse/partner) always, almost always, usually, sometimes or never agree about (READ ITEM)?

	Always	Almost Always	Usually	Some-times	Never	Not Sure
a. Managing the money	____ −4	____ −3	____ −2	____ −1	____ −0	____ −8
b. Cooking, cleaning, or repairing the house	____ −4	____ −3	____ −2	____ −1	____ −0	____ −8
c. Social activities and entertaining	____ −4	____ −3	____ −2	____ −1	____ −0	____ −8
d. Affection and sex re- lations	____ −4	____ −3	____ −2	____ −1	____ −0	____ −8

ASK IF CHILDREN IN Q.19, ELSE SKIP TO NEXT INSTRUCTION

e. Things about the children	____ −4	____ −3	____ −2	____ −1	____ −0	____ −8

IF NOT PARTNERED WITHIN THE PAST 12 MONTHS, SKIP TO Q.49.
I.E., ASK Q.35 IF (FTYPE = 1) OR IF (FTYPE = 3 and Q.10b2 = 2, 3, or 4), ELSE SKIP TO Q.49

35. No matter how well a couple gets along, there are times when they disagree, get annoyed with the other person or just have spats or fights because they're in a bad mood or tired or for some other reason. They also use many different ways of trying to settle their differences. I'm going to read some things that you and your partner might do when you have an argument. I would like you to tell me how many times (READ EACH ITEM) in the past 12 months you (READ LIST).

36. Thinking back over the last 12 months you've been together, was there ever an occasion when (your spouse/partner) (READ ITEM)? (READ ACROSS)

(IF EITHER "NEVER" OR "DON'T KNOW" ON ITEM FOR BOTH Q.35 AND Q.36, ASK Q.37 FOR THAT ITEM, THEN CONTINUE WITH LIST FOR Q.35.)

37. Has it ever happened?

							Q.35		
					Respondent			
READ LIST	Once	Twice	3–5 Times	6–10 Times	11–20 Times	More Than 20 Times	(DO NOT READ) Don't Know	(DO NOT READ) Never
a. Discussed an issue calmly	—1	—2	—3	—4	—5	—6	—8	—0
b. Got information to back up your/his/her side of things	—1	—2	—3	—4	—5	—6	—8	—0
c. Brought in or tried to bring in someone to help settle things	—1	—2	—3	—4	—5	—6	—8	—0
d. Insulted him or swore at him/ her/you	—1	—2	—3	—4	—5	—6	—8	—0
e. Sulked or refused to talk about an issue	—1	—2	—3	—4	—5	—6	—8	—0
f. Stomped out of the room or house or yard	—1	—2	—3	—4	—5	—6	—8	—0
g. Cried	—1	—2	—3	—4	—5	—6	—8	—0
h. Did or said something to spite him/her/you	—1	—2	—3	—4	—5	—6	—8	—0
i. Threatened to hit him/her or throw something at him/her/ you	—1	—2	—3	—4	—5	—6	—8	—0
j. Threw or smashed or hit or kicked something	—1	—2	—3	—4	—5	—6	—8	—0
k. Threw something at him/her/ you	—1	—2	—3	—4	—5	—6	—8	—0
L. Pushed, grabbed, or shoved him/her/you	—1	—2	—3	—4	—5	—6	—8	—0
m. Slapped him/her	—1	—2	—3	—4	—5	—6	—8	—0
n. Kicked, bit or hit him/her/you with a fist	—1	—2	—3	—4	—5	—6	—8	—0
o. Hit or tried to hit him/her/you with something	—1	—2	—3	—4	—5	—6	—8	—0
p. Beat him/her/you up	—1	—2	—3	—4	—5	—6	—8	—0
q. Choked him/her/you	—1	—2	—3	—4	—5	—6	—8	—0
r. Threatened him/her/you with a knife or gun	—1	—2	—3	—4	—5	—6	—8	—0
s. Used a knife or fired a gun	—1	—2	—3	—4	—5	—6	—8	—0

			Q.36							Q.37	
			Spouse							Ever Happen	
Once	Twice	3–5 Times	6–10 Times	11–20 Times	More Than 20 Times	(DO NOT READ) Don't Know	(DO NOT READ) Never	Yes	No	(DO NOT READ) Don't Know	
—1	—2	—3	—4	—5	—6	—8	—0	—1	—0	—8	
—1	—2	—3	—4	—5	—6	—8	—0	—1	—0	—8	
—1	—2	—3	—4	—5	—6	—8	—0	—1	—0	—8	
—1	—2	—3	—4	—5	—6	—8	—0	—1	—0	—8	
—1	—2	—3	—4	—5	—6	—8	—0	—1	—0	—8	
—1	—2	—3	—4	—5	—6	—8	—0	—1	—0	—8	
—1	—2	—3	—4	—5	—6	—8	—0	—1	—0	—8	
—1	—2	—3	—4	—5	—6	—8	—0	—1	—0	—8	
—1	—2	—3	—4	—5	—6	—8	—0	—1	—0	—8	
—1	—2	—3	—4	—5	—6	—8	—0	—1	—0	—8	
—1	—2	—3	—4	—5	—6	—8	—0	—1	—0	—8	
—1	—2	—3	—4	—5	—6	—8	—0	—1	—0	—8	
—1	—2	—3	—4	—5	—6	—8	—0	—1	—0	—8	
—1	—2	—3	—4	—5	—6	—8	—0	—1	—0	—8	
—1	—2	—3	—4	—5	—6	—8	—0	—1	—0	—8	
—1	—2	—3	—4	—5	—6	—8	—0	—1	—0	—8	
—1	—2	—3	—4	—5	—6	—8	—0	—1	—0	—8	
—1	—2	—3	—4	—5	—6	—8	—0	—1	—0	—8	

PAGE 13

**IF POSITIVE TO ANY ITEMS (K–S) IN Q.35 OR 36 ASK Q.38,
ELSE SKIP TO INSTRUCTION BEFORE Q.46a.**

38. You said there was a physical conflict between you and your (spouse, former spouse, partner). The next few questions are about those kinds of situations.

Try to think back to the very first time there was a physical fight between the two of you. About how long ago was that?

|___|___| years

Less than one year _____ − 00
Not sure   _____ − 98

IF INTERVIEW IS ABOUT A FORMER RELATIONSHIP (IF FTYPE = 3) ASK Q.39a, ELSE SKIP TO Q.40

39a. Do you think that physical fighting had anything to do with breaking up with your (spouse, partner)?

Yes   _____ − 1   (ASK Q.39b)

No   _____ − 0 ⎤ (SKIP TO Q.40)
Not sure/refused _____ − 9 ⎦

39b. Was it a main cause of the breakup?

Yes   _____ − 1
No   _____ − 0
Not sure/refused _____ − 9

SELECT HIGHEST LETTER (K–S) WITH ONE OR MORE TIMES IN Q.35 OR Q.36 AND ASK ABOUT THE MOST RECENT OCCURRENCE OF THAT INCIDENT

---

40. Let's talk about the last time you and your spouse/former spouse/partner/former partner got into a physical fight and (<u>MOST VIOLENT ACT</u>). In that particular instance, who started the physical conflict, you or your (spouse/partner)?

You   _____ − 1   (SKIP TO Q.42)

Spouse/partner _____ − 2 ⎤
Both (vol.)   _____ − 3 ⎥ (ASK Q.41)
Neither (vol.)   _____ − 0 ⎦

Not sure/refused _____ − 9   (SKIP TO Q.42)

*41. Which of the following describes what you did as a result?

a. Hit back or threw something _____ –1
b. Cried _____ –1
c. Yelled or cursed him (her) _____ –1
d. Ran to another room _____ –1
e. Ran out of the house _____ –1
f. Called a friend or relative _____ –1
g. Called the police _____ –1
h. Other (vol.) _____ –1
i. Refused _____ –1
j. Not sure _____ –1

* Q.41a TO Q.41j have been recoded into variables Q.41aR TO Q.41jR with two response categories, i.e., 0 = NO and 1 = YES.

42. Were either or both of you drinking right before the conflict started? (IF "YES")
Who was that?

No, neither was drinking _____ –0
Yes, male partner only was drinking _____ –1
Yes, female partner only was drinking _____ –2
Yes, both were drinking _____ –3
Not sure/refused _____ –9

43a. In the (last 12 months/last 12 months you were together) has either of you been hurt badly enough as a result of a conflict between you to need to see a doctor? (IF "YES") Who was that?

Neither did _____ –0   (SKIP TO Q.44a)

Female partner _____ –1 ⌐
Male partner _____ –2 | (ASK Q.43b)
Both _____ –3 ⌐

Not sure/refused _____ –9   (SKIP TO Q.44a)

43b. Did either of you actually go to a doctor? (IF YES:) Who was that?

Neither did _____ –0   (SKIP TO Q.44a)

Female partner _____ –1 ⌐
Male partner _____ –2 | (ASK Q.43c)
Both _____ –3 ⌐

Not sure/refused _____ –9   (SKIP TO Q.44a)

230

IF RESPONDENT WENT TO A DOCTOR IN Q.43b ASK 43c—ELSE SKIP TO Q.44a

*43c. Where did you go for treatment?

READ LIST— MULTIPLE RECORD	43c. Went to			43d. Number of Times
	Yes	No	Not Sure/ Refused	
1. Hospital emergency room	—1	—0	—9	
2. Hospital overnight	—1	—0	—9	
3. Hospital for a day or more	—1	—0	—9	
4. Clinic	—1	—0	—9	
5. Doctor's office	—1	—0	—9	
6. Anywhere else	—1	—0	—9	

*43d. (FOR EACH SOURCE OF CARE IN Q.43c). How many times did you go there for treatment in the (past year/last year you were together)? (RECORD ABOVE)

97 OR MORE TIMES = 97, NOT SURE = 98, and REFUSED = 99

* Q.43c (1 TO 6) AND Q.43d (1 to 6) have been recoded into Q.43CD (1 to 6)X. See page 34 for codes.

44a. Did you have a job for pay during the period that this occurred?

        Yes   —1   (ASK Q.44b)

        No   —0 (SKIP TO Q.45a)

        Not sure/refused —9

44b. How much did these incidents affect how well you could do your job: a lot, a little, or not at all?

        A lot   —2

        A little   —1

        Not at all   —0

        Not sure/refused —9

44c. Did you have to take time off from work because of these incidents?

        Yes   —1   (ASK Q.44d)

        No   —0 (SKIP TO Q.45a)

        Not sure/refused —9

44d. How many days in the past year/last year you were together?

        |___|___|___| days

        97 days or more   —97

        Not sure   —98

        Refused   —99

45a. Were the police called regarding these things in the last twelve months/12 months you were together?

Yes _____ −1 (ASK Q.45b)

No _____ −0 ⌉ (SKIP TO INSTRUCTION

Not sure _____ −8 ⌋ BEFORE Q.46a)

45b. How many times?

|__|__| times

97 or more _____ −97

Not sure _____ −98

Refused _____ −99

*45c. Did the police ever (READ LIST)?

1. Break up the fight (if it was still going on) _____ −1
2. Hit or push someone _____ −1
3. Try to calm everyone down _____ −1
4. Take time to listen to your story _____ −1
5. Give a warning _____ −1
6. Take information/file report _____ −1
7. Order you out of the house _____ −1
8. Order spouse/partner out of the house _____ −1
9. Threaten arrest right now _____ −1
10. Threaten arrest if it happened again _____ −1
11. Arrest you _____ −1
12. Arrest spouse/partner _____ −1
13. Other (SPECIFY)

    _____ _____ −1
14. Nothing _____ −1
15. Not sure _____ −1

* Q.45c1 TO Q.45c15 have been recoded into variables Q45C1R to Q45C15R with two response categories, i.e., 0 = NO and 1 = YES

45d. In general, do you think police should have been tougher, easier, or did they handle everything about right?

Should have been tougher _____ −3

Should have been easier _____ −1

About right _____ −2

Don't know _____ −8

232

45e. In general, how satisfied were you with the way the police handled the situation—
very satisfied, somewhat satisfied, somewhat dissatisfied, or very dissatisfied?

Very satisfied	_____ −4
Somewhat satisfied	_____ −3
Somewhat dissatisfied	_____ −2
Very dissatisfied	_____ −1
Not sure	_____ −8

45f. Did any case go to court in the last 12 months?

Yes	_____ −1	(ASK Q.45g)
No	_____ −0	(SKIP TO INSTRUCTION BEFORE Q.46a)
Not sure	_____ −9	

45g. How many cases went to court?

|___|___| cases

97 or more	_____ −97
Not sure	_____ −98

45h. How (was/were) the case(s) resolved? (What happened the last time?)

READ LIST   RECORD # OF TIMES

a. Case dismissed—nothing happened
b. A warning
c. Required to get counseling
d. A fine
e. Jail term
f. Suspended sentence
g. Other
h. Not sure (vol.)

97 OR MORE TIMES = 97, NOT SURE = 98, REFUSED = 99

45i. In general, how satisfied were you with the way these cases were resolved—very
satisfied, somewhat satisfied, somewhat dissatisfied, or very dissatisfied?

Very satisfied	_____ −4
Somewhat satisfied	_____ −3
Somewhat dissatisfied	_____ −2
Very dissatisfied	_____ −1
Not sure	_____ −8

*46a. In the past year, did your (husband, former husband, partner) ever try to, or force you to, have sexual relations by using physical force, such as holding you down, or hitting you, or threatening to hit you?

1. Attempted to _____ −1 | (ASK Q.46b)
2. Did force sex _____ −1 |

3. No _____ −1 | (SKIP TO Q.47) N.B.: This was
4. Not sure/refused _____ −1 | supposed to be Q.46c.

* Q.46a1 to Q.46a4 have been recoded into a single variable named Q.46aX. See page 34 for the categories and codes.

46b. How many times did this happen in the past year?

| | | |

Not sure _____ −98
Refused _____ −99

46c. Has this <u>ever</u> happened before this year? That is, did your (husband, former husband, partner) ever try to use physical force, or actually physically force you to have sex?

Attempted to _____ −1
Did force sex _____ −2
No _____ −0
Not sure/refused _____ −9

N.B.: The small sample asked this question is due to the error in the skip pattern noted for Q.46a.

47. Some women are afraid that their spouse (former spouse, partner) will hit them if they argue with him or do something he doesn't like. How much would you say you are afraid of this? (READ LIST)

Not at all _____ −0
A little _____ −1
Quite a bit _____ −2
Very afraid it will happen _____ −3
Not sure/refused _____ −9

IF ANY ACTS K–S IN Q.35 OR Q.36 AND RESPONDENT ACTED FIRST IN Q.40, ASK Q.48—ELSE SKIP TO Q.49

48. What do you think are the chances that you will (MOST VIOLENT ACT of K thru S) again in the next year? Please rate the chances on a scale from zero to 10. You should give a zero for something you think has no chance at all of happening, a 5 for something that you think has about a 50–50 chance of happening, and a 10 for something you think is sure to happen.

NO CHANCE   SURE
0 1 2 3 4 5 6 7 8 9 10

Not sure _____ – 98

ASK EVERYONE

49. Are there situations that you can imagine in which you would approve of a husband slapping his wife's face?

Yes _____ – 1
No _____ – 0
Not sure _____ – 8

50. Are there any situations that you can imagine in which you would approve of a wife slapping her husband's face?

Yes _____ – 1
No _____ – 0
Not sure _____ – 8

ASK IF CURRENTLY PARTNERED (FTYPE = 1), ELSE SKIP TO INSTRUCTION BEFORE Q.53

51. Suppose you hit your spouse/partner. I am going to read a list of things which might happen as a result. Please rate the chances of each result from 0 to 10. You should give a zero for something you think has no chance at all of happening, a 5 for something that you think has about a 50–50 chance of happening, and a 10 for something you think is sure to happen. From 0 to 10, how would you rate the chances of (RECORD BELOW)?

52. How bad would that be for you on a scale of 0 to 10 where 0 is not bad and 10 is extremely bad? (READ ACROSS)

NOT SURE = 98	Q.51 NO CHANCE ... SURE	Q.52 NOT BAD ... EXTREMELY BAD
a. Hitting you back and hurting you	0 1 2 3 4 5 6 7 8 9 10	0 1 2 3 4 5 6 7 8 9 10
b. Calling the police	0 1 2 3 4 5 6 7 8 9 10	0 1 2 3 4 5 6 7 8 9 10
c. You get arrested for it	0 1 2 3 4 5 6 7 8 9 10	0 1 2 3 4 5 6 7 8 9 10
d. He/she leaves or gets a divorce	0 1 2 3 4 5 6 7 8 9 10	0 1 2 3 4 5 6 7 8 9 10
e. Your friends or relatives disapprove or lose respect for you	0 1 2 3 4 5 6 7 8 9 10	0 1 2 3 4 5 6 7 8 9 10

235

IF ANY K–S IN Q.35, 36, OR 37 ASK Q.53—ELSE SKIP TO Q.55

53. Here are 8 things that some people have used to try to get their (spouses/partners) to stop hurting or threatening them.

Did you ever try (READ ITEM)?

54. (FOR EACH YES IN Q.53): How effective was it—very effective, somewhat effective, slightly effective, not effective, or made it worse? (READ ACROSS)

ASK Q.53 AND Q.54 ACROSS	Q.53 Did you ever?			Q.54 How effective Was It?					
	Yes	No	Not Sure/ Refused	Very Effec- tive	Some- what Effec- tive	Slightly Effec- tive	Not Effec- tive	Made It Worse	Not Sure/ Refused
a. Talking her/him out of it	__ –1	__ –0	__ –9	__ –5	__ –4	__ –3	__ –2	__ –1	__ –9
b. Getting him/her to prom- ise to stop	__ –1	__ –0	__ –9	__ –5	__ –4	__ –3	__ –2	__ –1	__ –9
c. Avoiding him/her or avoiding certain topics	__ –1	__ –9	__ –3	__ –5	__ –4	__ –3	__ –2	__ –1	__ –9
d. Hiding or going away when he/she hurts you	__ –1	__ –9	__ –3	__ –5	__ –4	__ –3	__ –2	__ –1	__ –9
e. Leaving home for two days or more	__ –1	__ –9	__ –3	__ –5	__ –4	__ –3	__ –2	__ –1	__ –9
f. Threatening to call the police	__ –1	__ –9	__ –3	__ –5	__ –4	__ –3	__ –2	__ –1	__ –9
g. Threatening to get a divorce	__ –1	__ –9	__ –3	__ –5	__ –4	__ –3	__ –2	__ –1	__ –9
h. Physically fighting back in any way you can	__ –1	__ –9	__ –3	__ –5	__ –4	__ –3	__ –2	__ –1	__ –9

ASK EVERYONE

55. In the past year, did you seek help for a family or personal problem from any of the following sources?

56. FOR EACH YES IN Q.55. How effective was it—very effective, somewhat effective, slightly effective, not effective, or made it worse? (READ ACROSS)

	Q.55 In the past year?			Q.56 How effective Was It?					
	Yes	No	Not Sure/ Refused	Very Effec- tive	Some- what Effec- tive	Slightly Effec- tive	Not Effec- tive	Made It Worse	Not Sure/ Refused
a. Relatives on your side of the family	—1	—0	—9	—5	—4	—3	—2	—1	—9
b. Your partner's relatives	—1	—0	—9	—5	—4	—3	—2	—1	—9
c. Friends and neighbors	—1	—0	—9	—5	—4	—3	—2	—1	—9
d. Minister, priest, rabbi	—1	—0	—9	—5	—4	—3	—2	—1	—9
e. Psychologist or psychia- trist	—1	—0	—9	—5	—4	—3	—2	—1	—9
f. Marriage or family coun- selor	—1	—0	—9	—5	—4	—3	—2	—1	—9
g. Alcohol and drug abuse treatment services	—1	—0	—9	—5	—4	—3	—2	—1	—9
h. Women's or men's sup- port group or hot line	—1	—0	—9	—5	—4	—3	—2	—1	—9
i. Battered women's shelter	—1	—0	—9	—5	—4	—3	—2	—1	—9
j. Community mental health center	—1	—0	—9	—5	—4	—3	—2	—1	—9
k. Other social service or counseling agency	—1	—0	—9	—5	—4	—3	—2	—1	—9
L. Police	—1	—0	—9	—5	—4	—3	—2	—1	—9
m. Doctors, nurses	—1	—0	—9	—5	—4	—3	—2	—1	—9
n. Lawyer, legal aid	—1	—0	—9	—5	—4	—3	—2	—1	—9
o. District attorney	—1	—0	—9	—5	—4	—3	—2	—1	—9

PAGE 22

ASK IF EVER PARTNERED, ELSE SKIP TO Q.59a
I.E., ASK IF FTYPE = 1 or 3, ELSE SKIP TO Q.59a.

57. Everyone gets angry or annoyed sometimes. How often in the last 12 months did you (READ ITEM) (READ RESPONSE CATEGORIES).

58. How often would you guess your (spouse, former spouse, partner) did that? Was it: (READ RESPONSE CATEGORIES)?

Never = 0
Once = 1
2 to 4 times = 2
5 to 9 times = 3
10 or more times = 4
Not Sure = 8

	Q.57 Respondent						Q.58 Spouse, Former Spouse, Partner					
	Never	Once	2–4	5–9	10+	Not Sure	Never	Once	2–4	5–9	10+	Not Sure
a. Get angry at someone who doesn't live here and yelled or shouted at them	0	1	2	3	4	8	0	1	2	3	4	8
b. Get angry at someone who doesn't live here and kicked or smashed something, slammed the door, punched the wall, etc.	0	1	2	3	4	8	0	1	2	3	4	8
c. Get into a fight with someone who doesn't live here and hit the person	0	1	2	3	4	8	0	1	2	3	4	8
d. Get into a fight with someone who doesn't live here and hurt that person badly enough to need to see a doctor	0	1	2	3	4	8	0	1	2	3	4	8

59a. Have you been arrested for anything in the past 12 months?

Yes _____ –1 (ASK Q.59b)

No _____ –0 ⎤ (SKIP TO INSTRUCTION BEFORE Q.60)
Not sure/refused_____ –9 ⎦

59b. What were you arrested for?

59b1. (first mention) _____

59b2. (second mention) _____

ASK IF ANY K–S IN Q.35 OR Q.36—ELSE SKIP TO Q.61

60. We would like you to compare your health and personal problems now with what things were like for you before you and your (spouse, former spouse, partner) started having physical fights. Let's start with (READ ITEM)? Do you think the fighting made (ITEM) much worse, a little worse, or did it have no effect as far as you can tell? (READ LIST)

	Much Worse	A Little Worse	No Effect	Not Sure/ Refused
a. Your health	−2	−1	−0	−9
b. The amount of stress you feel under	−2	−1	−0	−9
c. Feeling badly or depressed	−2	−1	−0	−9
d. Drinking or drug problems	−2	−1	−0	−9

PAGE 23

ASK EVERYONE

61. In general, would you say that your health is excellent, very good, good, fair or poor?

Excellent _____ −4
Very good _____ −3
Good _____ −2
Fair _____ −1
Poor _____ −0
Not sure/refused _____ −9

62. How many days have you spent in bed due to illness in the last month?

Not sure _____ −98

63. In the past year how often have you (READ ITEM)—never, almost never, sometimes, fairly often, or very often?

	Never	Almost Never	Sometimes	Fairly Often	Very Often	Not sure/ Refused
a. Had headaches or pains in the head	−0	−1	−2	−3	−4	−9
b. Been bothered by cold sweats	−0	−1	−2	−3	−4	−9
c. Felt nervous or stressed	−0	−1	−2	−3	−4	−9
d. Been bothered by feelings of sadness or depression	−0	−1	−2	−3	−4	−9
e. Felt difficulties were piling up so high that you could not overcome them	−0	−1	−2	−3	−4	−9
f. Felt very bad or worthless	−0	−1	−2	−3	−4	−9
g. Found that you could not cope with all of the things you had to do	−0	−1	−2	−3	−4	−9
h. Had times when you couldn't help wondering if anything was worthwhile anymore	−0	−1	−2	−3	−4	−9
i. Felt completely hopeless about everything	−0	−1	−2	−3	−4	−9
j. Thought about taking your own life	−0	−1	−2	−3	−4	−9

239

64. In the last year have you ever actually <u>tried</u> to take your own life?

Yes _____ −1
No _____ −0
Not sure/refused _____ −9

PAGE 24

65a. In general, how often do you consume alcoholic beverages—that is, beer, wine, or liquor—never, less than 1 day a month, 1 to 3 days a month, 1 to 2 days a week, 3 to 4 days a week, 5 to 6 days a week, or daily?

Never _____ −0 (SKIP TO Q.66)

Less than 1 day a month _____ −1
1 to 3 days a month _____ −2
1 to 2 days a week _____ −3
3 to 4 days a week _____ −4 (ASK Q.65b)
5 to 6 days a week _____ −5
Daily _____ −6
No answer _____ −9

65b. On a day when you do drink alcoholic beverages, on average, how many drinks do you have? By a "drink" we mean a drink with a shot of 1-and-½ ounces of hard liquor, 12 ounces of beer, or 5 ounces of wine.

|___|___| number of drinks
Not sure _____ −98
Refused _____ −99

ASK EVERYONE

66. In the past year, how often would you guess you (READ ITEM)?

NOT SURE = 998
REFUSED = 999

	Q.66 Respondent	Q.67 Spouse
a. Got drunk	|___|___|___|___|	|___|___|___|
b. Got high on marijuana or some other drug	|___|___|___|___|	|___|___|___|

ASK IF (FTYPE = 1) or IF (FTYPE = 3 AND Q.10B2 = 2, 3, OR 4), ELSE SKIP TO F1

67. In the past year, how often would you guess your spouse (READ ITEM)? (RECORD ABOVE)

240

ASK EVERYONE

F1. Including yourself, how many people live in this household?

97 OR MORE = 97
NOT SURE = 98
REFUSED = 99

|___|___|___| persons in household

F2a. Do you have any children who are <u>not</u> living with you

Yes, have   _____ −1   (ASK F2b)

No, don't   _____ −0

Not sure   _____ −8   (SKIP TO F3a)

No answer   _____ −9

F2b. How many?

|___|___|___|

Not sure   _____ −98

Refused   _____ −99

F3a. What is the last year or grade of school you completed?

	F3a Self	F3b Spouse/Partner
No formal schooling	_____ − 00	_____ − 00
First through 7th grade	_____ − 01	_____ − 01
8th grade	_____ − 02	_____ − 02
Some high school	_____ − 03	_____ − 03
High-school graduate	_____ − 04	_____ − 04
Some college	_____ − 05	_____ − 05
Four-year college graduate	_____ − 06	_____ − 06
Some post−B.A. training	_____ − 07	_____ − 07
Hold advanced degree	_____ − 08	_____ − 08
Refused	_____ − 99	_____ − 99
Not sure	_____ − 98	_____ − 98

ASK IF (FTYPE = 1 or FTYPE = 3), ELSE SKIP TO F4a

F3b. What is the last year or grade of school your (former/current) spouse/partner completed? **(RECORD ABOVE)**

F4a. What is your religious preference? **RECORD BELOW**

	F4a Self	F4b Spouse/Partner
Roman Catholic	_____ − 1	_____ − 1
Protestant (what denomination?)		

USE "PRINT METHODOLOGY" PROTESTANT LIST HERE

_____	_____ − 2	_____ − 2
Jewish	_____ − 3	_____ − 3
* Other (SPECIFY):		
_____	_____ − 4	_____ − 4
None	_____ − 0	_____ − 0
Not sure/refused	_____ − 9	_____ − 9

* NOTE: "Other" verbal descriptions are coded and recorded as variables. See page 32. F4AOTH and F4BOTH.

ASK IF EVER MARRIED OR PARTNERED, I.E., ASK IF FTYPE = 1 or FTYPE = 3

F4b. What is your (former/spouse's/partner's) religious preference? RECORD ABOVE

F5. In which of the following categories do you feel you belong? (READ CATEGORIES)

Pacific Islander	_____ − 1
American Indian or Alaskan native	_____ − 2
Asian (Oriental)	_____ − 3
Hispanic	_____ − 4
Hispanic/black	_____ − 5
White, but not Hispanic	_____ − 6
Black, but not Hispanic	_____ − 7
Not sure	_____ − 8
Refused	_____ − 9

N.B.: This question was asked as a screening question just before Q.6a for the black and Hispanic oversamples.

F6. For statistical purposes, we need to know which of these groups your total family income before taxes for (1984 or last year of relationship if formerly married/partnered) was in? Please include your own income and that of all members of your immediate family who are living with you, and any other sources of income you may have.

(INTERVIEWER: INCLUDE WELFARE PAYMENTS, SOCIAL SECURITY, INCOME FROM STOCKS, ETC.)

None	_____ −00
$5,000 or less	_____ −01
$5,001 to $10,000	_____ −02
$10,001 to $15,000	_____ −03
$15,001 to $20,000	_____ −04
$20,001 to $25,000	_____ −05
$25,001 to $30,000	_____ −06
$30,001 to $35,000	_____ −07
$35,001 to $40,000	_____ −08
$40,001 to $45,000	_____ −09
$45,001 to $50,000	_____ −10
More than $50,000	_____ −11
Refused	_____ −99
Not sure	_____ −98

PAGE 27

ASK EVERYONE

F7. In order to contact you about any follow-up study, I need your first name. I don't need your last name or address. I will record your first name and phone number on a separate sheet so that neither your name nor phone number will ever be attached to this interview. Your answers will still be completely anonymous and confidential.

Would you tell me your first name?

Yes _____ −1
No _____ −0

END OF INTERVIEW, SAY TO RESPONDENT: Thank you for your help; that concludes the inverview.

PAGE 28

Source of Interview (SOURCE) (From page A, Sample Point No.)

Cross-section	_____ −4
Cross-section	_____ −6
State oversample	_____ −7
Black oversample	_____ −8
Hispanic oversample	_____ −9

Size of Place (SIZE) (From page A, Sample Point No.)

Central City	_____	−1
Suburb of central city	_____	−2
City 2,500 outside urban area	_____	−3

State (STATEH) (From page A, Sample Point No.)

Alabama	−31	Illinois	−51
Alaska	−84	Indiana	−52
Arizona	−71	Iowa	−61
Arkansas	−41		
California	−81	Kansas	−62
		Kentucky	−34
Colorado	−72	Louisiana	−42
Connecticut	−11	Maine	−12
Delaware	−27	Maryland	−21
District of Columbia	−25		
Florida	−32	Massachusetts	−13
Georgia	−33	Michigan	−53
		Minnesota	−63
Hawaii	−85	Mississippi	−35
Idaho	−73	Missouri	−64

PAGE 29

Montana	−74	Rhode Island	−15
Nebraska	−65	South Carolina	−37
Nevada	−75		
New Hampshire	−14	South Dakota	−67
New Jersey	−22	Tennessee	−38
		Texas	−44
New Mexico	−76	Utah	−77
New York	−23	Vermont	−16
North Carolina	−36		
North Dakota	−66	Virginia	−39
Ohio	−54	Washington	−83
		West Virginia	−26
Oklahoma	−43	Wisconsin	−55
Oregon	−82	Wyoming	−78
Pennsylvania	−24		

244

RECORDING SHEET

Study No. 843007 (National Family Violence)   Sequence No: _____

                                                Sample Point No.: _____

Interviewer's Name: _____
                        (PLEASE PRINT)

Area Code: _____ Telephone No.: _____

Q.5 What kind of work do (did) you do?

ASK FOR JOB TITLE AND MAIN DUTIES—DESCRIBE IN DETAIL:

Q.9 What kind of work does your (spouse/partner) do?

ASK FOR JOB TITLE AND MAIN DUTIES—DESCRIBE IN DETAIL:

Q.15 What kind of work did your former spouse or partner do?

ASK FOR JOB TITLE AND MAIN DUTIES—DESCRIBE IN DETAIL:

Q.23 Other (SPECIFY) (The question is on page 7.)

_____

_____

_____

Q.45c Other (SPECIFY) (The question is on page 16.)

_____

_____

_____

Q.59b What were you arrested for? (The question is on page 22.)

Q.59b1 First mention

Driving while intoxicated	−01
Traffic violation	−02
Drug possession/dealing	−03
Resisting arrest	−04
Trespassing	−05
Assault	−06
Other	−11
Refused	−12

Q.59b2 Second mention

Driving while intoxicated	−01
Traffic violation	−02
Drug possession/dealing	−03
Resisting arrest	−04
Trespassing	−05
Assault	−06
Other	−11
Refused	−12

RECORDING SHEET (CONTINUED)

Fa, Fb Other (SPECIFY)

Self:

Jehovah Witness	−02	The variable name is F4AOTH
Holiness	−03	(The question is on page 26.)
Quaker	−04	
Agnostic	−06	
Other	−12	

Spouse/
Partner:

Jehovah Witness	−02	The variable name is F4BOTH
Holiness	−03	(The question is on page 26.)
Quaker	−04	
Agnostic	−06	
Other	−12	

N.B.: The following seven sample weights were constructed in order to allow the combining of various study subsamples in a statistically appropriate manner.

WEIGHT1   Cross Section + State Oversample
WEIGHT2   Cross Section + State Oversample + Black Oversample
WEIGHT3   Cross Section + State Oversample + Black Oversample
          + Hispanic Oversample
WEIGHT4   Cross Section + State Oversample + Hispanic Oversample
WEIGHT5   Cross Section + Black Oversample
WEIGHT6   Cross Section + Black Oversample + Hispanic Oversample
WEIGHT7   Cross Section + Hispanic Oversample

PAGE 33

Variable Q.10BX was created from variables Q.10b and Q.10b2 (see page 3).

Q10BX. How long ago did that (MOST RECENT) marriage or relationship end?

> Less than one month   = 0.1
> One month to six months = 0.4
> Six months to a year   = 0.7
> Number of years   = 1 to 99
> Not sure   = 108

Variable Q.13X was created from variables Q.13 and Q.13b (see page 4).

Q13X. Was your former (spouse/partner) employed full time, part time, unemployed, retired, a student, keeping house or something else?

> Employed full time   = 1
> Employed part time = 2
> Unemployed   = 3
> Retired   = 4
> Student   = 5
> Keeping house   = 6
> Disabled (vol.)   = 7
> Other   = 8
> Refused   = 9
> Not sure   = 109

Variable Q.19X was created from variables Q.19 and Q.19b (see page 5).

Q19X. In all, how many children under 18 do you (and your spouse) have living in this
household?

    None   = 0
    Number of children = 1 to 8 (8 = 8 or more)
    Not sure/refused   = 109

Variables Q.43CD1X to Q.43CD6X were created from Q.43c (1 TO 6) and Q.43d (1 to 6).

Original questions (see page 15).

Q.43c. Where did you go for treatment?

Q.43d. (FOR EACH SOURCE OF CARE IN Q.43c.) How many times did you go there for
treatment in the (past year/last year you were together)?

Variable and treatment location.

    Q43CD1X. Hospital emergency room
    Q43CD2X. Hospital overnight
    Q43CD3X. Hospital for a day or more
    Q43CD4X. Clinic
    Q43CD5X. Doctor's office
    Q43DC6X. Anywhere else

Response categories and codes for Q43CD1X to Q43CD6X.

    Didn't go to   = 0
    Went 1 to 96 times   = 1 to 96
    Went 97 or more times   = 97
    Not sure (Q43Dn)   = 98
    Refused (Q43Dn)   = 99
    Not sure/refused (Q43Cn) = 109

Variable Q46aX was created from variables Q46a (1 to 4). See page 18.

Q46aX. In the past year, did your (husband, partner) ever try to, or force you to, have
sexual relations by using physical force, such as holding you down, or hitting
you, or threatening to hit you?

    No   = 0
    Attempted to   = 1
    Did force sex   = 2
    Not sure/refused   = 101

248

Appendix C

Figures

Figure 1: Parent-to-Child Violence:
Comparison of Rates in 1975 and 1985

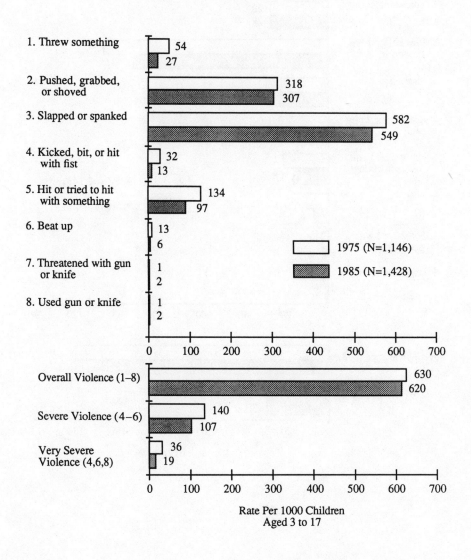

1. Threw something — 54 / 27
2. Pushed, grabbed, or shoved — 318 / 307
3. Slapped or spanked — 582 / 549
4. Kicked, bit, or hit with fist — 32 / 13
5. Hit or tried to hit with something — 134 / 97
6. Beat up — 13 / 6
7. Threatened with gun or knife — 1 / 2
8. Used gun or knife — 1 / 2

1975 (N=1,146)
1985 (N=1,428)

Overall Violence (1–8) — 630 / 620
Severe Violence (4–6) — 140 / 107
Very Severe Violence (4,6,8) — 36 / 19

Rate Per 1000 Children
Aged 3 to 17

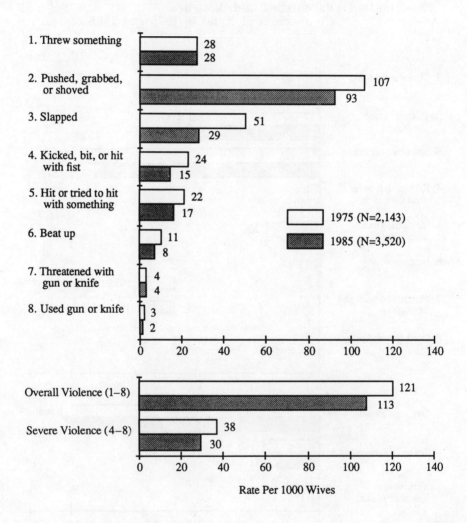

Figure 2: Husband-to-Wife Violence:
Comparison of Rates in 1975 and 1985

1. Threw something 28 28

2. Pushed, grabbed, or shoved 107 93

3. Slapped 51 29

4. Kicked, bit, or hit with fist 24 15

5. Hit or tried to hit with something 22 17

6. Beat up 11 8

7. Threatened with gun or knife 4 4

8. Used gun or knife 3 2

1975 (N=2,143)
1985 (N=3,520)

Overall Violence (1–8) 121 113

Severe Violence (4–8) 38 30

Rate Per 1000 Wives

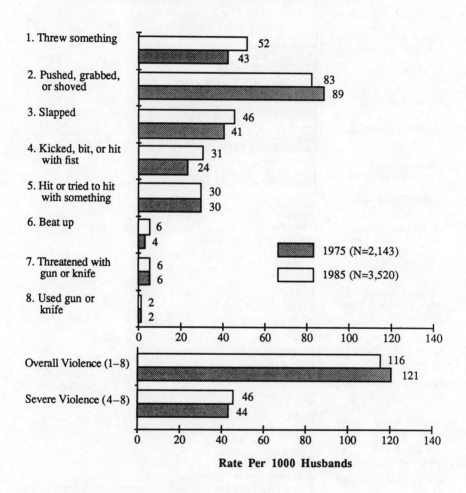

Figure 3: Wife-to-Husband Violence: Comparison of Rates in 1975 and 1985

1. Threw something — 52 / 43
2. Pushed, grabbed, or shoved — 83 / 89
3. Slapped — 46 / 41
4. Kicked, bit, or hit with fist — 31 / 24
5. Hit or tried to hit with something — 30 / 30
6. Beat up — 6 / 4
7. Threatened with gun or knife — 6 / 6
8. Used gun or knife — 2 / 2

1975 (N=2,143)
1985 (N=3,520)

Overall Violence (1–8) — 116 / 121
Severe Violence (4–8) — 46 / 44

Rate Per 1000 Husbands

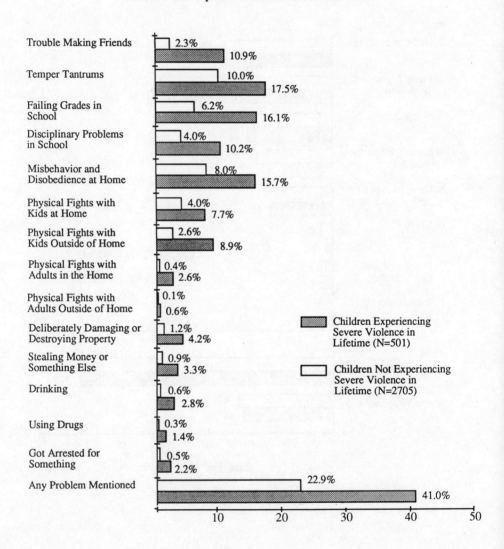

Figure 4: Relationship Between Experiencing Severe
Violence and Special Difficulties of the Child

Trouble Making Friends — 2.3% / 10.9%
Temper Tantrums — 10.0% / 17.5%
Failing Grades in School — 6.2% / 16.1%
Disciplinary Problems in School — 4.0% / 10.2%
Misbehavior and Disobedience at Home — 8.0% / 15.7%
Physical Fights with Kids at Home — 4.0% / 7.7%
Physical Fights with Kids Outside of Home — 2.6% / 8.9%
Physical Fights with Adults in the Home — 0.4% / 2.6%
Physical Fights with Adults Outside of Home — 0.1% / 0.6%
Deliberately Damaging or Destroying Property — 1.2% / 4.2%
Stealing Money or Something Else — 0.9% / 3.3%
Drinking — 0.6% / 2.8%
Using Drugs — 0.3% / 1.4%
Got Arrested for Something — 0.5% / 2.2%
Any Problem Mentioned — 22.9% / 41.0%

Children Experiencing Severe Violence in Lifetime (N=501)

Children Not Experiencing Severe Violence in Lifetime (N=2705)

252

Figure 5: The Perceived Effects of Violence Towards Wives

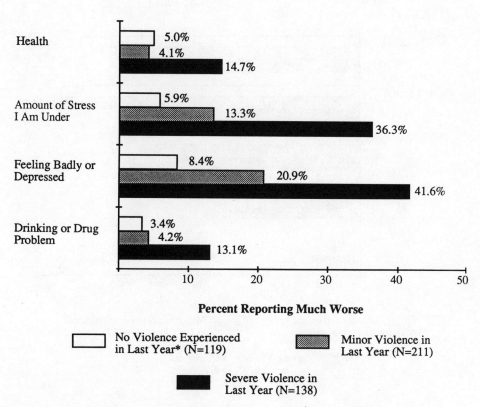

Health

5.0%
4.1%
14.7%

Amount of Stress
I Am Under

5.9%
13.3%
36.3%

Feeling Badly or
Depressed

8.4%
20.9%
41.6%

Drinking or Drug
Problem

3.4%
4.2%
13.1%

10   20   30   40   50

Percent Reporting Much Worse

No Violence Experienced
in Last Year* (N=119)

Minor Violence in
Last Year (N=211)

Severe Violence in
Last Year (N=138)

* Although they experienced no violence, these wives initiated violence in the last year.

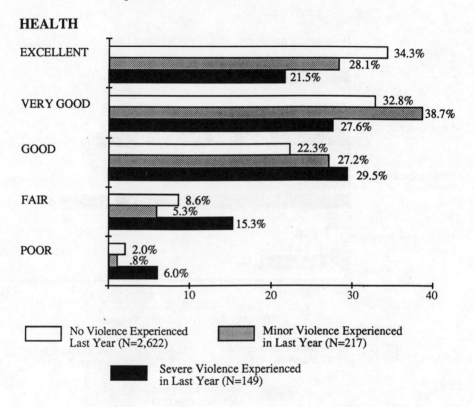

Figure 6: Relationship Between Health of Respondent and Experience with Violence in the Last Year

HEALTH

EXCELLENT
34.3%
28.1%
21.5%

VERY GOOD
32.8%
38.7%
27.6%

GOOD
22.3%
27.2%
29.5%

FAIR
8.6%
5.3%
15.3%

POOR
2.0%
.8%
6.0%

10   20   30   40

☐ No Violence Experienced Last Year (N=2,622)   ▨ Minor Violence Experienced in Last Year (N=217)

■ Severe Violence Experienced in Last Year (N=149)

Figure 7: Relationship Between Experiencing Violence in Last Year and Mean Number of Days in Bed Due to Illness in Last Month

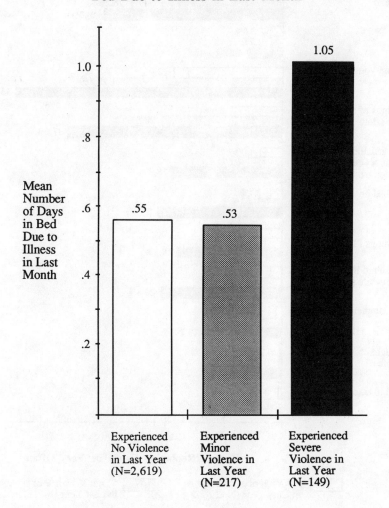

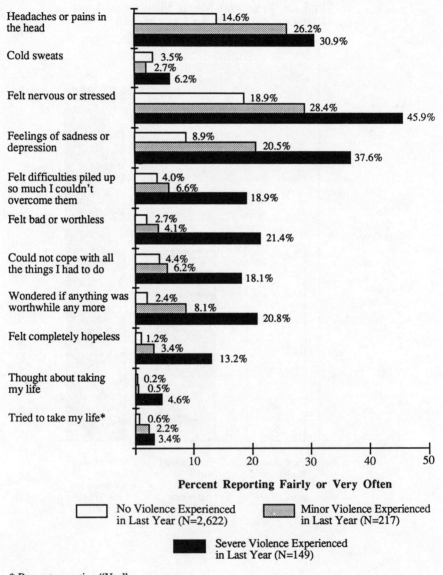

Figure 8:   Relationship Between Experiencing Violence in
Last Year and Psychological Distress

Headaches or pains in the head
14.6%
26.2%
30.9%

Cold sweats
3.5%
2.7%
6.2%

Felt nervous or stressed
18.9%
28.4%
45.9%

Feelings of sadness or depression
8.9%
20.5%
37.6%

Felt difficulties piled up so much I couldn't overcome them
4.0%
6.6%
18.9%

Felt bad or worthless
2.7%
4.1%
21.4%

Could not cope with all the things I had to do
4.4%
6.2%
18.1%

Wondered if anything was worthwhile any more
2.4%
8.1%
20.8%

Felt completely hopeless
1.2%
3.4%
13.2%

Thought about taking my life
0.2%
0.5%
4.6%

Tried to take my life*
0.6%
2.2%
3.4%

10   20   30   40   50

Percent Reporting Fairly or Very Often

No Violence Experienced in Last Year (N=2,622)

Minor Violence Experienced in Last Year (N=217)

Severe Violence Experienced in Last Year (N=149)

* Percent reporting "Yes"

Figure 9: Relationship Between Experiencing Violence in Last Year and Behavior

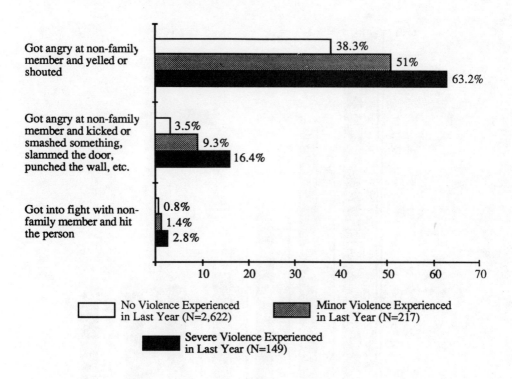

Figure 10: How Women Reacted to the Most Recent Incident of Violence

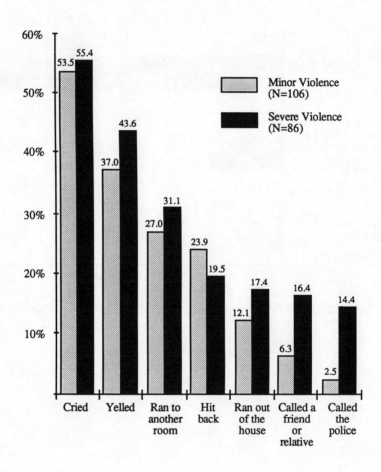

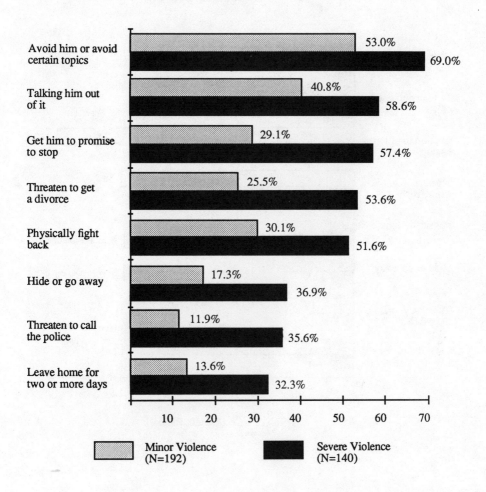

Figure 11: Strategies Used by Women
to end Violence

Avoid him or avoid certain topics	53.0% / 69.0%
Talking him out of it	40.8% / 58.6%
Get him to promise to stop	29.1% / 57.4%
Threaten to get a divorce	25.5% / 53.6%
Physically fight back	30.1% / 51.6%
Hide or go away	17.3% / 36.9%
Threaten to call the police	11.9% / 35.6%
Leave home for two or more days	13.6% / 32.3%

10 20 30 40 50 60 70

Minor Violence
(N=192)

Severe Violence
(N=140)

Figure 12: Ratio of Benefits to Costs for Strategies Used by Women to Try to End Violence

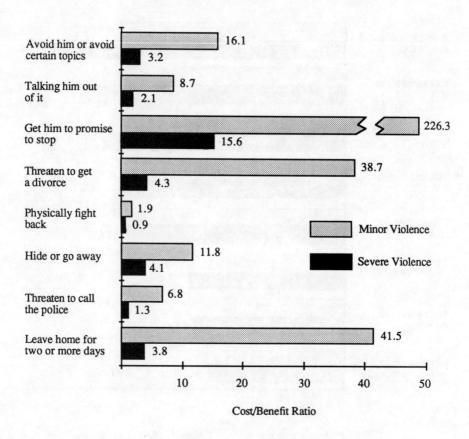

Cost/Benefit Ratio

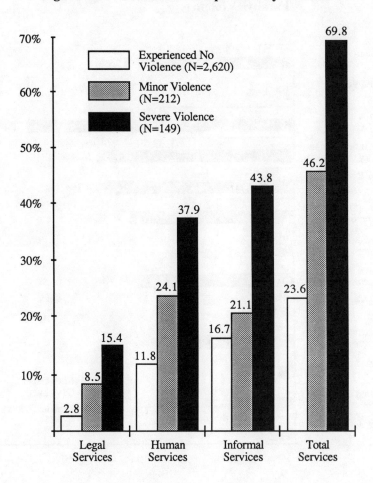

Figure 13: Sources of Help Used by Women

- Experienced No Violence (N=2,620)
- Minor Violence (N=212)
- Severe Violence (N=149)

70%
60%
50%
40%
30%
20%
10%

Legal Services: 2.8, 8.5, 15.4
Human Services: 11.8, 24.1, 37.9
Informal Services: 16.7, 21.1, 43.8
Total Services: 23.6, 46.2, 69.8

Figure 14: Police Intervention in Instances of Family Violence

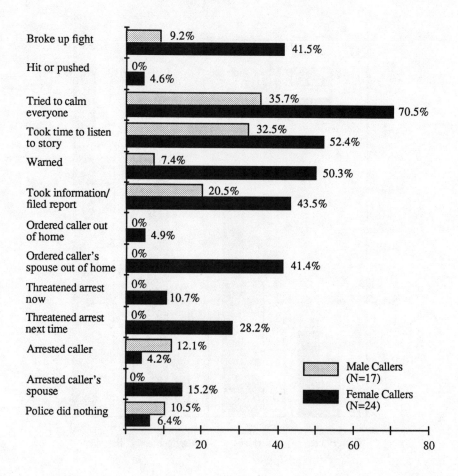

NOTES AND ELABORATIONS

CHAPTER ONE   BECAUSE THEY CAN

18: The Figgie Report: *The Figgie Report on Fear of Crime: America Afraid,* "Part I: The General Public" (Willoughby, Ohio: A-T-O Inc., 1980).

18: There are fifty-five million handguns: "Now Wake the Brave," *The Economist,* April 4, 1981, 11–12. This is probably an underestimate of the true total of handguns. In addition to handguns, there are an estimated ninety million rifles and shotguns. Also, see: James D. Wright and Peter H. Rossi, *Armed and Considered Dangerous: A Survey of Felons and Their Firearms* (Hawthorne, N.Y.: Aldine de Gruyter, 1986), 4, and James D. Wright, Peter H. Rossi, and Kathleen Daly, *Under the Gun: Weapons, Crime, and Violence in America,* (Hawthorne, N.Y.: Aldine de Gruyter, 1983).

18: the United States Department of Justice: Patrick Langan and Christopher Innes, *The Risk of Violent Crime* (Washington, D.C.: U.S. Department of Justice, May 1985).

18: the Federal Bureau of Investigation claims that: Albert Scardino, "Experts Question Data About Missing Children," *The New York Times,* August 18, 1985, 22. Actually, the Federal Bureau of Investigation does not tabulate official statistics on abducted children. When we called the FBI to confirm the fact that there were sixty-seven abductions, we were referred to the above article and to a second newspaper story which quoted the FBI as saying there were sixty-eight abductions in 1984 (Pinsky, Mark I., "Missing Laura: For parents there is no quitting," The *Los Angeles Times,* October 18, 1985, Section 1, page 1.) The National Center for Missing

and Exploited Children tells us that they are frequently misquoted regarding statistics on missing children. The only statistics they have are based on their own caseload. From June 18, 1985, until March 31, 1987, they had 13,508 cases of missing children. The National Center recognizes four categories of missing children: (1) runaways, (2) parental kidnappings, (3) other family member kidnappings, and (4) kidnappings. The center does not publish its caseload data. Callers seeking information on these statistics are referred to the center's media department. For an overview on the issue of missing children see: U.S. Attorney General's Advisory Board on Missing Children, *American's Missing & Exploited Children: Their Safety and Their Future*. (Washington, D.C.: U.S. Department of Justice, Office of Juvenile Justice and Delinquency Prevention, March 1986).

19: In May 1985: "Father Confesses to Killing Daughter after Leading Town Astray During Search," *Providence Journal Bulletin*, August 19, 1985, C4.

20: In our society, a person's: Murray A. Straus, Richard J. Gelles, and Suzanne K. Steinmetz, *Behind Closed Doors: Violence in the American Family* (Garden City, N.Y.: Anchor Books, 1980).

20: One of the first abusers we met: This case (and all other cases in the book) is a composite. Names and certain factual data have been altered slightly to protect the individuals involved.

22: The proposition that people hit family members: The notion that people hit family members because they can is fully outlined in Richard J. Gelles, "An Exchange/Social Control Theory," in David Finkelhor, Richard J. Gelles, Gerald T. Hotaling, and Murray A. Straus, eds., *The Dark Side of Families: Current Family Violence Research* (Beverly Hills, Calif.: Sage, 1983), 151–65. The theory draws from the following works on social exchange and criminal behavior: George C. Homans, "Fundamental Social Processes," in N. Smelser, ed., *Sociology: An Introduction* (New York: John Wiley, 1967), 27–78; Travis Hirschi, ed., *Causes of Delinquency* (Berkeley: University of California Press, 1969); F. Ivan Nye, "Choice, Exchange, and the Family," in W. R. Burr et al., eds., *Contemporary Theories About the Family*, vol. 2 (New York: Free Press, 1979), 1–41.

23: The National Institute of Justice reports: Joel Garner and Elizabeth Clemmer, "Danger to Police in Domestic Distrubances: A New Look," *Research in Brief*, November 1986, 3 (National Institute of Justice). See fig. 2.

23: Few police officers are rewarded: Jerome H. Skolnick, *Justice Without Trial: Law Enforcement in Democratic Society* (New York: John Wiley, 1966).

25: three basic propositions: See Gelles, "Control Theory."

26: More than 65 percent of Americans polled support the use of the death penalty: George Gallup, Jr., "7 in 10 Favor Death Penalty for Convicted Murderers," The Gallup Poll, March 2, 1986; Louis Harris, "Sizable Majorities Against Mandatory Death Penalty," The Harris Survey, February 10, 1983.

26: The U.S. Commission on the Causes and Prevention of Violence: The results of this survey are summarized in Rodney Stark and J. McEvoy, "Middle-Class Violence," *Psychology Today* 4 (November 1970): 52–54; 110–12.

27: About one in four wives and about a third of the husbands: Straus, Gelles, and Steinmetz, *Behind Closed Doors*.

28: For wife abuse, this has been labeled "burning bed" violence: The story of Francine Hughes was told in the book, *The Burning Bed: The True Story of Francine Hughes—A Beaten Wife Who Rebelled,* by Faith McNulty (New York: Harcourt Brace Jovanovich, 1980). The book was later made into a highly rated made-for-television movie of the same name starring Farah Fawcett.

28: Beatrice Whiting: Beatrice Whiting made this comment as a discussant at the Study Group on Recent Research on the Interaction Between Family and Society, sponsored by the Society for Research on Child Development, University of Michigan, Ann Arbor, 1975.

28: The social historian Barbara Laslett: Barbara Laslett, "The Family as a Public and Private Institution: A Historical Perspective," *Journal of Marriage and the Family* 35, no. 3 (1973): 480–92; and Barbara Laslett, "Family Membership, Past and Present," *Social Problems* 25, no. 5 (1978): 476–90.

29: The historian John Demos: John A. Demos, *A Little Commonwealth* (New York: Oxford, 1970).

31: The sociologist Lenore Weitzman: Lenore J. Weitzman, *The Marriage Contract: Spouses, Lovers and the Law* (New York: Free Press, 1981).

31: The sociologists Russell and Rebecca Dobash: R. Emerson Dobash and Russell Dobash, *Violence Against Wives* (New York: Free Press, 1979).

31: The expression "rule of thumb": Sir W. Blackstone, *Commentaries on the Laws of England* (London: Houghton Mifflin, 1968).

32: Dair Gillespie points out: Dair Gillespie, "Who Has the Power? The Marital Struggle," *Journal of Marriage and the Family* 33 (August 1971): 445–58.

32: James Q. Wilson and Richard J. Herrnstein: James Q. Wilson and Richard J. Herrnstein, *Crime and Human Nature* (New York: Simon and Schuster, 1986).

33: The sociologist William Goode: William J. Goode, "Force and Violence in the Family," *Journal of Marriage and the Family* 33 (November 1971): 624–36.

CHAPTER TWO   PEOPLE OTHER THAN US: PUBLIC PERCEPTIONS OF FAMILY VIOLENCE

39: A. A. Milne, in his popular children's book: The story of the Woozle is told in A. A. Milne, *Winnie-the-Pooh* (New York: Dell, 1926), in chapter 3 titled, "In Which Pooh and Piglet Go Hunting and Nearly Catch a Woozle." Beverly Houghton first applied what she called "The Woozle Effect" in her paper, "Research of Research on Woman Abuse" (Paper presented at the annual meetings of the American Society of Criminology, Philadelphia, 1979).

40: Myth 1: These myths have been elaborated from the first presentation in Richard J. Gelles and Claire Pedrick-Cornell, *Intimate Violence in Families* (Beverly Hills, Calif.: Sage, 1985).

40: Public and professional attention: An excellent examination of the increase in public and professional attention to child abuse can be found in Barbara J. Nelson, *Making an Issue of Child Abuse: Political Agenda Setting for Social Problems* (Chicago: University of Chicago Press, 1984). Another review of the development of professional attention is Stephen J. Pfohl, "The 'Discovery' of Child Abuse," *Social Problems* 24, no. 3 (1977): 310–23.

40: in 1962 Dr. C. Henry Kempe and his colleagues: C. H. Kempe, F. N. Silverman, B. F. Steele, W. Droegemueller, and H. K. Silver, "The Battered-Child Syndrome," *Journal of the American Medical Association* 181 (July 7, 1962): 17–24.

40: The article was accompanied by an editorial: "The Battered-Child Syndrome," editorial, *Journal of the American Medical Association* 181 (July 7, 1962): 42.

40: In our first effort to study: The results of this research were reported in Richard J. Gelles, *The Violent Home: A Study of Physical Aggression Between Husband and Wives* (Beverly Hills, Calif.: Sage, 1974).

41: Finally, in 1977: Roger Langley and Richard C. Levy, *Wife Beating: The Silent Crisis* (New York: E. P. Dutton, 1977).

41: The political scientist, Barbara Nelson: Barbara Nelson, *Making an Issue of Child Abuse* (Chicago: University of Chicago Press, 1984).

41: A number of years ago we were panelists on the David Susskind show: The show aired in April 1976.

42: With the exception of a few television docudramas: This point was investigated by Murray A. Straus and Suzanne K. Steinmetz and discussed in the article, "The Family as Cradle of Violence," *Society* 10 (September–October 1973): 50–56.

42: The theory that abusers are sick is often supported by a: This discussion is derived from Richard J. Gelles, "Child Abuse as Psychopathology: A Sociological Critique and Reformulation," *American Journal of Orthopsychiatry* 43 (July 1973): 611–21.

43: In fact, only about 10 percent of abusive incidents: This figure is presented by both Murray A. Straus, "A Sociological Perspective on the Causes of Family Violence," in Maurice Green, ed., *Violence and the Family* (Boulder, Colo.: Westview Press, 1980), 7–31; and Brandt F. Steele, "The Child Abuser," in I. Kutash, S. Kutash, and L. Schlesinger, eds., *Violence: Perspectives on Murder and Aggression* (San Francisco: Jossey-Bass, 1978), 285–300.

43: The actor David Soul: Brad Darrach, "The Souls' Dark Night," *People Weekly*, April 18, 1983, 30–35.

43: The sociologists Patrick Turbett and Richard O'Toole: Patrick Turbett and Richard O'Toole, "Physicians' Recognition of Child Abuse" (Paper presented at the annual meetings of the American Sociological Association, New York, 1980).

45: Craig MacAndrew and Robert Edgerton: Craig MacAndrew and Robert B. Edgerton, *Drunken Comportment: A Social Explanation* (Chicago: Aldine, 1969).

46: A series of experiments conducted by the social psychologist: Lang and his colleagues reasoned that if drinking behavior was learned, one could manipulate a situation to produce drunken behavior even if people were not drinking alcohol. Lang set up a laboratory experiment. He chose to use vodka as the alcoholic beverage because its taste could not be differentiated from tonic water that has been decarbonated. The experiment calls for the subjects to be randomly assigned to four groups. Two groups receive the tonic water, while the other two groups receive the vodka and tonic mix. One set of groups (tonic only, vodka and tonic) is accurately told what they are drinking. The other two groups are misled so that the tonic drinkers believe they have vodka and tonic while the vodka and tonic drinkers believe their glasses contain only decarbonated tonic.

Lang and his coexperimenters measured aggression by assessing the intensity and duration of shocks subjects believed they were delivering to Lang's associates (actually no shocks were delivered—this is a standard design that psychologists have used to measure aggression in the laboratory). Lang found that aggression was related to drinking only as a function of expectancy. The most aggressive subjects were those who thought they were drinking alcohol, regardless of the content of their drinks. Lang has also reviewed the results of numerous other laboratory experiments, and concludes that it is expectancy which determines how people behave when they are (or believe they are) drinking.

The series of research projects that used vodka and tonic water are reviewed in Alan R. Lang, "Drinking and Disinhibition: Contributions from Psychological Research" (Paper presented at the Social Research Group of the University of California at Berkeley School of Public Health and the National Institute on Alcohol Abuse and Alcoholism-sponsored conference on "Alcohol Disinhibition: The Nature and Meaning of the Link," Berkeley, Calif., February 11–13, 1981).

46: Research by the psychologist Morton Bard: See Morton Bard and J. Zacker, "Assaultiveness and Alcohol Use in Family Disputes: Police Perceptions," *Criminology* 12 (1974): 181–92.

46: Finally, our own investigations have discovered: Our second survey, conducted in 1985, collected information from a nationally representative sample of families. This survey used more sophisticated measures of drinking and produced dramatic evidence of an association between the frequency of drinking and wife abuse. Whereas those who do not drink or drink infrequently have a rate of wife assault of 77 per 1,000 households, the binge drinkers (those who drink from once a month to one to two times a week, five or more drinks per day) had a rate of wife abuse of 203 per 1,000 households. Yet, in spite of this strong association, we believe that the association we found does not support the theory that the chemical properties of alcohol produce violent behavior. This is because we found that alcohol *was not* used immediately prior to violent conflict in most (nearly 75 percent) of the situations. We conclude that although drinking and alcohol are often found to be associated with violence in the home, drinking, and even excessive drinking, does not usually result in wife abuse. Glenda Kaufman Kantor and Murray A. Straus, "The Drunken Bum Theory of Wife Beating" (Paper presented at the National Alcoholism Forum Conference on Alcohol and the Family, San Francisco, April 18, 1986).

46: In our survey of family violence: Diane H. Coleman and Murray A. Straus, "Alcohol Abuse and Family Violence," in E. Gottheil, K. A. Drueley, T. E. Skoloda, and H. M. Waxman, eds., *Alcohol, Drug Abuse and Aggression* (Springfield, Ill.: Charles C. Thomas, 1983), 104–24.

46: The sociologist Howard Becker: Howard S. Becker, *Outsiders: Studies in the Sociology of Deviance* (New York: Free Press, 1963).

47: Reviews of the different forms of drugs: See Roger N. Johnson, *Aggression in Man and Animals* (Philadelphia: W. B. Saunders, 1972), 174–78, for a review of drugs and aggressive behavior.

47: The primatologist Neil Smith: Euclid O. Smith and Larry D. Byrd, "External and Internal Influences on Aggression in Captive Group-Living Monkeys," in Richard J. Gelles and Jane B. Lancaster, eds., *Child Abuse and Neglect: Biosocial Dimensions* (Hawthorne, N.Y.: Aldine de Gruyter, 1987), 175–99.

48: The book, *Fatal Vision:* Joseph McGinnis, *Fatal Vision* (New York: G. P. Putnam Sons, 1983).

49: Even the evidence that supports the claim: The psychologists Sharon Herzberger and Deborah Potts investigated the claim that abuse leads to abuse. They amassed all the articles that stated what they referred to as "the cross-generational pattern of child rearing." Herzberger and Potts found, for example, that an author will list numerous other articles to support the claim for the intergenerational transmission theory. When Herzberger and Potts checked the articles cited, they found more articles cited—few actually reported—the results of scientific research. The claim that abuse leads to abuse has been repeated so often that it has evolved into the status of a law. At worst, about half of abused children grow up to be abusive. This is, on the one hand, quite a bit less than being preprogrammed for abuse, but, on the other hand, it is a much greater risk than if one grew up in a nonviolent home. Deborah Potts and Sharon Herzberger, "Child Abuse: A Cross-Generational Pattern of Child Rearing?" (Paper presented at the annual meeting of the Midwestern Psychological Association, Chicago, May 1979).

50: The physicians Barton Schmitt and C. Henry Kempe: Barton D. Schmitt and C. Henry Kempe, "Neglect and Abuse of Children," in V. Vaughan and R. McKay, eds., *Nelson Textbook on Pediatrics,* 10th ed. (Philadelphia: W. B. Saunders, 1975), 107–11.

51: The greatest function served by the seven myths: The idea of myths about child abuse and family violence serving as a smoke screen was originally developed by David Gil in his book, *Violence Against Children: Physical Child Abuse in the United States* (Cambridge, Mass.: Harvard University Press, 1970).

CHAPTER THREE FROM SPANKINGS TO MURDER: DEFINING AND STUDYING INTIMATE VIOLENCE

52: The United States Supreme Court Justice Potter Stewart: *Jacobelis* v. *Ohio,* 1964.

53: Parents have told us again and again that their kids: Richard J. Gelles, *The Violent Home: A Study of Physical Aggression Between Husbands and Wives* (Beverly Hills, Calif.: Sage, 1974); Murray A. Straus, Richard J. Gelles, and Suzanne K. Steinmetz, *Behind Closed Doors: Violence in the American Family* (Garden City, N.Y.: Anchor Books, 1980).

54: we stated that violence was an act: Richard J. Gelles and Murray A. Straus, "Determinants of Violence in the Family: Toward an Integrated Theory," in W. Burr, R. Hill, F. I. Nye, and I. Reiss, eds., *Contemporary Theories About the Family*, vol. 1 (New York: Free Press, 1979), 549–81.

55: Kempe and his coauthors: C. H. Kempe, F. N. Silverman, B. F. Steele, W. Droegmueller, and H. K. Silver, "The Battered-Child Syndrome," *Journal of the American Medical Association* 181 (July 7, 1962): 17–24.

55: The social policy expert and noted researcher on child abuse, David Gil: David Gil presented this anecdote at the Harvard Interfaculty Seminar on Child Abuse, October 1973.

57: The National Center on Child Abuse and Neglect defines: This definition appears in the Child Abuse Prevention and Treatment Act of 1974 (PL–93–237).

57: David Gil takes this formal definition much further: David Gil, "Unraveling Child Abuse," *American Journal of Orthopsychiatry* 45 (April 1975): 346–56.

58: The classic case is that of Baby Jane Doe: E. Salholz, "Baby Doe's Legal Fate," *Newsweek* 102 (November 14, 1983): 84; A. Press, "The Case of Baby Jane Doe," *Newsweek* 102 (November 28, 1983): 45–46; T. Morganthau, "The Case of Baby Jane Doe, Continued," *Newsweek* 102 (December 12, 1983): 47; *The New York Times*, October 14, 1984, sec. 1, p. 56.

59: An intensive examination of the definitions of child abuse: Jeanne Giovannoni and Rosina Becerra, *Defining Child Abuse* (New York: Free Press, 1979).

59: In point of fact, the most common form of intimate violence: Straus, Gelles, and Steinmetz, *Behind Closed Doors*, chap. 4; Richard J. Gelles and Claire Pedrick-Cornell, *Intimate Violence in Families* (Beverly Hills, Calif.: Sage, 1985), chap. 5.

60: The sociologist Suzanne Steinmetz: Suzanne K. Steinmetz, *The Cycle of Violence: Assertive, Aggressive, and Abusive Family Interaction* (New York: Praeger, 1977).

61: The physician Henry Harbin and his colleague Dennis Madden: Henry Harbin and Dennis Madden, "Battered Parents: A New Syndrome," *Journal of Psychiatry* 136 (October 1979): 1288–91.

61: The sociologist Carol Warren: Carol Warren, "Battered Parents: Adolescent Violence in the Family" (Paper presented at the annual meetings of the Pacific Sociological Association, 1978).

61: Our own survey of family violence found that: Straus, Gelles, and Steinmetz, *Behind Closed Doors*.

62: Harbin and Madden note: Harbin and Madden, "Battered Parents."

62: A study of the reporting of elder abuse: Legal Research and Services for the Elderly, "Elder Abuse in Massachusetts: A Survey of Professionals and Paraprofessionals" (Boston, 1979).

63: There are varying estimates of the extent of elder abuse: For a review of the estimates and problems with each estimate, see Claire Pedrick-Cornell and Richard J. Gelles, "Elder Abuse: The Status of Current Knowledge," *Family Relations* 31 (July 1982): 457–65.

63: The most recent and reliable study of the extent of elder abuse: Karl A. Pillemer and David Finkelhor, "The Prevalence of Elder Abuse: A Random Sample Survey" (Paper presented at the annual meetings of the Gerontological Society of America, Chicago, November 1986).

63: Experts feel that the most likely victim of elder abuse: For a review of the factors related to elder abuse see, Pedrick-Cornell and Gelles, "Elder Abuse."

63: A variety of studies of dating and violence find that: R. M. Cate, J. M. Henton, J. Koval, F. S. Christopher, and S. Lloyd, "Premarital Abuse: A Social Psychological Perspective," *Journal of Family Issues* 3 (March 1982): 79–90; J. M. Henton, R. Cate, J. Koval, S. Lloyd, and F. S. Christopher, "Romance and Violence in Dating Relationships," *Journal of Family Issues* 4 (September 1983): 467–82; James Makepeace, "Courtship Violence Among College Students," *Family Relations* 30 (January 1981): 97–102; James Makepeace, "Social Factors and Victim-Offender Differences in Courtship Violence," *Family Relations* 36 (January 1987): 87–91; M. R. Laner and L. Thompson, "Abuse and Aggression in Courting Couples," *Deviant Behavior* 3 (1982): 229–44; K. E. Lane and P. A. Gwartney-Gibbs, "Violence in the Context of Dating and Sex," *Journal of Family Issues* 6 (1985): 45–59.

64: The sociologist June Henton and her colleagues: Henton et al., "Romance and Violence."

64: Kempe defined sexual abuse: C. H. Kempe, "Sexual Abuse, Another Hidden Pediatric Problem: The 1977 C. Anderson Aldrich Lecture," *Pediatrics* 62 (September 1978): 382–89.

64: An editorial in *The New Republic:* "Greasy Kid Stuff," *The New Republic* 192 (May 13, 1985): 4ff.

65: The American Humane Association recorded: American Humane Association, *National Study on Child Neglect and Abuse Reporting 1984* (Denver: American Humane Asscociation, 1986).

65: The Child Welfare League of America: Child Welfare League, *Too Young to Run: A Research Study* (Washington, D.C.: Child Welfare League, 1986), 12.

65: The sociologist Diana Russell surveyed: Diana Russell, *Sexual Exploitation: Rape, Child Sexual Abuse, and Workplace Harassment* (Beverly Hills, Calif.: Sage, 1984); Also see, "Incidence and Prevalence of Intrafamilial and Extrafamilial Sexual Abuse of Children," *Child Abuse and Neglect: The International Journal* 7 (1983): 133–46.

65: Russell found that: Russell, *Sexual Exploitation*.

65: David Finkelhor surveyed: David Finkelhor, *Sexually Victimized Children* (New York: Free Press, 1979).

67: Today, according to the National Clearinghouse on Marital Rape: National Clearinghouse on Marital Rape, 2325 Oak Street, Berkeley, Calif. 94708.

67: David Finkelhor and Kersti Yllo: David Finkelhor and Kersti Yllo, *License to Rape: Sexual Abuse of Wives* (New York: Holt, Rinehart & Winston, 1985).

67: Diana Russell's survey in San Francisco: Diana Russell, *Rape in Marriage* (New York: Macmillan, 1982).

69: the rather bizarre practice of Munchausen Syndrome: Roy Meadow, "Muchausen Syndrome by Proxy: The Hinterland of Child Abuse," *Lancet* (August 13, 1977), 343–45.

70: Henry Kempe's first article on the battered child: Kempe et al., "Battered-Child Syndrome."

70: The first published article on wife abuse: Leroy Schultz, "The Wife Assaulter," *Journal of Social Therapy* 6, no. 2 (1960): 103–12.

70: Another clinical investigation was the 1964 article: J. E. Snell, R. J. Rosenwald, and A. Robey, "The Wifebeater's Wife: A Study of Family Interaction," *Archives of General Psychiatry* 11 (August 1964): 107–12.

71: Physicians Brandt F. Steele and Carl B. Pollock: Brandt F. Steele and Carl B. Pollock, "A Psychiatric Study of Parents Who Abuse Infants and Small Children," in Ray Helfer and C. Henry Kempe, eds., *The Battered Child* (Chicago: University of Chicago Press, 1968): 103–47.

71: A number of books and articles on battered women: See, for example: R. Emerson Dobash and Russell Dobash, *Violence Against Wives: The Case Against Patriarchy* (New York: Free Press, 1979); Mildred Pagelow, *Women Battering— Victims and Their Experiences* (Beverly Hills, Calif.: Sage, 1981; Lenore Walker, *The Battered Woman* (New York: Harper & Row, 1979).

71: Perhaps the major drawback of: A piece of research not related to violent behavior can be used to illustrate the problem of selecting an inappropriate comparison group. A few years ago the *New England Journal of Medicine* published an article which claimed that heavy coffee drinkers were more likely to contract pancreatic cancer than individuals who did not drink as much coffee. The researchers examined the coffee-drinking patterns of a hospitalized group of patients who suffered from pancreatic cancer and a matched group of patients who did not have the cancer. They found heavy coffee drinking among the cancer patients. Although the clinical investigation included a comparison group, the group was inappropriate and may have led to an inaccurate interpretation of the data. Among the comparison group who did not have cancer were a number of patients who had been admitted to the hospital for gastrointestinal problems. A physician who wrote to the *New England Journal of Medicine* noted that it would not be unusual for the physicians of the patients with stomach problems to recommend that they cease drinking coffee. The writer noted that if one removed from the comparison group all the individuals with stomach problems, the resulting comparison would reveal no difference in coffee-drinking patterns. Coffee drinking could lead to pancreatic cancer, but because the clinical study included the wrong comparison group, the study was not useful for answering the question about factors leading to risk of cancer. Brian MacMahon, Stella Yen, Dimitrios Trichopoulos, Kenneth Warren, and George Nardi, "Coffee and Cancer of the Pancreas," *New England Journal of Medicine* 305 (March 12, 1981): 630–33; Harvey R. Goldstein, "No Association Found Between Coffee and Cancer of the Pancreas." Letter to the Editor, *New England Journal of Medicine* 306 (April 22, 1982): 997.

72: When Saleem Shah, the former chief: Saleem Shah, *Report on the XYY Chromosomal Abnormality,* National Institute of Mental Health conference report (Chevy Chase, M.D.: National Institute of Mental Health Center for Studies of Crime and Delinquency. [For sale by the Superintendent of Documents, U.S. Government Printing Office])

73: Child abuse is not only tabulated at the state level: The Association for the Protection of Children, a division of the American Humane Association in Denver, publishes an annual summary report on Child Neglect and Abuse Reporting.

73: The federal government fielded its own national: The final results of the government survey of child maltreatment reporting can be found in K. Burgdorf, *Recognition and Reporting of Child Maltreatment* (Rockville, Md.: Westat, 1980).

73: The American Humane Association: American Humane Association, *National Study on Child Neglect.*

73: We had the unusual opportunity to examine the child abuse: The results of our examination are published in A. Carr, "Reported Child Maltreatment in Florida: The Operation of a Public Child Protective Service System (Kingston: University of Rhode Island, 1978, Mimeographed).

74: Yet, Kinsey, Masters and Johnson, Shere Hite, and others: See A. Kinsey, B. Wardell, and C. Martin, *Sexual Behavior in the Human Male* (Philadelphia, W. B. Saunders, 1948); William Masters and Virginia Johnson, *Human Sexual Response* (Boston: Little, Brown, 1966); Shere Hite, *The Hite Report: A Nationwide Study of Female Sexuality* (New York: Macmillan, 1976).

74: The sociologist Laud Humphreys: Laud Humphreys, *Tearoom Trade: Impersonal Sex in Public Places* (Chicago: Aldine, 1970).

CHAPTER FOUR   PROFILING VIOLENT FAMILIES

77: If we reject the notion that violence and abuse: Two articles that critique the theory that abuse is the product of mental illness or psychopathology are: Richard J. Gelles, "Child Abuse as Psychopathology: A Sociological Critique and Reformulation," *American Journal of Orthopsychiatry* 43 (July 1973): 611–21; and J. Spinetta and D. Rigler, "The Child-Abusing Parent: A Psychological Review," *Psychological Bulletin* 77 (April 1972): 296–304.

78: There are a number of distinct organizational characteristics: The organizational characteristics of the family that promote both intimacy and conflict were first described in Richard J. Gelles and Murray A. Straus, "Determinants of Violence in the Family: Towards an Integrated Theory," in Wesley Burr, Reuben Hill, F. Ivan Nye, and Ira L. Reiss, eds., *Contemporary Theories About the Family,* vol. 1. (New York: Free Press, 1979), 549–81. These ideas were further developed in Murray A. Straus and Gerald T. Hotaling, eds., *The Social Causes of Husband-Wife Violence* (Minneapolis: University of Minnesota Press, 1980); and Richard J. Gelles and Claire Pedrick-Cornell, *Intimate Violence in Families* (Beverly Hills, Calif.: Sage, 1985).

81: Half of all households have children under eighteen years of age: U.S. Bureau of the Census, *Statistical Abstract of the United States: 1987,* 107th ed. (Washington, D.C.: Government Printing Office, 1986), chart 45; U.S. Bureau of the Census, *Current Population Report,* ser. P-20, no. 411.

81: When someone is blocked from doing something that he or she: This is the classic statement of psychological frustration/aggression theory. The theory has been articulated by J. C. Dollard, L. Doob, N. Miller, O. Mowrer, and R. Sears, *Frustration and Aggression* (New Haven, Conn.: Yale University Press, 1939); and N. E. Miller, "The Frustration-Aggression Hypothesis," *Psychological Review* 48, no. 4 (1941): 337–42. A sociological formulation of the notion that blocked goals can be frustrating can be found in Robert K. Merton, "Social Structure and Anomie," *American Sociological Review* 3 (October 1938): 672–82.

82: You can be an ex-husband or an ex-wife: This idea was first presented by Alice Rossi in her article, "Transition to Parenthood," *Journal of Marriage and the Family* 30 (February 1968): 26–39.

84: The earliest students of child and wife abuse: See, for example: Vincent J. Fontana, *The Maltreated Child: The Maltreatment Syndrome in Children* (Springfield, Ill.: Charles C. Thomas, 1971); Richard Galdston, "Observations on Children Who Have Been Physically Abused and Their Parents," *American Journal of Psychiatry* 122, no. 4 (1965): 440–43; Leroy G. Schultz, "The Wife Assaulter," *Journal of Social Therapy* 6, no. 2 (1960): 103–12; Brandt F. Steele and Carl B. Pollock, "A Psychiatric Study of Parents Who Abuse Infants and Small Children," in R. Helfer and C. Henry Kempe, eds., *The Battered Child* (Chicago: University of Chicago Press, 1968), 103–47; and S. R. Zalba, "Battered Children," *Transaction* 8 (July–August 1971): 58–61.

84: Later, those who studied violence and abuse: See Gelles, "Child Abuse"; and David Gil, "Violence Against Children," *Journal of Marriage and the Family* 33 (November 1971): 637–48.

84: Still others chose to study violence: See R. Emerson Dobash and Russell Dobash, *Violence Against Wives: The Case Against Patriarchy* (New York: Free Press, 1979).

84: there are a multitude of factors: For a review of the factors related to family violence, see Richard J. Gelles, "Family Violence," in Ralph H. Turner and James F. Short, eds., *Annual Review of Sociology,* vol. 11 (Palo Alto, Calif.: Annual Reviews, Inc, 1985), 347–67; Marc F. Maden and D. F. Wrench, "Significant Findings in Child Abuse Research," *Victimology* 2 (1977): 196–224; and Suzanne

K. Steinmetz, "Violence Between Family Members," *Marriage and Family Review* 1 (1978):, 1–16.

85: If one had to come up with a profile of the prototypical: The profile that is presented is a statistical profile. It would be incorrect to assume that someone who does not fit this profile would not be an abuser. Similarly, someone who fit the profile is likely to abuse, but is not always an abuser. The profile was developed in Murray A. Straus, Richard J. Gelles, and Suzanne K. Steinmetz. *Behind Closed Doors: Violence in the American Family* (Garden City, N.Y.: Anchor Books, 1980).

85: Our 1976 survey of violence: The survey is reported in Straus, Gelles, and Steinmetz, *Behind Closed Doors*. The measure of stress was adapted from T. H. Holmes and R. H. Rahe, "The Social Readjustment Rating Scale," *Journal of Psychosomatic Research* 11 (1967): 213–18.

86: It was apparent that the extensive social: Straus, Gelles, and Steinmetz, *Behind Closed Doors;* and Noel Cazenave and Murray A. Straus, "Race, Class, Network Embeddedness and Family Violence: A Search for Potent Support Systems," *Journal of Comparative Family Studies* 10 (Autumn 1979): 281–300.

87: Low birth weight babies: A review of child factors that are related to physical abuse can be found in W. N. Friedrich and J. A. Boriskin, "The Role of the Child in Abuse: A Review of the Literature," *American Journal of Orthopsychiatry* 46 (October 1976): 580–90.

88: If there is a typical wife beater: The profile of wife beaters is a statistical profile and was first presented in Straus, Gelles, and Steinmetz, *Behind Closed Doors*.

88: Researchers have found that status inconsistency: C. A. Hornung, B. C. McCullough, and T. Sugimoto, "Status Relationships in Marriage: Risk Factors in Spouse Abuse," *Journal of Marriage and the Family* 43 (August 1981): 675–92.

89: Victims of wife beating are often found to be dependent: Lenore Walker, *The Battered Woman* (New York: Harper & Row, 1979).

89: Pregnant women often report: Richard J. Gelles, "Violence and Pregnancy: A Note on the Extent of the Problem and Needed Services," *Family Coordinator* 24 (January 1975): 81–86.

89: Pregnancy, however, does not make women vulnerable: When we analyzed the results of the Second National Family Violence Survey, we did find that the rates of violence and abuse were higher among pregnant women than women who were not pregnant. However, when we controlled for age, the differences disappeared. Women under the age of twenty-four years old experienced high rates of violence and abuse, but the rates were the same for pregnant and nonpregnant women. Women over twenty-four years old experienced lower rates of violence, and again, there were no differences between pregnant and nonpregnant women. Thus, the relationship between violence and pregnancy which we first reported in 1975 (Gelles, "Violence and Pregnancy") and which others have reported, turns out to be spurious.

90: Since 1975 at least ten additional investigations: Michael David Allan Freeman, *Violence in the Home: A Socio-legal Study* (Farnborough, England: Saxon House, 1979); Richard J. Gelles, *The Violent Home: A Study of Physical Aggression Between Husbands and Wives* (Beverly Hills, Calif.: Sage, 1974); Morgan E. Scott, "The Battered Spouse Syndrome," *Virginia Medical* 107 (January 1980): 41–43; Suzanne Sedge, "Spouse Abuse," in Marilyn R. Block and Jan D. Sinnott, eds., *The Battered Elder Syndrome: An Exploratory Study* (College Park, Md.: Center on Aging, 1979), 33–48; Suzanne K. Steinmetz, "The Battered Husband Syndrome," *Victimology* 2 (1978): 499–509; Straus, Gelles, and Steinmetz, *Behind Closed Doors;* Mary Warren, "Battered Husbands," in Margaret E. Ankeney, ed., *Family Violence: A Cycle of Abuse* (Laramie, Wyo.: College of Education, University of Wyoming, 1979), 76–78.

91: The sociologists Debra Kalmuss and Judith Seltzer: Debra Kalmuss and Judith A. Seltzer, "A Test of Social Learning and Stress Models of Family Violence." (Paper presented at the annual meetings of the American Sociological Association, New York, 1986).

93: The criminologist Marvin Wolfgang: Marvin Wolfgang, *Patterns in Criminal Homicide* (Philadelphia: University of Pennsylvania Press, 1958).

94: After 8:00 P.M.: This analysis was first presented in Gelles, *Violent Home,* chap. 4.

CHAPTER FIVE   HOW VIOLENT ARE AMERICAN FAMILIES?

99: it has to harm a significant number of people in order: The notion that something has to harm a significant number of people in order to attract public attention is drawn from the literature on the sociology of social problems. One definition of social problems is a condition affecting a significant number of people in ways considered undesirable, about which it is felt something can be done through collective action. This definition was developed by Paul B. Horton and Gerald R. Leslie, *The Sociology of Social Problems,* 3d ed. (New York: Appelton, Century, Crofts, 1965).

99: "One million children are abused each year": This figure is used by the National Center on Child Abuse and Neglect. The estimate of one million abused children was used by the National Committee for Prevention of Child Abuse in its print and television public service announcements which were created by the Ad Council.

99: "A woman is battered by her husband every 18 seconds": This estimate is frequently attributed to the Federal Bureau of Investigation. In point of fact, the FBI arrived at this figure by taking the data on wife abuse from Murray A. Straus, Richard J. Gelles, and Suzanne Steinmetz's book, *Behind Closed Doors: Violence in the American Family* (Garden City, N.Y.: Anchor Books, 1980), chap. 2, and simply dividing this figure (two million) by the number of seconds in a year.

99: Lois Haight Herrington: Nadine Broznan, "An Expert Looks at Family Violence," *The New York Times,* May 20, 1984, sec. 1, p. 62.

100: The National Center on Child Abuse and Neglect: As we noted above, the figure of one million abused children is used often by officials of the National Center on Child Abuse and Neglect.

100: national opinion survey carried out by David Gil: David Gil, *Violence Against Children: Physical Child Abuse in the United States* (Cambridge, Mass.: Harvard University Press, 1970).

101: the statistician Richard Light: Richard Light, "Abused and Neglected Children in America: A Study of Alternative Policies," *Harvard Educational Review* 43 (November 1973): 556–98.

101: The American Humane Association has conducted: American Association for Protecting Children, Inc., *Highlights of Official Child Neglect and Abuse Reporting, 1984* (Denver: American Humane Association, 1986).

101: A similar number of physically assaulted children: Kenneth Burgdorf, *Recognition and Reporting of Child Maltreatment* (Rockville, Md.: Westat, 1980).

101: the U.S. Justice Department published: Harold R. Lentzer, *Intimate Victims: A Study of Violence Among Friends and Relatives* (Washington, D.C.: Department of Justice, Bureau of Justice Statistics, 1980); P. A. Klaus and M. R. Rand, *Family Violence* (Washington, D.C.: Government Printing Office, 1984).

102: We conducted the First National Family Violence Survey in 1976: The results are published in: Straus, Gelles, and Steinmetz, *Behind Closed Doors;* Richard J. Gelles, "Violence Towards Children in the United States," *American Journal of Orthopsychiatry,* 48 (October 1978): 580–92; Murray A. Straus, "Wife Beating: How Common and Why," *Victimology* 2, no. 3/4 (1978): 443–58.

103: *Violence Toward Children:* The detailed results appear in Gelles, "Violence Towards Children."

104: *Violence Between Partners:* The detailed results appear in Straus, "Wife Beating."

104: In 1978 our colleague: Suzanne K. Steinmetz, "The Battered Husband Syndrome," *Victimology* 2, no 3-4 (1978): 499–509.

105: United Press International headlined: *Chicago Daily News,* August 31, 1977.

105: *Time* magazine devoted: "The Battered Husbands," *Time,* March 20, 1978, 69.

105: Dr. Joyce Brothers mentioned: Joyce Brothers, "Husbands Can Be Battered," *Bergen Record,* July 13, 1978.

105: When journalist Langley wrote: Roger Langley, "Battered Husbands" (New York) *Daily News Magazine,* July 2, 1978, 7ff.

105: The same study that found that forty-six men in one thousand: Richard J. Gelles, "The Myth of Battered Husbands—and New Facts About Family Violence," *Ms.* magazine 8 (October 1979): 65–73.

106: Critics of the statistics are: An example of this criticism can be found in an editorial by Jetse Sprey, then the editor of the *Journal of Marriage and the Family*. In reviewing the data on violence in the family, Sprey added that . . . "behind the spectre of these phantom legions of the domestically abused lies the largely over-looked fact that the same data seem to indicate that in more than 90% of families children are not abused, nor do spouses seem to beat up on one another." Jetse Sprey, "Editorial Comments," *Journal of Marriage and the Family* 47 (February 1985):3.

106: Ten years ago only one in ten Americans: Edward Magnuson, "Child Abuse: The Ultimate Betrayal," *Time,* September 5, 1983, 20–22. The Harris poll was conducted in the fall of 1982.

107: They point incorrectly to the supposed rise in the divorce rate: U.S. National Center for Health Statistics, 1985. A current review of the statistics on chang-ing divorce rates are discussed in Arthur J. Norton and Jeanne E. Moorman, "Current Trends in Marriage and Divorce Among American Women," *Journal of Marriage and the Family* 49 (February 1987): 3–14.

107: Lloyd DeMause examined: Lloyd DeMause, ed., *The History of Childhood* (New York: Psychohistory Press, 1974); Lloyd DeMause, "Our Forebears Made Childhood a Nightmare," *Psychology Today* 8 (April 1975): 85–87.

107: Women, Russell and Rebecca Dobash note: R. Emerson Dobash and Rus-sell Dobash, *Violence Against Wives: A Case Against Patriarchy* (New York: Free Press, 1979).

107: Couples in the 1980s are marrying later, having fewer children: U.S. Bureau of the Census, *Statistical Abstract of the United States, 1985* (Washington, D.C.: Government Printing Office, 1985), tables 120, 92, 63, and 97. See also: Norton and Moorman, "Current Trends"; U.S. Bureau of the Census, *1980 Census of Population, Subject Reports 2, Marital Characteristics* (Washington, D.C.: U.S. Department of Commerce, Bureau of the Census [for sale by the Superintendent of Documents, Government Printing Office], 1985); U.S. Bureau of the Census, *House-holds, Families, Marital Status, and Living Arrangements,* Current Population Re-ports, Series P-20, Population Characteristics; No. 391 (Washington, D.C.: Government Printing Office, 1985).

107: The American Association for Protecting Children: American Association for Protecting Children, *Highlights of Official Child Neglect,* 1986.

108: We were surprised in 1976: See Straus, Gelles, and Steinmetz, *Behind Closed Doors;* Gelles, "Violence Towards Children"; Straus, "Wife Beating."

108: We were shocked in 1985: The full results of the survey are published in: Murray A. Straus and Richard J. Gelles, "Societal Change and Change in Family Violence from 1975 to 1985 as Revealed by Two National Surveys," *Journal of Marriage and the Family* 48 (August 1986): 465–79; and Richard J. Gelles and Murray A. Straus, "Is Violence Towards Children Increasing? A Comparison of 1975 and 1985 National Survey Rates," *Journal of Interpersonal Violence* 2 (June 1987): 212–22.

109: a *New York Times* editorial: "On Hitting Children," *The New York Times,* November 27, 1985, A22.

109: The *Christian Science Monitor* reported: Cheryl Sullivan, "2 Researchers Say Family Violence Has Plunged in Last 10 Years, but . . ." *Christian Science Monitor,* November 18, 1985, 3–4.

109: Dr. Frederick Green: Marilyn Gardner, "Professionals Broaden Efforts to Prevent Child Abuse," *Christian Science Monitor,* November 19, 1985, 39.

109: The sociologist Richard Berk: Sullivan, "2 Researchers Say."

110: Yet, had Berk consulted the Uniform Crime Reports: *Uniform Crime Reports for the United States, 1986* (Washington, D.C.: U.S. Department of Justice, Federal Bureau of Investigation [for sale by the Superintendent of Documents, Government Printing Office], 1986).

111: However, our colleagues at Louis Harris and Associates. Discussions with David Neft, former chief financial officer and John Boyle, former vice president at Louis Harris and Associates, revealed that coverage of telephone interviews is essentially the same as in-person interviews. This statement was backed up in a paper by Alfred C. Marcus and Lori A. Crane, "Telephone Surveys in Public Health Research," *Medical Care* 24, no. 2 (1986): 97–112.

112: The average age a man and a woman first get married: Norton and Moorman, "Current Trends"; Bureau of the Census, *Statistical Abstract, 1985.*

112: For intact families, the economic climate of the country: Data on the decline in unemployment can be found in Bureau of the Census, *Statistical Abstract, 1985,* tables 680–687.

113: There has been tremendous growth in paid employment of married women: Bureau of the Census, *Statistical Abstract, 1985,* tables 669–672.

113: States have increased their staffs of protective service workers: Calls to several federal and private organizations concerned with child abuse revealed that no national statistics are available on the number of child protective service (CPS) workers. However, some indication of the magnitude of change can be gleaned from data on the New England states: In Connecticut the number of caseworkers assigned to children's services increased from 244.5 full-time equivalent workers in 1976 to 308 in 1985, an increase of 26 percent. In Maine the number of CPS workers increased from 163 in 1977 to 238 in 1985, an increase of 46 percent. In Massachusetts the budget for child protective services increased from $120 million in 1980 to $293 million in 1985, a 144 percent increase. In New Hampshire the number of state social workers increased from 95 in 1972 to 136 in 1985, an increase of 43 percent. In Rhode Island the number of CPS workers increased from 12 in 1974 to 125 in 1985, a 792 percent increase.

113: Membership in the American Association of Marital and Family Therapists: Membership increased from 3,373 in 1975 to 12,302 in 1985.

114: the training manual prepared by the International Association of Chiefs of Police: International Association of Chiefs of Police, *Wife Beating. Training Key 245* (Gaithersburg, Md., 1976).

114: Shortly after we published our results: This information was reported to us by Peter B. Morgan, Regional Program Manager, Child and Family Services, Region I, Augusta, Maine.

CHAPTER SIX   THE IMPACT OF INTIMATE VIOLENCE

121: Henry Kempe and Barton Schmitt claimed: Barton D. Schmitt and C. Henry Kempe, "Neglect and Abuse of Children," in V. Vaughan and R. McKay, eds., *Nelson Textbook on Pediatrics,* 10th ed. (Philadelphia: W. B. Saunders, 1975), 107–11.

121: On the other side is the child development expert Edward Zigler: Joan Kaufman and Edward Zigler, "Do Abused Children Become Abusive Parents?" (Mimeographed, 1987). Zigler and his colleague, Joan Kaufman, reviewed the available empirical evidence on the intergenerational link. Data came from four primary sources—case study materials, social agency records, clinical interviews, and self-report questionnaires or interviews. For the most part, Kaufman and Zigler dismiss the evidence derived from case histories by noting that the flaws and shortcomings mean that these data should be interpreted with extreme caution if not totally ignored. Agency data are equally flawed. Clinical interviews without comparison groups yield findings which are impossible to interpret. One simply cannot know whether the experiences of the subjects are unique to abusive parents or common to all adults who seek and receive psychological services.

Self-report studies typically have the advantage of larger samples and comparison groups. These studies all find that a history of child abuse is more common among parents who maltreat their children than among parents who do not report that they are abusing their children. The strength of the association, however, differs from study to study. The researchers Rosemary Hunter and Nancy Kilstrom studied 282 parents of newborns who were admitted to a regional intensive care nursery for premature and ill infants. The rate of intergenerational transmission in this study was 18 percent—nine of forty-nine parents who reported a history of maltreatment were identified as maltreaters.

One of the most carefully conducted studies that examined the theory of the intergenerational cycle of abuse is Byron Egeland's Mother-Child Project at the University of Minnesota. In 1975 Egeland enrolled a sample of 267 mothers in the last trimester of pregnancy. The mothers, who were patients at the Minneapolis Public Health Clinics, were considered high risk for caretaking problems. Their risk factors included low income, youth (some were as young as twelve years of age), marital status (more than half were not married when their child was born), and the fact that the pregnancy was unplanned. Few of the mothers were prepared for the birth of their firstborn. They had not bought clothes, cribs, or other baby necessities. Few had actually made arrangements for a place in which the baby could sleep. The lives of the mothers were characterized by chaos, disruption, and stress.

Egeland has followed the mothers and their children for more than a decade. He has seen many mothers raise their children without neglect and violence, and he has seen a number of children maltreated and abused. Egeland believes his research strongly supports the notion of the intergenerational transmission of abuse. Of the mothers in his group who had been abused as children, 70 percent mistreated their own children.

Our own 1976 National Survey of Family Violence also assessed the possibilities of violence begetting violence. Of those who had experienced physical punishment as adolescents, nearly 18 percent (17.6 percent) reported using severe violence toward their children as adults. See Kaufman and Zigler, "Abusive Parents"; R. Hunter and N. Kilstrom, "Breaking the Cycle in Abusive Families," *American Journal of Psychiatry* 136 (October 1979): 1320–22; Byron Egeland, D. Jacobvitz, and K. Papatola, "Intergenerational Continuity of Abuse," in Richard J. Gelles and Jane Lancaster eds., *Child Abuse and Neglect: Biosocial Dimensions* (Hawthorne, N.Y.: Aldine De Gruyter, 1987), 255–76; Murray A. Straus, Richard J. Gelles, and Suzanne K. Steinmetz, *Behind Closed Doors: Violence in the American Family* (Garden City, N.Y.: Anchor Press, 1980), chap. 5.

121: Zigler and his colleague Joan Kaufman believe: Kaufman and Zigler, "Abused Children."

122: Kaufman and Zigler believe: Kaufman and Zigler, "Abused Children."

122: The researchers Rosemary Hunter and Nancy Kilstrom reported: Hunter and Kilstrom, "Abusive Families."

122: The psychologist Byron Egeland has also examined: Egeland, Jacobvitz, and Papatola, "Continuity of Abuse."

122: One of the subjects in Egeland's research: Egeland, Jacobvitz, and Papatola, "Continuity of Abuse."

124: a number of investigators have collected data: See, for example, E. Baher, C. Hyman, C. Jones, R. Jones, A. Kerr, and R. Mitchell, *At Risk: An Account of the Work of the Battered Child Research Department* (London: Routledge & Kegan Paul, 1976); E. Elmer and G. S. Gregg, "Developmental Characteristics of Abused Children," *Pediatrics* 40 (1967): 596–602; Elizabeth Elmer, *Children in Jeopardy: A Study of Abused Minors and Their Families* (Pittsburgh: University of Pittsburgh Press, 1967); David Gil, *Violence Against Children: Physical Child Abuse in the United States* (Cambridge, Mass.: Harvard University Press, 1970); Harold P. Martin, "The Child and His Development," in C. H. Kempe and R. Helfer, eds., *Helping the Battered Child and His Family* (Philadelphia: Lippincott, 1972), 93–114; Harold P. Martin, P. Beezley, E. F. Conway, and C. H. Kempe, "The Development of Abused Children," *Advances in Pediatrics* 21 (1974): 25–73; C. Morse, O. J. Z. Sahler, and S. Friedman, "A Three-Year Follow-up Study of Abused and Neglected Children," *American Journal of the Disabilities of Children* 120 (November 1970): 439–46; A. Sandgrund, R. Gaines, and A. Green, "Child Abuse and Mental Retardation: A Problem of Cause and Effect," *American Journal of Mental Deficiency* 79, no. 3 (1975): 327–30.

124: Research conducted by Roy and Ellen Herrenkohl: Roy C. Herrenkohl, Ellen C. Herrenkohl, Brenda P. Egolf, and Monica Sibley, *Child Abuse and Social Competence,* vol. 1, *Executive Summary* (Bethlehem, Pa.: Lehigh University Center for Social Research, March 1984).

125: Researchers and clinicians list several characteristics: See, for example, Martin et al., "Development of Abused Children."

125: E. Milling Kinard reviewed: E. Milling Kinard, "The Psychological Consequences of Abuse for the Child," *Journal of Social Issues* 35, no. 2 (1979): 82–100.

125: The psychiatrist Brandt Steele: Brandt F. Steele, "The Child Abuser," in Irwin L. Kutash, Samuel B. Kutash, Louis B. Schlesinger, & Associates, eds., *Violence: Perspectives on Murder and Aggression* (San Francisco: Jossey-Bass, 1978), 285–300.

125: A variety of data points to the fact that abused children: See, for example, C. P. Smith, D. J. Berkman, and W. M. Fraser, *A Preliminary National Assessment of Child Abuse and Neglect and the Juvenile Justice System: Shadows of Distress* (Washington, D.C.: Law Enforcement Assistance Administration, U.S. Department of Justice, 1980); J. Alfaro, "Report on the Relationship Between Child Abuse and Neglect and Later Socially Deviant Behavior" (Paper presented at a symposium, Exploring the Relationship Between Child Abuse and Delinquency, University of Washington, Seattle, 1977); F. G. Bolton, J. Reich, and S. E. Guiterres, "Delinquency Patterns in Maltreated Children and Siblings," *Victimology* 2 (1977): 349–57.

126: One investigation in New York State tracked children: Alfaro, "Report on the Relationship."

126: Of the more than two thousand family homicides: Federal Bureau of Investigation, *Crime in the United States* (Washington, D.C.: Department of Justice, 1985).

126: Late in 1982 Richard Jahnke: For details on the killing of Richard Jahnke and the subsequent trial of his son and daughter, see, Greggory W. Morris, *The Kids Next Door: Sons and Daughters Who Kill Their Parents* (New York: William Morrow, 1985); "It Made Terrible Sense," *Time,* December 13, 1982, 34.

127: Three and one-half years after Richard Jahnke was murdered: The details on the killing of James Pierson by his daughter's boyfriend are found in Dena Kleiman, "Murder on Long Island," *The New York Times Magazine,* September 14, 1986, 52, 56 ff.; and Marica Chambers, "Children Citing Self-Defense in Murder of Parents," *The New York Times,* October 12, 1986, 38.

127: As one of Richard Jahnke's neighbors said: *Time,* December 13, 1982, 34.

129: Brandt Steele notes that many famous figures: Brandt Steele, "Notes on the Lasting Effects of Early Child Abuse Throughout the Life Cycle," *Child Abuse and Neglect: The International Journal* 10, no. 3 (1986): 283–91.

130: research conducted by Byron Egeland: Egeland, Jacobvitz, and Papatola, "Continuity of Abuse."

131: The psychologist Lenore Walker: Lenore Walker, *The Battered Woman* (New York: Harper & Row, 1979).

131: Clinicians who have worked with and studied: Walker, *Battered Woman.*

132: Clinicians note that battered women: Walker, *Battered Woman.*

133: In 1984, 806 women killed their husbands: Federal Bureau of Investigation, *Crime in the United States.*

133: On the evening of March 9, 1977: The story of Francine Hughes is told in *The Burning Bed: The True Story of Francine Hughes—a Beaten Wife Who Rebeled,* by Faith McNulty (New York: Harcourt Brace Jovanovich, 1980). Additional details can be found in Ann Jones, *Women Who Kill* (New York: Holt, Rinehart, & Winston, 1980).

134: Early in the morning of January 28, 1977: Information about the case of Joyce Hawthorne was obtained directly from Joyce Hawthorne and her family. Richard Gelles served as an expert witness during Joyce Hawthorne's second trial for murdering her husband.

134: A third case that captured some national attention: For information on the case of Roxanne Gay, see Jones, *Women Who Kill.*

137: We adapted a "Psychiatric Symptom Check List": The items in the checklist were derived from the following: Sheldon Cohen, Tom Kamarack, and Robin Mermelstein, "A Global Measure of Perceived Stress," *Journal of Health and Social Behavior* 24 (1983): 385–96; Bruce P. Dohrenwend, Patrick E. Shrout, Gladys Egri, and Frederick S. Mendleson, "Nonspecific Psychological Distress and Other Dimensions of Psychopathology," *Archives of General Psychiatry* 37 (1980): 1229–36; and Joy P. Newman, "Sex Differences in Depressive Symptoms" (Madison: University of Wisconsin, Department of Psychiatry, n.d., Mimeographed).

CHAPTER SEVEN   COPING WITH VIOLENCE

141: At the conclusion of her third trial: *State of Florida* v. *Joyce Bernice Hawthorne,* Case No. 77-235-C. July 1982.

141: the psychologist, Lenore Walker: Lenore Walker is the author of two major books on spouse abuse: *The Battered Woman* (New York: Harper & Row, 1979), and *The Battered Women Syndrome* (New York: Springer, 1984).

142: The appeals court, however: *Joyce Bernice Hawthorne* v. *State of Florida,* District Court of Appeal, First District, State of Florida, Case No. AN-435.

142: Walker's theory of learned helplessness: Walker, *Battered Woman;* Lenore E. Walker, "Battered Women and Learned Helplessness," *Victimology* 2, no. 3/4 (1977–78): 525–34; Walker, *Battered Women Syndrome,* chap. 9.

142: the experimental psychologist, Martin Seligman: Martin E. P. Seligman, *Helplessness: On Depression, Development, and Death* (San Francisco: W. H. Freeman, 1975); M. E. P. Seligman, "Comment and Integration," *Journal of Abnormal Psychology* 87, no. 1 (1978): 165–79.

143: One of the first essays on the subject: Elizabeth Truninger, "Marital Violence: The Legal Solutions," *Hastings Law Review* 23 (November 1971): 259–76.

143: In our own research: Richard J. Gelles, "Abused Wives: Why Do They Stay?" *Journal of Marriage and the Family* 38 (November 1976): 659–68.

144: The sociologist Mildred Pagelow: Mildred Pagelow, *Women Battering: Victims and Their Experiences* (Beverly Hills, Calif.: Sage, 1981).

144: The sociologists Michael Strube and Linda Barbour: Michael J. Strube and Linda S. Barbour, "The Decision to Leave an Abusive Relationship: Economic Dependence and Psychological Commitment," *Journal of Marriage and the Family* 45 (November 1983): 785–93.

145: the sociologist Lee Bowker: Lee H. Bowker, *Beating Wife Beating* (Lexington, Mass.: Lexington Books, 1983).

146: As one of Bowker's respondents said: Bowker, *Beating Wife Beating*, 126.

CHAPTER EIGHT   COMPASSION OR CONTROL:
LEGAL, SOCIAL, AND MEDICAL SERVICES

160: On June 10, 1983, Charles Thurman, Sr.: For details on the case of Tracy Thurman see: Jamie M. Moore, "Landmark Court Decision for Battered Women," *Response* 8 (Fall 1985): 5–8; "Battered Woman Wins Landmark Case Against Police," *Sanenews* 3 (September 1985): 1–2; "The Tracy Thurman Case: A Precedent Setter for Victims of Domestic Violence." *Sanenews* 4 (February 1986): 1ff; "Jury Awards Abused Wife $2.3 Million, Blasts Police," *Providence Journal-Bulletin*, June 26, 1985, A4; Dirk Johnson, "Abused Women Get Leverage in Connecticut," *The New York Times*, June 15, 1986, sec. 4, p. 8; *Thurman* v. *City of Torrington*, 595 F. Supp. 1521 (1984); *Thurman* v. *City of Torrington*, USDC DConn, No. H-84-120, June 25, 1985.

161: Three years to the day after Tracy Thurman: Johnson, "Abused Women."

162: to the U.S. attorney general and the U.S. surgeon general: *Attorney General's Task Force on Family Violence: Final Report* (Washington, D.C.: Government Printing Office, September 1984); *Surgeon General's Workshop on Violence and Public Health: Report*, Leesburg, Va., October 27–29, 1985 (Washington, D.C.: Health Resources and Services Administration, U.S. Public Health Service, U.S. Department of Health and Human Services, 1986).

163: Two judges in Massachusetts: "Judge Defends Domestic Violence Decision," *The Westerly Sun*, November 13, 1986, 19.

164: According to the physicians Alvin Rosenfeld and Eli Newberger: Alvin A. Rosenfeld and Eli H. Newberger, "Compassion vs. Control: Conceptual and Practical Pitfalls in the Broadened Definition of Child Abuse," *Journal of the American Medical Association* 237 (1977): 2086–88.

165: In December 1976: *Bruno* v. *Codd*, New York Supreme Court, City of New York, Index No. 21946/76, consent decree.

165: In 1974, a class-action suit was filed: *Raguz* v. *Chandler*, Case No. C74-1064, Complaint, at 4-8; see also, "Battered Women Press Police for Equal Protection," *Response* 2, no. 6 (1979): 3–24.

165: In Oakland, California: *Scott* v. *Hart*, C76-2395.

165: of the Minneapolis Police Experiment: Lawrence W. Sherman and Richard A. Berk. "The Minneapolis Domestic Violence Experiment," *Police Foundation Reports* 1 (1984): 1–8; Lawrence W. Sherman and Richard A. Berk, "The Specific

Deterrent Effects of Arrest for Domestic Violence," *American Sociological Review* 49, no. 2 (1984): 261–72.

166: Sherman, quoted in *The New York Times:* Philip M. Boffey, "Domestic Violence Study Favors Arrest," *The New York Times,* April 5, 1983, C1 ff.

166: Ten days after the Sherman and Berk study was reported: James LeMoyne, "A Firmer Response to Domestic Strife," *The New York Times,* April 15, 1984, E7.

166: the United States Attorney General's Task Force: *Attorney General's Task Force,* 1984.

168: Eli Newberger, a leading voice: Eli H. Newberger, "Prosecutions: A Problematic Approach to Child Abuse," *Journal of Interpersonal Violence* 2 (March, 1987): 112–117.

168: Prosecution, according to Newberger, can: Newberger, "Prosecutions."

169: Morton Bard was the pioneer student of police intervention: See: Morton Bard and Harriet Connolly, "The Police and Family Violence: Policy and Practice," in U.S. Commission on Civil Rights, *Battered Women: Issues of Public Policy* (Washington, D.C.: U.S. Commission on Civil Rights, 1978), 304–26; Morton Bard and Joseph Zacker, "Assaultiveness and Alcohol Use in Family Disputes: Police Perceptions," *Criminology* 12 (1974): 281–92; Morton Bard, and Joseph Zacker, "The Prevention of Family Violence: Dilemmas of Community Interaction," *Journal of Marriage and the Family* 33, no. 4 (1971): 677–82; Morton Bard, "Family Crisis Intervention: From Concept to Implementation," in Maria Roy, ed., *Battered Women: A Psychosociological Study of Domestic Violence* (New York: Van Nostrand Reinhold, 1977): 172–93.

169: Elizabeth Truninger observed: Elizabeth Truninger, "Marital Violence: The Legal Solutions," *Hastings Law Review* 23 (November 1971): 259–76.

169: Martha and Henry Field: Martha Field and Henry Field, "Marital Violence and the Criminal Process: Neither Justice nor Peace," *Social Science Review* 47, no. 2 (1973): 221–40.

170: By the mid-1980s more than two-thirds: G. Gallop, "7 in 10 Favor Death Penalty for Convicted Murderers," The Gallop Poll, released March 2, 1986; Louis Harris, "Sizable Majority Against Mandatory Death Penalty," The Harris Survey, released February 10, 1983; H. Erskine, "The Polls: Capital Punishment," *Public Opinion Quarterly* 34, no. 2 (1970): 290–307.

172: The sociologist David Ford: David Ford, personal communication.

173: The psychologist James Kent: James T. Kent, "A Follow-up Study of Abused Children," *Journal of Pediatric Psychology* 1 (1976): 25–31.

174: Pizzey authored one of the first books: Erin Pizzey, *Scream Quietly or the Neighbors Will Hear* (London: Penguin Books, 1974).

175: According to the sociologists Rebecca and Russell Dobash: R. E. Dobash and Russell Dobash, *Violence Against Wives: A Case Against Patriarchy* (New York: Free Press, 1979).

175: Some claim that the first shelter: Jane O'Reilly, "Wife Beating: The Silent Crime." *Time,* September 5, 1983, 23 ff.

176: A recent study by the sociologists Richard Berk: Richard A. Berk, Phyllis J. Newton, and Sarah Fenstermaker Berk, "What a Difference a Day Makes: An Empirical Study of the Impact of Shelters for Battered Women," *Journal of Marriage and the Family* 48 (August 1986): 481–90.

177: since Kempe and his colleagues: C. H. Kempe, F. N. Silverman, B. F. Steele, W. Droegemueller, and H. K. Silver, "The Battered-Child Syndrome," *Journal of the American Medical Association* 181 (July 7, 1962): 17–24.

177: Eli Newberger and Stephen Bittner: Stephen Bittner and Eli H. Newberger, "Pediatric Understanding of Child Abuse and Neglect," in Eli H. Newberger, ed., *Child Abuse* (Boston: Little, Brown, 1982), 137–57.

178: Newberger and Bittner offer seven axioms: Bittner and Newberger, "Pediatric Understanding."

178: The sociologist Evan Stark and his wife: Evan Stark and Anne Flitcraft, "Social Knowledge, Social Policy, and the Abuse of Women: The Case Against Patriarchal Benevolence," in David Finkelhor, Richard J. Gelles, Gerald T. Hotaling, and Murray A. Straus, eds., *The Dark Side of Families: Current Family Violence Research* (Beverly Hills, Calif.: Sage, 1983), 330–48.

179: An official with the federal Security and Exchange Commission: "John E. Fedders, head of enforcement at the Security and Exchange Commission since 1981, resigned amid widespread publicity that he beat his wife," from: "SEC Enforcer Quits After Wife-beating Story," *Providence Evening Bulletin,* February 27, 1985, C18.

180: Michael Strube and Linda Barbour: Michael J. Strube and Linda S. Barbour, "The Decision to Leave an Abusive Relationship: Economic Dependence and Psychological Commitment," *Journal of Marriage and the Family* 45 (November 1983): 785–93.

180: Social scientists have found that individuals who have: See Howard B. Kaplan, "Toward a General Theory of Psychosocial Deviance: The Case of Aggressive Behavior," *Social Science and Medicine* 6, no. 5 (1972): 593–617.

180: The sociologist Kathleen Ferraro: Kathleen Ferraro, "Police Response to Domestic Violence" (Paper presented at the annual meetings of the American Sociological Association, Washington, D.C., August 1985).

181: Ferraro continues: Ferraro, "Police Response."

181: Family system interventions are a controversial form: See Richard J. Gelles and Peter E. Maynard, "A Structural Family Systems Approach in Cases of Family Violence," *Family Relations* 36 (1987): 270–75.

182: Rosenfeld and Newberger advise: Rosenfeld and Newberger, "Compassion vs. Control."

CHAPTER NINE   MAKING IT SO PEOPLE CAN'T: TREATING
AND PREVENTING FAMILY VIOLENCE

184: We often wait for the babies and women to die: The two cases that follow
illustrate the point that the flaws of the child and adult protection systems are rarely
uncovered until after there has been a fatality. In both cases, deaths of children led
to the formation of a state commission to investigate the operation of the child
protection system. In both cases the director of the child protection system resigned
and was replaced. Also, in both cases state funding for protective services was
dramatically increased after the deaths of children.

186: National social work guidelines recommend that protective service workers: *Child Welfare League of America Standards for Child Protective Services*
(1972), sec. 5.15, p. 60. The standards are currently being revised.

187: Eli Newberger calls: E. H. Newberger, "The Helping Hand Strikes Again:
Unintended Consequences of Child Abuse Reporting," in Eli H. Newberger and
Richard Bourne, eds., *Unhappy Families* (Littleton, Mass.: PSG Publications, 1985),
171–78.

188: The sociologist Kai Erikson once said: Kai Erikson, "Notes on the Sociology of Deviance," *Social Problems* 9 (Spring 1962): 307–14.

189: Child abuse researchers are convinced that if an unwanted baby: See, for
example: E. Bennie and E. Sclare, "The Battered Child Syndrome," *American Journal of Psychiatry* 125, no. 7 (1969): 975–79; Richard J. Gelles, "Child Abuse as
Psychopathology: A Sociological Critique and Reformulation," *American Journal
of Orthopsychiatry* 43 (July 1973): 611–21; Murray A. Straus, Richard J. Gelles,
and Suzanne K. Steinmetz, *Behind Closed Doors: Violence in the American Family*
(Garden City, N.Y.: Anchor Books, 1980); S. Wasserman, "The Abused Parent of
the Abused Child," *Children* 14 (September–October, 1967): 175–79; S. Zalba,
"Battered Children," *Transaction* 8 (July–August, 1971): 58–61.

189: I was called to testify before the U.S. Senate: Richard J. Gelles, "Violence
Towards Children in the United States," testimony before the U.S. Senate Subcom-
mitee on Child and Human Development, April 1977.

191: Perhaps only a third of all instances of child abuse: K. Burgdorf, *Recognition and Reporting of Child Maltreatment* (Rockville, Md.: Westat, 1980).

191: Eli Newberger and his colleague: Robert L. Hampton and Eli H. Newberger, "Child Abuse Incidence and Reporting by Hospitals: Significance of Severity,
Class, and Race," *American Journal of Public Health* 75, no. 1 (1985): 56–60.

193: Henry Kempe and his colleagues: J. D. Gray, C. A. Cutler, J. G. Dean, and
C. H. Kempe, "Prediction and Prevention of Child Abuse and Neglect," *Child
Abuse and Neglect: The International Journal* 1, no. 1 (1977): 45–58.

195: As a country, Sweden represents a pioneer in the Western world: For an
overview of the steps Sweden has taken to reduce the cultural norm of violence see:
Richard J. Gelles and Ake W. Edfeldt, "Violence Towards Children in the United
States and Sweden," *Child Abuse and Neglect: The International Journal* 10, no. 4

(1986): 501–10; J. Vinocur, "Sweden's Anti-Spanking Law Seems to Be a Success," *The New York Times,* October 19, 1980, sec 1, p. 22.

195: Psychological research has: For a review of the research on the effectiveness of punishment see: Jane Ritchie and James Ritchie, *Spare the Rod* (Boston: George Allen & Unwin, 1981); R. Johnson *Aggression in Man and Animals* (Philadelphia: W. B. Saunders, 1972).

196: What are the alternatives to using spanking: For an excellent review of the alternatives to spanking, see Ritchie and Ritchie, *Spare the Rod,* chap. 7.

197: The average child watches: D. M. Zuckerman and B. S. Zuckerman, "Television's Impact on Children," *Pediatrics* 75 (February 1985): 233–40; M. B. Rothenberg, "Effect of Television Violence on Children and Youth," *Journal of the American Medical Association* 234 (1975): 1043–46.

197: Among the most violent television programs: National Coalition on Television Violence, *NCTV News* 9 (January–February 1987).

198: According to the National Coalition on Television Violence: National Coalition on Television Violence, Press Release, Monday, November 24, 1986.

199: Parent education programs such as PET: PET stands for Parent Effectiveness Training; see T. Gordon, *Parent Effectiveness Training* (New York: Wyden, 1970).

200: The majority of family homicides involves guns: M. Riedel, M. Zahn, and Lois F. Mock, *The Nature and Patterns of American Homicide* (Washington, D.C.: U.S. Department of Justice, National Institute of Justice, 1985).

206: "People are not for hitting." The phrase, "people are not for hitting" was coined by Dr. John Valusek, Wichita, Kansas.

APPENDIX A   HOW THE STUDIES WERE DONE

207: We began our research on family violence early: The first three publications in our program of research on family violence were: Murray A. Straus, "Some Social Antecedents of Physical Punishment: A Linkage Theory Interpretation," *Journal of Marriage and the Family* 33 (November 1971): 658–63; Suzanne K. Steinmetz and Murray A. Straus, *Violence in the Family* (New York: Harper and Row, 1974); Suzanne K. Steinmetz and Murray A. Straus, "The Family as Cradle of Violence," *Society* 10 no. 6 (1973): 50–56.

207: The Conflict Tactics Scales: A complete discussion of the Conflict Tactics Scales can be found in Murray A. Straus, "Measuring Intrafamily Conflict and Violence: The Conflict Tactics (CT) Scales," *Journal of Marriage and the Family* 41 (February 1979): 75–88; Murray A. Straus, Richard J. Gelles, and Suzanne K. Steinmetz, *Behind Closed Doors: Violence in the American Family* (Garden City, N.Y.: Anchor, 1980): Appendix B.

208: Our first studies found that family violence: Straus, 1971.

208: Thus, we sent questionnaires home to the parents: Richard Bulcroft and Murray A. Straus, "Validity of Husband, Wife, and Child Reports of Intrafamily Violence and Power," University of New Hampshire, mimeographed.

208: The second line of work was a bit more difficult: The second line of research consisted of in-depth interviews with eighty family members. The results of these interviews are reported in Richard J. Gelles, *The Violent Home* (Beverly Hills, Ca.: Sage Publications, 1974).

208: Overall, nearly half of those: Gelles, 1974.

209: In 1976 we embarked on our most ambitious survey: The results of the survey are reported in Straus, Gelles, and Steinmetz, 1980.

209: Our most recent survey was conducted in 1985: The survey methodology report presents a complete overview of the survey: Louis Harris and Associates, *Second National Family Violence Survey: Survey Methodology*. Available from Richard J. Gelles, Office of the Dean, College of Arts and Sciences, University of Rhode Island, Kingston, RI 02881. There is a $15 charge for this report.

211: As of the end of 1986, there were more than: A partial listing of these studies includes: Craig Allen and Murray A. Straus, "Resources, Power and Husband-Wife Violence," in Murray A. Straus and Gerald T. Hotaling, eds., *The Social Causes of Husband-Wife Violence* (Minneapolis: University of Minnesota Press, 1980): 188–210; Judith Brutz and Bron B. Ingoldsby, "Conflict Resolution in Quaker Families," *Journal of Marriage and the Family* 46 (1984): 21–26; Rodney M. Cate, June M. Henton, James Koval, F. Scott Christopher, and Sally Lloyd, "Premarital Abuse: A Social Psychological Perspective," *Journal of Family Issues* 3 (1982): 79–90; Jean Giles-Sims, *Wife Battering: A Systems Theory Approach* (New York: Guilford Press, 1983); Carlton A. Hornung, B. Claire McCullough, and Taichi Sugimoto, "Status Relationships in Marriage: Risk Factors in Spouse Abuse," *Journal of Marriage and the Family* 43 (1981): 675–92; Stephen R. Jorgensen, "Social Class Heterogamy, Status Striving, and Perception of Marital Conflict: A Partial Replication and Revision of Pearlin's Contingency Hypothesis," *Journal of Marriage and the Family* 39 (1977): 653–61; Mary R. Laner and Jeannie Thompson, "Abuse and Aggression in Courting Couples," *Deviant Behavior: An Interdisciplinary Journal,* 3 (1982): 229–44; James M. Makepeace, "Life Events Stress and Courtship Violence," *Family Relations* 32 (1983): 101–9.

INDEX

About

the Authors

Richard J. Gelles is Dean of the College of Arts and Sciences and professor of Anthropology and Sociology at the University of Rhode Island. In 1984, *Esquire* named him one of the men and women under the age of forty who are "changing America."

Murray A. Straus is professor of Sociology and Director of the Family Research Laboratory at the University of New Hampshire.